abandon—*Syn.* desert, relinquish, give up, let go, surrender, resign, discontinue, vacate. *Ant.* keep, maintain, uphold, support, adopt, occupy.
abase—*Syn.* disgrace, debase, lower, cast down, confound, expose. *Ant.* uplift, praise, cherish, honor, elevate, dignify.
abash—*Syn.* discourage, disconcert, discompose, confound, embarrass, humiliate. *Ant.* encourage, embolden, hearten, praise, uphold, cheer, buoy, rally.
abate—*Syn.* moderate, mitigate, diminish, reduce, restrain, assuage. *Ant.* extend, increase, magnify, amplify, aggravate, enhance, intensify, prolong.
abatement—*Syn.* lessening, diminution, mitigation. *Ant.* increase.
abbreviate—*Syn.* Shorten, curtain, condense, contract, reduce. *Ant.* lengthen, enlarge, increase, expand, extend.
abbreviation—*Syn.* abridgment, contraction, shortening. *Ant.* enlargement, expansion, extension.
abdicate—*Syn.* resign, abandon, forsake, renounce, quit, forego. *Ant.* claim, defend, hold, maintain, retain.
abet—*Syn.* aid, assist, help, incite, stimulate, promote, uphold. *Ant.* discourage, impede, obstruct, frustrate, hinder, resist, deter, oppose.
abettor—*Syn.* assistant, helper, accomplice, accessory, associate. *Ant.* opponent, antagonist, resister, adversary.
abeyance—*Syn.* suspension, inaction, adjournment. *Ant.* enforcement, renewal, exercise, revival, action, resuscitation.
abhor—*Syn.* hate, loathe, detest, despise, dislike, scorn. *Ant.* love, cherish, esteem, like, desire, admire, love.
abide—*Syn.* live, stay, inhabit, reside, continue, wait, remain. *Ant.* go, move, depart, migrate, proceed.
ability—*Syn.* capacity, skill, aptitude, faculty, talent. *Ant.* incompetency, weakness, inability, limitation.
abject—*Syn.* despicable, worthless, servile, base, low, contemptible, absurd. *Ant.* exalted, proud, imposing, excellent, worthy, praiseworthy, commendable, lofty.
abjure—*Syn.* forswear, recant, retract, disclaim, renounce, repudiate, dismiss, deny. *Ant.* maintain, approve, certify, sanction, ratify, assent, justify.
able—*Syn.* robust, stalwart, powerful, vigorous, qualified, capable, competent. *Ant.* weak, infirm, ineffective, useless, powerless.
abominable—*Syn.* odious, hateful, detestable, disgusting, horrible, repugnant, revolting, infamous, loathsome, foul. *Ant.* likable, enjoyable, pleasant, sweet, pleasing.
abomination—*Syn.* disgust, nuisance, pest, horror, evil, corruption, hatred, wickedness, anathema. *Ant.* cleanliness, beauty, loveliness, affection, gratification, satisfaction, delight, treat, happiness.
abortive—*Syn.* vain, ineffective, useless, futile, fruitless. *Ant.* effectual, efficient, efficacious, productive.
abound—*Syn.* teem, swarm, flow, flourish, swell, stream. *Ant.* want, lack, fail, deficient, destitute, need, short of.
about—*Syn.* concerning, regarding, respecting, around, nearly. *Ant.* unlike, remote, afar, separated, distant.
abridgment—*Syn.* outline,, digest, synopsis, abstract, abbreviation, presis. *Ant.* enlargement, extension, addition, expansion, increase.
accord, *n.*—*Syn.* agreement, harmony, acquiescence. *Ant.* disagreement, discord, denial, denunciation.
accost—*Syn.* salute, greet, address, approach. *Ant.* shun, avoid, ignore, evade, dodge, eschew.
account—*Syn.* description, recital, rehearsal, detail, relation, report, statement, explanation, moneys, bill, reckoning.
accountable—*Syn.* responsible, amendable, liable, guilty. *Ant.* irresponsible, unreliable.
accumulate—*Syn.* amass, gather, hoard, assemble, aggregate. *Ant.* scatter, dissipate, disperse, parcel, portion.
accumulation—*Syn.* mass, store, aggregation, concentration, stock, bulk. *Ant.* scattering, division, separation, dissipation.
accurate—*Syn.* correct, trustworthy, minute, conclusive, just, certain, reliable. *Ant.* erroneous, doubltful, wrong, false, questionable, inaccurate, unjust, erring, uncertain, vague.
achieve—*Syn.* accomplish, perform, execute, conquer, act, effect, gain. *Ant.* fail, neglect, retreat, foresake, lose.
achievement—*Syn.* accomplishment, deed, exploit, feat, performance. *Ant.* failure, cessation, negligence, carelessness, loss, deprivation.
acknowledge—*Syn.* confess, concede, allow, grant, recognize, accept, certify, endorse. *Ant.* deny, decline, refuse, ignore, renounce, repudiate.
acquaint—*Syn.* inform, apprise, notify, announce. *Ant.* deceive, delude, mislead.
acquaintance—*Syn.* friendship, familiarity, intimacy, association, knowledge, experience. *Ant.* unfamiliarity, ignoring, inexperience, strangeness.
acquit—*Syn.* pardon, free, clear, discharge, absolve, liberate, exculpate, release, exonerate. *Ant.* condemn, bind, hold, keep, defeat, reprove, reject, repudiate, blame.
acrimony—*Ayn.* acerbity, tartness, harshness, bitterness, hatred, anger, irascibility, acridity, pungency, unkindness. *Ant.* amiability, smoothness, sweetness, kindness, courtesy.
act, *v.*—*Syn.* do, perform, play, enact, operate, effect, execute, transact, accomplish, enforce. *Ant.* refrain, idle, halt, stop, cease, give up, abstain.
action—*Syn.* achievement, feat, battle, engagement, motion, operation, work, activity, exertion, movement, alertness, doing. *Ant.* inertia, inactivity, inaction, sluggishness, rest, rest, idleness, ennui, lassitude.
active—*Syn.* quick, sharp, brisk, spry, bustling, energetic, vigorous *Ant.* inactive, idle, slow, dull, sluggish, inert, quiet.
activity—*Syn.* business, action, motion, vigor, quickness, agility, readiness. *Ant.* inactivity, sluggish, inertia.
actual—*Syn.* real, positive, certain, certified, undoubted. *Ant.* false, doubtful, spurious, unreliable, counterfeit.
acumen—*Syn.* insight, keenness, penetration, sagacity, perpicacity. *Ant.* obtuseness, apathy, insensibility.
adapt—*Syn.* fit, conform, accommodate, set, regulate, adjust. *Ant.* confuse, disarrange, misfit, disturb.
add—*Syn.* increase, extend, augment, attach, append, adjoin. *Ant.* subtract, diminish, lessen, reduce.
addicted—*Syn.* attached, devoted, prone, given, inclined. *Ant.* averse, unaccustomed, disinclined.
addition—*Syn.* increase, accession, appendage, adjunct, increment, annexation. *Ant.* subtraction, abstraction, decrease, diminution, lessening.
address, *v.*—*Syn.* speak to, greet, salute, hail, accost, approach. *Ant.* overlook, ignore, pass, shun, elude, cut, avoid, dodge.
abscond—*Syn.* run off, run away, decamp, depart, retreat, flee, disappear, leave, bolt, hide, steal away, withdraw. *Ant.* remain, stay, continue, stop, endure, emerge.
absent—*Syn.* inattentive, abstracted, listless, dreamy, heedless, thoughtless, abosrbed, oblivious. *Ant.* present, attentive, mindful, thoughtful, interested.
absolute—*Syn.* entire, complete, unrestricted, unqualified, arbitrary, exacting, positive, dogmatic, commanding, unlimited. *Ant.* mild, meek, gentle, lowly, submissive, yielding, compliant, limited, lenient, tractable.
absolve—*Syn.* pardon, exonerate, forgive, overlook, clear, exempt, liberate, discharge, expulpate. *Ant.* bind, charge, accuse, compel, inculpate.
absorb—*Syn.* imbibe, consume, exhaust, engross, merge, engulf. *Ant.* disgorge, eject, emit, dissipate, disperse.
abstinence—*Syn.* temperance, continence, moderation, self-denial, self-control, sobriety, fasting. *Ant.* excess, intoxication, self-indulgence, intemperance.
abstract—*Syn.* steal, appropriate, purloin, remove, divert, separate, distract, take away. *Ant.* restore, unite, add, fill up, increase.
absurd—*Syn.* stupid, senseless, ridiculous, foolish, nonsensical, unreasonable, ludicrous, crazy, mistaken. *Ant.* reasonable, logical, wise, sound, sensible, true, undeniable, indubitable, incontestable, indisputable, infallible, unquestionable, certain, sagacious, demonstrated.
abuse, *v.*—*Syn.* ill-treat, damage, disparage, defame, violate, injure, harm, hurt, malign, slander, revile, vilify, reproach, depreciate, maltreat, misuse, wrong. *Ant.* praise, laud, extol, shield, uphold, favor, benefit, sustain, protect, respect, commend.
abyss—*Syn.* depth, pit, gulf, chasm, void. *Ant.* height, hill, eminence, elevation, summit.
academic—*Syn.* learned, scholarly, lettered, literary, bookish, Platonic. *Ant.* ignorant, illiterate, unlettered, uninstructed, untaught.
accede—*Syn.* assent, comply, concur, agree, approve. *Ant.* protest, dissent, deny, refuse, denounce, withhold.
accelerate—*Syn.* hurry, expedite, hasten, push, facilitate. *Ant.* hinder, defer, obstruct, impede.
accept—*Syn.* take, acquire, admit, get, gain, agree, assent, concur. *Ant.* discard, deny, disagree, dispute, renounce, yield, reject.
accessory—*Syn.* ally, assistant, partner, aide, helper, accomplice, abettor, henchman, follower, companion, colleague. *Ant.* opponent, enemy, foe, adversary.
accident—*Syn.* casualty, mishap, hazard, happening, chance, misadventure, disaster, misfortune, hazard. *Ant.* plan, purpose, fate, decree, provision, ordinance, calculation.
accommodate—*Syn.* serve, oblige, adapt, aid, suit, adjust, supply, reconcile, arrange, conform, *Ant.* impede, bar, unsuit, disoblige, hinder, embarrass, ob-struct, limit, prevent.
accomplice—*Syn.* ally, helper, assistant, coworker, associate, abettor, supporter, aide. *Ant.* opponent, objector, destroyer, opposer, enemy.
accomplish—*Syn.* perform, carry out, succeed, attain, effect, execute, perfect, complete, finish, manage. *Ant.* fail, undo, deter, block, nullify, forsake, disappoint, give up.
accomplishment—*Syn.* performance, completion, acquisition. *Ant.* defeat, failure, nullification.
accord, *v.*—*Syn.* admit, acquiesce, give, permit, agree, harmonize, assent. *Ant.* refuse, disagree, disallow, relinquish, disbar, question, challenge, controvert, oppose.
address, *n.*—*Syn.* speech, discourse, oration, ability, dexterity, courtesy, adroitness. *Ant.* rudeness, clumsiness, awkwardness, folly, unmannerliness.
adduce—*Syn.* allege, advance, assign, mention, urge, affirm. *Ant,* fail, bungle, botch, hesitate.
adequate—*Syn.* adapted, suitable, sufficient, satisfactory, enough, ample. *Ant.* unsuited, unfit, insufficient, poor.
adhere—*Syn.* stick, cling, join, fasten, attach. *Ant.* separate, loosen, divide
adherent—*Syn.* follower, partisan, comrade, aid, helper, disciple, accomplice. *Ant.* opponent, adversary.
adhesion—*Syn.* attachment, connection, union, cohesion. *Ant.* separation, division, unattachment, disruption, disconnection.
adhesive—*Syn.* sticky, viscous, cohesive, gummy, gelatinous. *Ant.* free, loose, apart.
adjacent—*Syn.* adjoining, near,

beside, next, close, bordering, abutting. *Ant.* distant, beyond, detached, disconnected, separate.
adjourn—*Syn.* defer, postpone, put off, delay, suspend, protract, interrupt, withhold. *Ant.* begin, continue, keep on, keep up, prolong.
adjudge—*Syn.* assign, decide, decree, determine, settle, award. *Ant.* postpone, dodge, shun, decline.
adjunct—*Syn.* addition, appendage, appurtenance, help, complement, dependency, auxiliary. *Ant.* subtraction, lessening, removal, separation.
adjust—*Syn.* arrange, adapt, fit, settle, accommodate, classify, suit. *Ant.* disarrange, confuse, mix, mingle, disorder, derange, jumble.
administer—*Syn.* dispense, distribute, execute, furnish, control, supply, discharge, provide, disburse. *Ant.* neglect, refuse, restrain, deny, oppose, mullify.
admirable—*Syn.* worthy, attractive, striking, enticing, winsome, wonderful, good, excellent, desirable, praiseworthy. *Ant.* repelling, repulsive, detestable, unworthy, contemptible, disgusting, censurable.
admiration—*Syn.* wonder, appreciation, praise, respect, regard, esteem. *Ant.* hatred, detestation, disapproval, disregard, aversion.
admire—*Syn.* appreciate, approve, applaud, laud, praise, boost, honor, respect, esteem. *Ant.* condemn, censure, protest, detest, scorn, abhor, dislike.
admissible—*Syn.* worthy, proper, right, suitable, passable, allowable, possible, permitted, approved. *Ant.* unworthy, wrong, unsuitable, inadmissible.
admission—*Syn.* allowance, confession, acknowledgement, access, entrance, charge. *Ant.* denial, refusal, repudiation, disallowance, rejection, expulsion.
admit—*Syn.* allow, open, suffer, acknowledgement, avow, grant, concede, tell. *Ant.* deny, refuse, shut, dismiss, dissent, reject.
admonish—*Syn.* warn, advise, counsel, reprove, censure, forewarn, reprimand, dissuade. *Ant.* approve, laud, applaud, praise.
adore—*Syn.* worship, honor, praise, extol, love. *Ant.* despise, hate, detest, abhor.
adorn—*Syn.* ornament, beautify, embellish, garnish, decorate. *Ant.* mar, spoil, deface, deform, tarnish.
adroit—*Syn.* clever, proficient, dexterous, expert, artful. *Ant.* unskilled, awkward, dull, clumsy.
advance—*Syn.* go, move, proceed, progress, continue, improve, accelerate, allege. *Ant.* recede, turn, return, yield, stop, stand, halt, hesitate, withdraw.
advancement—*Syn.* promotion, progress, progression, gain, knowledge, improvement, proficiency, elevation. *Ant.* retrogression, decline, descent, return, reversion, retreat, withdrawal, halt.
alike—*Syn.* like, resembling, akin, kindred, similar, uniform. *Ant.* unlike, dissimilar, different, opposite, diverse.
alive—*Syn.* live, existent, subsisting, active, lively, animated, brisk, agile. *Ant.* dead, lifeless, inanimate, defunct, dull, morose, sluggish.
allay—*Syn.* soothe, pacify, tranqualize, mollify, calm, alleviate. *Ant.* agitate, excite, stir, fan.
allege—*Syn.* aver, state, cite, declare, affirm, advance, assert. *Ant.* deny, conceal, dissent, object.
allegiance—*Syn.* loyalty, submission, subjection, homage, devotion, fealty, obedience. *Ant.* dissatisfaction, disloyalty, sedition, treason, rebellion.
alleviate—*Syn.* mitigate, lessen, moderate, abate, lighten, relieve, remove. *Ant.* intensify, heighten, magnify, augment, aggravate.
alliance—*Syn.* union, fusion, federation, confederation, coalition, partnership. *Ant.* separation, discord, antagonism.
allot—*Syn.* give, grant, distribute, divide, award, arrange, allocate, collocate. *Ant.* keep, deny, reject, cast aside, disallow, resist, dissent.
allow—*Syn.* assent, authorize, accord, empower, license, warrant, permit, let, grant, sanction, yield, consent, tolerate. *Ant.* deny, forbid, disallow, reject, withstand.
allure—*Syn.* coax, cajole, attract, draw, tempt, seduce, invite. *Ant.* repel, warn, deter, hinder.
alter—*Syn.* change, vary, modify, diversify, turn, reconstruct. *Ant.* keep, retain, maintain, hold, stay, refrain.
altercation—*Syn.* controversy, contention, quarrel, wrangle, dispute, fracas, strife, argument. *Ant.* union, harmony, agreement, unanimity.
alternative—*Syn.* option, preference, choice, pick. *Ant.* necessity, compulsion, constraint, restraint.
amass—*Syn.* heap, store, gather, collect, accumulate. *Ant.* disperse, scatter, spend, dissipate.
amateur—*Syn.* novice, beginner, learner. *Ant.* professional, savant.
amazement—*Syn.* suprise, wonder, astonishment, bewilderment. *Ant.* steadiness, stoicism, cool, calmness, composure.
ambition—*Syn.* aspiration, enterprise, desire, striving, eagerness, earnestness. *Ant.* indifference, humility, placidity, laziness.
amend—*Syn.* improve, correct, rectify, mend, mitigate, ameliorate. *Ant.* harm, impair, tarnish, corrupt, deteriorate, debase, injure, aggravate, reduce, alloy.
amiable—*Syn.* pleasing, kindly, agreeable, pleasant, attractive, winning, engaging, pleasing, charming, good-tempered. *Ant.* dour, morose, testy, crusty, grouchy, troublesome, peevish, ill-tempered, surly, sad, disagreeable, ill-humored.
amplify—*Syn.* enlarge, increase, magnify, extend, widen, expand, augment. *Ant.* reduce, summarize, curtail, abridge, condense, lessen, compress.
anger—*Syn.* ire, wrath, indignation, resentment, fury, rage, irritation, temper, animosity. *Ant.* meekness, mildness, gentility, calmness, gentleness, placidity, peace.
announce—*Syn.* speak, tell, deliver, reveal, report, state, proclaim, say, notify, communicate. *Ant.* hold, refrain, keep silent, hide, depress, forbid, muzzle, restrain, quash, stifle, bottle up.
anticipation—*Syn.* expectancy, hope, foreboding, forecast, expectation, presentiment, prevision. *Ant.* fear, doubt, dread, despair, sensation, surprise.
antipathy—*Syn.* hatred, hostility, enmity, aversion, repugnance, abhorrence, repulsion, antagonism, opposition, disklike, ill-will. *Ant.* admiration, love, approval, approbation, esteem, commendation, appreciation.
antique—*Syn.* ancient, old-fashioned, superannuated, time-worn, primitive. *Ant.* new, modern, recent, stylish, fresh, modish, fashionable.
advantage—*Syn.* benefit, gain, help, vantage, expediency, superiority. *Ant.* loss, drawback, disadvantage, incumbrance, burden.
advantageous—*Syn.* beneficial, useful, gainful, helpful, favorable, good. *Ant.* hurtful, harmful, injurious, unfavorable, detrimental.
adventure—*Syn.* happening, event, occurrence, circumstance, pursuit, trial, experiment. *Ant.* passiveness, inaction, inertia, latency, passivity.
adversary—*Syn.* opponent, antagonist, competitor, rival. *Ant.* aid, assistant, friend, co-worker, contributor, backer.
adverse—*Syn.* contrary, unfortunate, against, opposing, unlucky, untoward, conflicting, unfavorable, calamitous. *Ant.* favorable, lucky, fortunate, good, desirable.
adversity—*Syn.* misfortune, ill-luck, calamity, distress, opposition. *Ant.* help, aid, assistance, encouragement, favor, fortune.
advice—*Syn.* counsel, guidance, instruction, suggestion, exhortation, charge, lesson, caution. *Ant.* deception, misrepresentation, falsification, delusion.
advise—*Syn.* counsel, inform, tell, apprise, acquaint, warn, instruct, suggest, show. *Ant.* lead astray, deceive, betray, trick, hoax, fool.
affable—*Syn.* easy, kindly, polite, courteous, gracious, pleasing. *Ant.* grouchy, impolite, haughty, arrogant, surly.
affection—*Syn.* love, friendship, goodwill, friendliness, kindness, tenderness. *Ant.* dislike, hatred, enmity, unkindness, discouragement.
affectionate—*Syn.* caring, solicitous, tender, fond, warm. *Ant.* unkind, careless, neglectful, morose, cold, antagonistic.
affront—*Syn.* insult, annoy, vex, taunt, provoke, exasperate, offend, displease, reproach. *Ant.* placate, conciliate, appease, mollify, assuage.
afraid—*Syn.* timid, scared, alarmed, frightened, terrified, fearful, timorous, faint-hearted, anxious. *Ant.* fearless, courageous, valiant, bold, brave, confident, undaunted, venturesome, audacious, collected, calm, composed, confident.
aggrandize—*Syn.* exalt, enrich, augment, advance, elevate, dignify, expand, magnify. *Ant.* humble, lower, reduce, shame, disgrace, degrade, depress, abase.
agree—*Syn.* comply, concur, approve, accept, admit, acquiesce, coincide, accord, match. *Ant.* decline, refuse, demur, disagree, dissent, oppose, differ, dispute, contradict.
agreeable—*Syn.* pleasant, pleasing, charming, inviting, ready, acceptable, suitable, consistent. *Ant.* disagreeable, unpleasant, harsh, unsuitable, offensive, contentious.
aim—*Syn.* goal, mark, object, aspiration, intention, purpose. *Ant.* aimlessness, oversight.
air—*Syn.* manner, look, appearance, style, mien, demeanor, carriage, behavior, port, way, sort, fashion, expression, bearing.
alacrity—*Syn.* speed, swiftness, briskness, quickness, readiness, liveliness, agility, promptness, alertness. *Ant.* apathy, laziness, indifference, slowness, reluctance, sluggishness, aversion, inertness.
alarm—*Syn.* terror, fright, fear, dismay, consternation, affright, disquietude, apprehension, misgiving, solicitude. *Ant.* repose, quiet, security, assurance, confidence, peace.
alert—*Syn.* active, lively, nimble, ready, brisk, wide-awake, vigilant, watchful. *Ant.* heavy, drowsy, dull, slow, sluggish, inactive, lethargic, weary.
alien, *a.*—*Syn.* strange, opposed, distant, remote, unlike, extraneous. *Ant.* alike, corresponding, appropriate, relevant, friendly.
alien, *n.*—*Syn.* foreigner, outlander, outsider, stranger. *Ant.* native, citizen.
anxiety—*Syn.* care, concern, foreboding, worry, trouble, apprehension, dread, misgiving, fear. *Ant.* ease, tranquillity, peace, contentment, calmness, apathy, assurance, satisfaction, nonchalance, indifference, unconcern.
apathy—*Syn.* unconcern, indifference, passiveness, stoicism, composure, calmness, lethargy, quietness, unfeelingness, sluggishness. *Ant.* care, emotion, passion, fury, frenzy, disturbance, distress, feeling, vehemence, violence, turbulence, sensibility, alarm, agitation, anxiety, excitement, eagerness.
apology—*Syn.* excuse, plea, defense, justification, exculpation, evasion, subterfuge, entreaty, evasion, pretext, pretense, supplication. *Ant.* accusation, charge, censure, arraignment, imputation, offense, wrong, injury, insult.
apparent—*Syn.* likely, probable, presumable, seeming, evident, obvious, clear, plain, visible. *Ant.* unlikely, indistinct, improbable, doubtful, dubious, unimaginable, wavering, uncertain, fluctuating, equivocal, ambiguous, questionable.
appeal—*Syn.* call upon, request, invoke, plead, ask, beg, beseech, entreat, supplicate, apply. *Ant.* deny, disclaim, disavow, recant, renounce, revoke, forswear.
appendage—*Syn.* appendix, supplement, addition, adjunct, appurtenance, extension, auxiliary, attachment, addendum, accompaniment. *Ant.* whole, all, entirety, bulk, mass, body.
appetite—*Syn.* craving, desire, liking, relish, longing, thirst, zest, proclivity, propensity. *Ant.* aversion, distaste, repulsion, revulsion, detestation, disgust, repugnance, anorexia.
appropriate, *v.*—*Syn.* take, arrogate, usurp, seize. *Ant.* give, bestow, set aside, return, abandon.
appropriate, *a.*—*Syn.* fitting, suitable, becoming, proper, meet, fit,

apt, applicable, opportune. *Ant.* unfitting, unsuitable, improper, contrary.
argue—*Syn.* dispute, debate, differ, discuss, reason, contest, battle, wrangle. *Ant.* ignore, overlook, scorn, despise, repudiate, reject, pass by.
arraign—*Syn.* charge, cite, censure, summon. *Ant.* discharge, exonerate, overlook, release, excuse, condone, pardon.
arrange—*Syn.* adjust, assort, classify, group, set, sort, marshal, array. *Ant.* disorder, scatter, jumble, disarrange, disturb.
artifice—*Syn.* ruse, stratagem, trick, wile, maneuver, contrivance, invention, subterfuge, fraud, cunning, finesse, blind. *Ant.* innocence, candor, honesty, sincerity, truth, fairness, artlessness, guilelessness, simplicity.
ask—*Syn.* entreat, demand, solicit, supplicate, request, petition. *Ant.* refuse, repudiate, deny.
associate, *v.*—*Syn.* ally, combine, link, unite, connect, affiliate. *Ant.* part, separate, sever, divide, dissociate.
associate, *n.*—*Syn.* companion, comrade, helpmate, partner, auxiliary, colleague, consort, ally, accomplice. *Ant.* opponent, rival, enemy.
association—*Syn.* lodge, club, combination, company, partnership, confederation, connection, community, alliance. *Ant.* separation, disintergration, rupture, division.
assurance—*Syn.* self-reliance, self-confidence, trust, assumption, assertion. *Ant.* distrust, misgiving, timidity, hesitancy, shyness, consternation.
astute—*Syn.* clever, smart, intelligent, crafty, cunning, shrewd, sagacious, keen, discerning, sharp, knowing. —*Syn.* shallow, shortsighted, dull, obtuse, noncomprehensive, unintelligent, stolid.
attach—*Syn.* fasten, secure, stick, fix, unite, join, connect, append. *Ant.* sever, separate, detach, cut.
attachment—*Syn.* friendship, esteem, respect, regard, affection, adhesion. *Ant.* aversion, opposition, separation, detachment, severance, distance.
attack, *v.*—*Syn.* assil, assault, encounter, combat, besiege, storm, invade, charge, encroach, infringe, seize, violate. *Ant.* protect, defend, cover, uphold, resist, shield, withstand.
attack, *n.*—*Syn.* invasion, assault, aggression, intrusion, trespass, infringement, inroad, charge. *Ant.* defense, repulsion, resistance, submission.
attain—*Syn.* get, gain, obtain, win, secure, achieve, procure, acquire, reach, accomplish. *Ant.* give up, let go, surrender, discard, forfeit, lose, miss, fail.
audacity—*Syn.* boldness, effrontery, presumption, arrogance, assurance, brazenness. *Ant.* meekness, mildness, humility, gentility, yielding.
austere—*Syn.* rigid, rigorous, severe, stern, harsh, unrelenting, keen, strict, exacting. *Ant.* mild, meek, gentle, kind, encouraging, bland, placid, soft, quiet, peaceful, soothing, indulgent.
authentic—*Syn.* real, genuine, reliable, trustworthy, certain, accepted, legitimate, authoritative, sure. *Ant.* spurious, false, fictitious, conterfeit.
auxiliary—*Syn.* helper, aid, assistant, confederate, accomplice, associate, companion. *Ant.* opponent, opposer, competitor, rival.
avaricious—*Syn.* miserly, parsimonious, niggardly, penurious, sordid, stingy, greedy, close. *Ant.* generous, liberal, free, bountiful, munificent.
aversion—*Syn.* antipathy, dislike, opposition, hatred, repugnance, detestation, abhorrence. *Ant.* love, affection, care, solicitude, fondness, kindness, tenderness.
avow—*Syn.* own, acknowledge, profess, testify, aver, declare, proclaim, witness, confess, declare. *Ant.* disown, disclaim, repudiate, renounce, deny, contradict, ignore.
awe—*Syn.* dread, fear, reverence, respect, veneration. *Ant.* familiarity, fellowship, friendship, buoyancy, enthusiasm, coolness, steadiness.
awkward—*Syn.* ungainly, gawky, clumsy. *Ant.* adroit, clever, handy, apt.
axiom—*Syn.* maxim, proverb, aphorism, byword, saying, motto. *Ant.* absurdity, paradox, sophism, blunder.

B

bad—*Syn.* evil, vile, wrong, corrupt, ill, vicious, abominable. *Ant.* good, true, honest, sincere, right, valid.
baffle—*Syn.* confound, outfit, foil, elude. *Ant.* abet, help, support, succor, cooperate.
barbarous—*Syn.* savage, barbaric, uncivilized, cruel, tyrannical, brutal, untamed. *Ant.* civilized, humane, cultured, refined, gentle.
barrier—*Syn.* bulwark, obstacle, rampart, obstruction, prohibition, barricade, restraint. *Ant.* entrance, opening, road, way, transit.
base—*Syn.* mean, corrupt, low, vulgar, contemptible, dishonorable, worthless. *Ant.* noble, superior, exalted, illustrious.
battle—*Syn.* conflict, fight, combat, skirmish, strife. *Ant.* truce, suspension, harmony, agreement.
bear—*Syn.* convey, transport, support, sustain, endure, maintain, yield, produce. *Ant.* evade, dodge, shun, avoid, refuse, cast aside.
beastly—*Syn.* brutal, cruel, brutish, coarse, carnal, vile. *Ant.* lofty, superior, pure, chaste, magnanimous, generous, exalted.
beat—*Syn.* strike, batter, bruise, crush, thrash, chastise, hit, defeat. *Ant.* defend, protect, guard, shield, aid, assist, succor, submit, fail, give up, surrender, relinquish, cede.
beautiful—*Syn.* pretty, lovely, elegant, attractive, captivating. *Ant.* ugly, homely, offensive, repulsive, revolting, unattractive.
beg—*Syn.* implore, ask, supplicate, entreat, crave, solicit, petition. *Ant.* give, bestow, grant, favor.
beginning—*Syn.* origin, source, start, commencement, inception, opening, outset. *Ant.* finish, completion, goal, consummation, conclusion, result, expiration.
behavior—*Syn.* manners, bearing, breeding, conduct, demeanor, action, bearing, attitude, management, tactics, policy, strategy.
beneficent—*Syn.* generous, liberal, kind, charitable, benevolent. *Ant.* miserly, grasping, uncharitable, close-fisted, greedy.
benefit—*Syn.* advantage, kindness, utility, profit. *Ant.* injury, harm, hurt, obstacle.
benevolence—*Syn.* beneficence, benignity, humanity, kindness, charity, generosity. *Ant.* malevolence, envy, malignity, selfishness, unkindness, inhumanity.
bind—*Syn.* chain, band, gird, tie, fasten, hitch, secure, moor, restrain, tether. *Ant.* loose, untie, free, unfasten.
blame—*Syn.* censure, reprove, reproach, unbraid, condemn, accuse. *Ant.* praise, laud, boost, commend, applaud.
bleak—*Syn.* bare, chill, unsheltered, dismal, gloomy, dreary, desolate, exposed. *Ant.* cheerful, pleasant, comforting, bright, balmy, appealing.
blemish—*Syn.* flaw, fleck, spot, stain, mark, defect, fault, smirch, dent, deformity, tarnish. *Ant.* adornment, embellishment, decoration, purity.
blind—*Syn.* sightless, careless, heedless, obtuse. *Ant.* cunning, farsighted, penetrative, quick, keen.
blot—*Syn.* smudge, stain, smirch, darken, foul, blotch, erase, efface, obliterate, delete, destroy. *Ant.* cleanse, purify, restore, record, enter, retain, keep, note.
blow—*Syn.* box, stroke, rap, knock, lash, hit, calamity, disaster, misfortune. *Ant.* caress, embrace, clasp, smile, salute, hug, kindness.
bluff—*Syn.* rough, bold, brazen, impolite, inconsiderate, rude, discourteous, blustering, coarse, outspoken, frank. *Ant.* polite, refined, courteous, genial, kindly, bland, pleasant.
body—*Syn.* frame, trunk, system, carcass, form, organism, stem.
body—*Syn.* mass, collection, assemblage, association, organization, corporation, whole, all, density, opacity. *Ant.* nothing, unreality ethereality, concept, immateriality, imponderability.
bold—*Syn.* brave, courageous, dermined, intrepid, daring, valiant, confident, pert. *Ant.* timid, gentle, shy, reticent, silent, quiet, unobtrusive.
border—*Syn.* brim, brink, edge, margin, rim, verge, boundary, confine, frontier, limit. *Ant.* center, inside, territory.
bound, *v.*—*Syn.* circumscribe, limit, define, measure, confine, restrain, leap, jump, spring. *Ant.* widen, extend, liberate, free, stand.
bound, *a.*—*Syn.* confined, tied, trussed, restrained, obliged, compelled. *Ant.* free, loose, untied, unrestricted.
boundary—*Syn.* limit, border, brink, confines, margin, enclosure, edge, line, barrier, landmark. *Ant.* inside, interior, center, middle, beginning.
brave—*Syn.* fearless, gallant, heroic, valiant, bold, courageous, unafraid, daring, intrepid, firm. *Ant.* cowardly, skulking, timid, fearful, afraid.
brave, *v.*—*Syn.* confront, challenge, defy, dare, object, reject, scorn, command. *Ant.* run, renounce, hide, dodge skip, implore, grovel, whine.
bravery—*Syn.* courage, temerity, valor, daring, boldness. *Ant.* cowardice, timidity, weakness, dismay.
break—*Syn.* smash, shatter, split, burst, rupture, batter, tear, curb. *Ant.* mend, join, bind, attach, adhere.
bright—*Syn.* brilliant, shining, gleaming, glowing, luminous, radiant, sunny, shiny, glittering, glossy, sparkling, dazzling, burning, twinkling. *Ant.* dark, gloomy, threatening, cloudy, shady, obscure, dull, murky, swart, dim, opaque, shadowy, dismal, sombre, depressing, dreary, doleful, horrid, dreadful, indistinct, overcast, faded, tarnished.
brim—*Syn.* edge, verge, rim, lip, border, top, brink, margin, line. *Ant.* center, interior, foot, base, side.
bring—*Syn.* carry, bear, convey, induce, cause, move, transmit, transport. *Ant.* leave, relinquish, refuse, abandon, drop, desist.
brittle—*Syn.* fragile, weak, delicate, frail, breakable. *Ant.* strong, tough, unbreakable, resistible, enduring.
broad—*Syn.* wide, large, extensive, ample, open, clear, comprehensive. *Ant.* narrow, short, abbreviated. conservative, close.
broken—*Syn.* separated, parted, severed, rocky, unsettled, tamed, reduced, wretched, crushed. *Ant.* smooth, easy, joined, united, staid, steady, untamed, honored.
brutish—*Syn.* brutal, coarse, beastly, savage, barbarous, cruel, tyrannical, revolting, vile, depraved, stolid. *Ant.* kind, considerate, humane, gentle, mild.
build—*Syn.* erect, construct, raise, frame, establish, make, manufacture. *Ant.* destroy, demolish, raze, dismantle, overthrow.
burn—*Syn.* consume, ignite, char, singe, kindle, scorch. *Ant.* cool, smother, subdue, extinguish, stifle.
business—*Syn.* occupation, profession, duty, work, transaction, trade, barter, vocation, craft, concern, trading. *Ant.* sloth, passivity, inertness, inactivity, non-employment.
bustle—*Syn.* hurry, action, haste, flurry, fuss, tumult, stir. *Ant.* slowness, inertia, inaction, sluggishness, quiet repose.
butcher—*Syn.* kill, slay, destroy, maim, massacre, slaughter, mangle, tear, slice, mutilate. *Ant.* preserve, guard, tend, nourish, nurture, heal, cure, repair, mend, revive.
buy—*Syn.* purchase, procure, acquire, obtain, secure, negotiate, bribe, influence, corrupt, pervert.

C

cabal—*Syn.* gang, combine, combination, confederacy, conspiracy, conclave.
calamity—*Syn.* misfortune, mishap, distress, misery, adversity, trouble, grief, sadness, tribulation, trial. —*Syn.* benefit, happiness, joy, rejoicing.
calculate—*Syn.* estimate, enumerate, consider, deem, number, account, count, compute.
call—*Syn.* exclaim, bellow, yell, roar, clamor, shriek, command, summon, designate. *Ant.* list, listen, refrain, suppress, restrain, stifle.
callous—*Syn.* unfeeling, indifferent, insensible, obdurate, hard. *Ant.* feeling, compassionate, tender, soft, indulgent.
calm—*Syn.* cool, collected, quiet, reserved, unruffled, serene, tranquil, dispassionate, gentle, smooth. *Ant.* rough, boisterous, excited, agitated, inflamed, angry, fierce, furious, roused, stormy, wild, turbulent.
calumny—*Syn.* slander, defamation, libel, detraction, lying, aspersion, distortion, scandal. *Ant.* charity, praise, laudation, commendation, goodwill, friendliness, kindness.
cancel—*Syn.* annul, abolish, rescind, remove, erase, abrogate, void, vacate. *Ant.* approve, uphold, sustain, record, enforce, ratify, keep, endorse.
candid—*Syn.* sincere, frank, fair, unbiased, unprejudiced, open, simple, ingenuous, straightforward. *Ant.* intriguing, shrewd, tricky, wily, designing, insincere, cunning, maneuvering, subtle, crafty.
candor—*Syn.* sincerity, fairness, openness, ingenuousness. *Ant.* deception, falsehood, partiality, unfairness, trickery, fraud.
capable—*Syn.* able, competent, qualified, suitable. *Ant.* incompetent, unqualified, unable, disqualified, inefficient.
caprice—*Syn.* freak, crotchet, whim, humor, inclination. *Ant.* steadiness, thoroughness, dependability, firmness., deliberation.
captious—*Syn.* fretful, cross, petulant, censorious, touchy, testy, irritable, critical, hypersensitive, cynical, carping. *Ant.* considerate, appreciative, approving, encouraging, commendatory, complimentary, laudatory, thoughtful.
captivate—*Syn.* enchant, charm, bewitch, fascinate, entrance, capture, subdue. *Ant.* hate, disillusion, offend, displease.
captivity—*Syn.* confinement, servitude, slavery, imprisonment, subjection. *Ant.* freedom, liberty, independence.
care—*Syn.* concern, attention, heed, solicitude, anxiety, caution, vigilance, worry, management, charge, bother. *Ant.* carelessness, neglect, disregard, omission, slight, indifference.
career—*Syn.* life, progress, course, way, pursuit, walk, line, experience, occupation, vocation. *Ant.* inactivity, idleness, torpor, inertia, sloth, stupor, ergophobia, indolence, lethargy.
careless—*Syn.* heedless, inattentive, negligent, thoughtless, unconcerned, incautious, imprudent, improvident. *Ant.* careful, mindful, thoughtful.
caress—*Syn.* pamper, fondle, embrace, cuddle, flatter, hug. *Ant.* neglect, buffet, beat, strike, lash, scourge, irritate, annoy, displease, aggravate.
caricature—*Syn.* exaggeration, parody, travesty, imitation, copy, mimicry,ridicule. *Ant.* truth, fact, reality, exactness, accuracy, precision.
carnival—*Syn.* festivity, feasting, revel, merrymaking, rout.
carousal—*Syn.* revelry, orgy, spree, debauch, carnival. *Ant.* austerity, sobriety, temperance, abstinence.
carriage—*Syn.* walk, pace, gait, manner, deportment, demeanor, behavior, bearing.
carry—*Syn.* transport, bear, convey, take, move, transmit, bring, lift, sustain, support. *Ant.* throw off, cast off, shake off, let go, drop.
caste—*Syn.* rank, class, race, blood, lineage, order, descent, ancestry.
catastrophe—*Syn.* calamity, misfortune, disaster, mishap, revolution, blow, affliction, cata-clysm, reverse. *Ant.* blessing, bene-fit, favor, prosperity, comfort, suc-cess, privilege, boon, pleasure, hap-piness.
catch—*Syn.* grasp, clasp, capture, seize, take, grip, clutch, secure, apprehend, comprehend, entrap, ensnare, discover. *Ant.* lose, miss, fail, restore, release.
cause—*Syn.* agent, source, origin, spring, fountain, object, purpose, reason, inducement, condition, power, precedent, motive, occasion. *Ant.* effect, result, outcome, development, consequence, end, issue, product.
caution—*Syn.* care, heed, vigilance, prudence, watchfulness, warning, reason, injunction, precept, advice, exhortation, notice. *Ant.* neglect, imprudence, carelessness, thoughtlessness, rashness.
cautious—*Syn.* watchful, circumspect, careful, prudent, attentive, thoughtful. *Ant.* impetuous, rash, headstrong, hasty, heedless, unwary, inattentive.
cavity—*Syn.* hole, cavern, ravine, depth, cave, depression, excavation, chasm, opening, cleft, breach, burrow, bore, aperture, gap, indentation, perforation, dent, gorge, mine, shaft. *Ant.* mound, hill, hillock, peak, knoll, height, prominence, projection, rising, elevation, proturberance.
cease—*Syn.* stop, quit, terminate, finish, end, conclude, refrain, desist, discontinue, withdraw, pause. *Ant.* begin, start, commence, initiate, institute, inaugurate, originate, continue.
celebrate—*Syn.* observe, commemorate, praise, extol, glorify, honor. *Ant.* overlook, neglect, disregard, ignore.
celebration—*Syn.* commemoration, observance, glorification, festivity, gaiety, frolic, hilarity, mirth. *Ant.* sadness, solemnity, sorrow, grief, mourning, lamentation, melancholy, depression.
celebrity—*Syn.* fame, honor, glory, renown, notoriety, distinction, reputation. *Ant.* dishonor, discredit, ignominy, opprobrium, censure.
censure, *v.*—*Syn.* criticize, judge, blame, reprove, reprimand, upbraid, denounce, condemn. *Ant.* praise, laud, commend, sanction, promote, admire.
certain—*Syn.* sure, indubitable, incontrovertible, undeniable, unfailing, secure, reliable, real, true, genuine. *Ant.* uncertain, unreliable, wavering, doubtful, dubious, questionable, vague, obscure.
certify—*Syn.* declare, testify, assure, inform, demonstrate, attest, prove, aver, acknowledge, state, proclaim. *Ant.* deny, deprecate, repudiate, disavow.
cessation—*Syn.* intermission, stop, discontinuance, halt, armistice. *Ant.* continuance, prolongation, advancement, extension, perpetuation, continuity.
chagrin—*Syn.* vexation, mortification, shame, humiliation, dismay, disappointment, confusion, discomposure. *Ant.* delight, triumph, glorification, rapture, exultation, rejoicing, gladness.
chance—*Syn.* fate, fortune, hazard, risk, casualty, luck, random, venture. *Ant.* design, certainty, intention, aim, purpose, plan, scheme, assurance, stability.
change, *n.*—*Syn.* alteration, mutation, variety, transformation, modification, transition, vicissitude, deviation, conversion. *Ant.* firmness, permanency, constancy, steadiness, stability, certainty, durability.
change, *v.*—*Syn.* barter, exchange, substitute, vary, alter, turn, veer, shift, diversify, innovate, convert, commute, transform. *Ant.* hold, keep, stay, remain, retain, wait, tarry, bide, persist, dwell.
character—*Syn.* personality, disposition, reputation, constitution, temperament, nature, spirit, repute, estimation, record, standing, species, symbol, mark, letter, type.
characteristic—*Syn.* personality, peculiarity, singularity, diagnosis, distinction, individuality, manners, bearing, attitude, specialty, trait, mark, attribute, feature, property, quality, sign, trace, mark, indication, character.
charm—*Syn.* captivate, enchant, fascinate, attract, bewitch, allure, delight, please, control. *Ant.* frighten, repulse, repel, offend, provoke.
charming—*Syn.* bewitching, captivating, fascinating, delightful, winning, ravishing, irresistible, attractive, alluring, pleasing. *Ant.* disgusting, repellent, repugnant, horrid, forbidding, deterrent, awful, shocking, offensive, unpleasant, disagreeable.
chaste—*Syn.* pure, virtuous, undefiled, innocent, immaculate, unstained, uncontaminated, unaffected, uncorrupted, unsullied, unblemished. *Ant.* unchaste, lewd, lascivious, libidinous, lustful, corrupt, defiled, sullied, licentious, dissolute, profligate, voluptuous.
chasten—*Syn.* humble, subdue, chastise, punish, correct. *Ant.* encourage, uplift, help, assist, incite, inspirit, animate, cheer, stimulate, impel, comfort.
cheap—*Syn.* inexpensive, common, low-priced, mean, worthless, petty, shabby, valueless, paltry. *Ant.* dear, costly, valuable, expensive, worthy.
check—*Syn.* curb, repress, hinder, impede, repress, restrain, moderate, control, obstruct, reduce. *Ant.* abet, assist, help, encourage, expedite, accelerate, allow, loosen, indulge, instigate.
cheer—*Syn.* festivity, gaiety, mirth, comfort, happiness, hope, liveliness, fun, frolic, hilarity. *Ant.* gloom, sadness, depression, heaviness, seriousness, gravity.
cheerful—*Syn.* gay, sprightly, buoyant, spirited, joyous, lively, happy, joyful. *Ant.* dull, weary, sad, gloomy, melancholy, mournful, sorrowful, heavy.
cheerfulness—*Syn.* jollity, liveliness, gaiety, gladness, happiness. *Ant.* anxiety, sorrow, discontent, melancholy, gloom, sadness.
cherish—*Syn.* indulge, nurse, nurture, foster, encourage, shelter, harbor, protect, value. *Ant.* abandon, renounce, desert, forsake, repudiate, cast off, denounce, scold, upbraid, discard.
chief—*Syn.* principal, leader, head, ruler, king, commander, master. *Ant.* subordinate, retainer, minion, vassal, underling, follower, adherent.
childish—*Syn.* childlike, simple, silly, foolish, infantile, paltry, petty, ludicrous. *Ant.* wise, timely, appropriate, proper, sophisticated.
choose—*Syn.* pick, select, cull, prefer, elect, adopt, collect, remove, arrange. —*Syn.* discard, reject, refuse, dismiss, repudiate, decline, leave.
circumlocution—*Syn.* verbiage, redundancy, diffuseness, surplus, verbosity, tediousness. *Ant.* conciseness, terseness, condensation, compression, directness, brevity, succinctness.
circumstance—*Syn.* fact, incident, occurrence, situation, accompaniment, event, item, detail, point, position.
cite—*Syn.* call, name, summon, quote, mention, arraign, convoke, invite, nofify, warn. *Ant.* ignore, neglect, disregard.
class—*Syn.* degree, order, rank, standing, grade, caste, set, clan, division, category, kind, group, association, club, company, tribe.
clean—*Syn.* pure, unmixed, purified, spotless. *Ant.* dirty, impure, stained.
cleanse—*Syn.* clean, purify, wash, mop, brush, sponge. *Ant.* soil, defile, pollute, taint, stain, besmirch, debase, corrupt, deprave, contaminate, spoil.
clear—*Syn.* vivid, lucid, pure, transparent, apparent, plain, unmistakable, unequivocal, obvious, evident, free, distinct, explicit, definite, straightforward. *Ant.* opaque, dark, obscure, shaded, shadowy, muddy, dim, gloomy, cloudy, amgiguous, vague, indistinct.
clever—*Syn.* able, adroit, skillful, apt, bright, capable, smart, talented, ingenious, sharp, intelligent, keen, quick. *Ant.* dull, stupid, slow, perverse, bungling, clumsy, awkward.
cloister—*Syn.* monastery, priory, convent, nunnery, abbey, seclusion, retirement, isolation, meditation, solitude.

clothes—*Syn.* rainment, clothing, garments, garb, vesture, dress, attire, apparel.
coalition—*Syn.* alliance, confederacy, union, compact. *Ant* separation, disagreement, difference, contrariety.
coax—*Syn.* flatter, appeal, persuade, cajole, entice, fawn. *Ant.* scorn, jeer, sneer, deride, ridicule, reproach, taunt, delude, impel, flout, insult.
cold—*Syn.* frigid, wintry, cool, frosty, bleak, indifferent, unconcerned, stoical, distant, unfeeling, forbidding, apathetic, lifeless. *Ant.* warm, glowing, fiery, ardent, hot, fervid, enthusiastic, zealous, eager, interested, affectionate, excited.
colleague—*Syn.* partner, associate, companion, ally, contributor. *Ant.* opponent, antagonist, foe, enemy, detractor.
collect—*Syn.* obtain, get, gather, accumulate, assemble, amass, congregate, convene, aggregate, summon, reap, gain. *Ant.* scatter, disperse, dissipate, strew, throw away, divide, disseminate, dispel, dispense.
collision—*Syn.* clash, contact, shock, encounter, meeting, concussion, conflict. *Ant.* concurrence, agreement, harmony, conformity, union, concert, coincidence, opposition.
color, *n.*—*Syn.* stain, tint, tinge, pigment, paint, hue, shade, tincture.
color, *v.*—*Syn.* paint, tinge, tint, stain, dye, flush, blush, redden.
combination—*Syn.* union, association, alliance, league, cabal, plot, party. *Ant.* separation, division, severance, detachment, partition.
comely—*Syn.* handsome, pretty, seemly, pleasing, graceful, prepossessing, agreeable, beautiful. *Ant.* offensive, plain, unattractive, uninviting.
comfort—*Syn.* consulation, solace, encouragement, support, help, assistance, succor, relief. *Ant.* aggravation, annoyance, trouble, grief.
comfortable—*Syn.* genial, satisfied, satisfactory, warm, commodious, convenient, agreeable, cozy. *Ant.* uncomfortable, neglected.
command—*Syn.* order, decree, precept, mandate, power, authority, charge. *Ant.* countermand, revocation, contradiction, opposition, recall, reversal, entreaty, supplication.
commit—*Syn.* entrust, confide, relegate, delegate, assign, consign, enact, perpetrate, act, transact, perform, discharge. *Ant.* stop, cease, be inactive, stand still, rest.
commodious—*Syn.* suitable, comfortable, roomy, convenient, accomodating. *Ant.* unsuitable, uncomfortable, inconvenient, cramped, confined.
commodity—*Syn.* articles, merchandise, wares, stock, materials, possessions, property, chattels, assets, belongings.
common—*Syn.* ordinary, customary, usual, frequent, low, mean, vulgar, depraved. —*Syn.* rare, unusual, scarce, superior, refined, cultured, uncommon.
commotion—*Syn.* excitement, agitation, tumult, turmoil, disturbance, emotion. *Ant.* calm, quiet, peace, tranquility, placidity, stillness.
communicate—*Syn.* write, convey, announce, state, publish, divulge, disclose, reveal, enlighten. *Ant.* conceal, suppress, withhold, cloak, cover, reserve.
communion—*Syn.* fellowship, agreement, concord, union, brotherhood, harmony, friendship, association, relationship, bond. *Ant.* separation, division, antagonism, enmity, disagreement.
companion—*Syn.* associate, friend, comrade, consort, fellow, follower. *Ant.* stranger, antagonist, outsider, rival.
company—*Syn.* assembly, assemblage, meeting, congregation, convention, collection, group. *Ant.* loneliness, seclusion, solitude, privacy, dispersion, diffusion, dissemination.
compassion—*Syn.* sympathy, pity, clemency, kindness, commiseration. *Ant.* cruelty, severity, persecution.
compel—*Syn.* force, enforce, coerce, necessitate, oblige, constrain, drive, make, influence. *Ant.* thwart, resist, retard, prevent, impede, interrupt, obstruct, block, check, counteract, embarrass, delay, prolong, oppose, encumber, defer, foil.
compensation—*Syn.* remuneration, recompense, satisfaction, amends, reward, gain. *Ant.* loss, deprivation.
complain—*Syn.* lament, murmur, grunt, bemoan, bewail, deplore. *Ant.* praise, laud, commend, approve, applaud, confirm.
complete—*Syn.* execute, consummate, accomplish, terminate, finish, conclude, end, effect, realize, achieve. *Ant.* leave, halt, abandon, withdraw, begin.
complex—*Syn.* involved, complicated, intricate, tangled, compound. *Ant.* easy, simple, plain, clear, obvious, direct, apparent.
compliment—*Syn.* laud, praise, sanction, endorse, confirm, gratify. *Ant.* disparage, criticize, censure, blame, denounce, reproach.
comply—*Syn.* accede, conform, yield, concur, agree, assent. *Ant.* refuse, reject, repell, rebuff.
compose—*Syn.* form, make, fashion, formulate, arrange, construct. *Ant.* break, scatter, destroy, ruin, disarrange, disperse, agitate, rouse, taunt, annoy, disturb.
compound, *a.*—*Syn.* complex, mixed, combined, composite. *Ant.* simple, elemental, plain.
comprehend—*Syn.* embrace, grasp, understand, perceive, encompass, contain, involve, conceive. *Ant.* exclude, misunderstand, misinterpret, miscalculate, except.
comprise—*Syn.* contain, embrace, include, imply, involve. *Ant.* lack, want, fail, exclude, except, reject.
compromise—*Syn.* adjustment, arrangement, conciliation, arbitration, concession, accommodation. *Ant.* disagreement, altercation, strife, dissension, controversy, contention.
compulsion—*Syn.* constraint, force, coercion. *Ant.* freedom, liberty, entreaty, craving, appeal.
conceal—*Syn.* hide, secrete, screen, cover, bury, disguise, mask. *Ant.* uncover, open, reveal, expose, strip, show, disclose, divulge, impart.
concede—*Syn.* assent, yield, permit, grant, allow, surrender, admit, acknowledge. *Ant.* deny, refuse, disallow, dissent, reject.
conclusion—*Syn.* result, end, consequence, decision, resolution. *Ant.* preface, beginning, prelude, preamble, introduction, origin, start.
concur—*Syn.* agree, join, unite, approve, endorse, certify, approve. *Ant.* disagree, differ, disapprove, dissent, object, oppose.
condemn—*Syn.* convict, doom, denounce, blame, reprove. *Ant.* approve, praise, justify, exonerate, laud, applaud, release, discharge.
conduct, *v.*—*Syn.* direct, guide, lead, govern, regulate, manage, behave, act. *Ant.* desert, abandon, forsake, resign, refuse, leave, quit, relinquish, forswear, abjure, discontinue, retire (from), renounce, forego.
confess—*Syn.* concede, disclose, acknowledge, admit, allow, avow. *Ant.* dissemble, hide, screen, conceal, cover, cloak, deny, repudiate, disavow, veil.
confirm—*Syn.* prove, corroborate, approve, attest, ratify, assure, sustain, uphold, support, affirm, substantiate. *Ant.* upset, annul, cancel, void, abrogate, contradict, oppose, deny.
conflict—*Syn.* combat, contest, contention, struggle, battle, fight. *Ant.* peace, tranquility, calm, harmony, concord.
conquer—*Syn.* subdue, overcome, defeat, overthrow, overpower, subjugate, vanquish, rout, humble, mount. *Ant.* yield, succumb, surrender, forfeit, retreat, lose, fail, cede, capitulate.
conscious—*Syn.* aware, cognizant, informed, certain, apprised, assured, felt, advised. *Ant.* unconscious, unaware, ingnorant, cold, indifferent, unfeeling, dead.
consent—*Syn.* agree, compliance, accord, ratification, approval, indorsement, affirmation, aggreement. *Ant.* dissent, refusal, noncompliance, disagreement, objection.
consent, *v.*—*Syn.* accede, agree, assent, comply, permit, approve, acquiesce, concur. *Ant.* refuse, disagree, withdraw, dissent, differ, stop, demur, object.
consequence—*Syn.* effect, result, outgrowth, upshot, outcome. *Ant.* origin, beginning, start.
consider—*Syn.* ponder, examine, contemplate, regard, reflect, deliberate. *Ant.* dismiss, ignore, pass, neglect, abandon, leave.
considerate—*Syn.* kind, charitable, thoughtful, prudent, cautious, unselfish. *Ant.* unkind, uncharitable, harsh, mean, overbearing, selfish, imperious.
consideration—*Syn.* attention, kindness, friendliness, motive, heed, caution. *Ant.* disregard, thoughtlessness, negligence, heedlessness.
consistent—*Syn.* according, equable, uniform, same. *Ant.* inconsistent, varying, incongruous.
console—*Syn.* comfort, ease, sympathize, encourage, gladden, support. *Ant.* depress, sadden, grieve, trouble, discourage, dishearten.
consolidate—*Syn.* unite, combine, compact, condense, compress. *Ant.* sever, separate, part, divide.
conspicuous—*Syn* visible, outstanding, distinguished, noted, illustrious, prominent, well-known. *Ant.* hidden, concealed, unseen, secret, covered, obscure, unknown.
consternation—*Syn.* dismay, fear, wonder, surprise, astonishment, amazement. *Ant.* tranquility, peace, quiet, calm, repose, stillness, rest.
constrain—*Syn.* prevent, urge, drive, restrain, press, repress. *Ant.* ask, request, beg, implore, coax.
construct—*Syn.* erect, build, form, compose, fabricate, invent, create, produce. *Ant.* demolish, destroy, break, burst, raze, ruin.
consume—*Syn.* absorb, expend, squander, spend, imbibe, swallow. *Ant.* hoard, accumulate, collect, gather, store, amass.
contaminate—*Syn.* corrupt, pollute, infect, taint, tarnish, vitiate, debase, spoil, defile. *Ant.* improve, better, ameliorate, freshen, ennoble, heal, cure.
contemplate—*Syn.* consider, study, ponder, muse, design. *Ant.* disregard, discard, disdain, scorn.
contempt—*Syn.* disdain, scorn, derision, mockery, disregard, disrespect, slight, slur. *Ant.* regard, respect, praise, approval, honor.
contemptible—*Syn.* vile, despicable, base, mean, worthless. *Ant.* good, worthy, respectable, decent, honorable, admired, loved, obliging.
contend—*Syn.* compete, contest, battle, fight, struggle, combat, cope. *Ant.* cede, cease, stop, halt, desist.
contention—*Syn.* contest, struggle, quarrel, conflict, feud, enmity, competition, disagreement, discord. *Ant.* affection, regard, amity, consideration, kindness.
contest, *v.*—*Syn.* dispute, debate, object, oppose, tackle, contend, fight, battle, struggle, strain, strive. *Ant.* cease, abandon, retire, forsake, resign, relinquish.
contest, *n.*—*Syn.* conflict, battle, engagement, altercation, controversy, dispute, feud, competition. *Ant.* peace, quiet, quietness, calm, stillness.
continual—*Syn.* constant, continuous, incessant, unvarying, regular, unbroken, ceaseless, unremitting. *Ant.* intermittent, broken, interrupted, periodic.
continue—*Syn.* persist, persevere, proceed, advance, keep going, go on. *Ant.* stop, halt, cease, desist, end, interrupt.
contract—*Syn.* convenant, agreement, compact, stipulation, engagement, obligation, guarantee, pledge, cartel, bargain, pact.
contradict—*Syn.* deny, impugn, correct, deny, disclaim, check, denounce. *Ant.* agree, acquiesce, indorse, confirm, approve, verify, sanction, support.
contrary—*Syn.* opposite, dissimilar, opposed, conflicting, contradictory. *Ant.* similar, agreeing, harmonious, resembling, alike, obliging.
contrast, *v.*—*Syn.* differentiate, compare, oppose, discriminate, distinguish. *Ant.* coincide, concur, accord, be identical, be equal.
contribute—*Syn* give, cooperate, assist, supply, help, aid, furnish. *Ant.* ignore, neglect, shun, withhold, oppose.

contrive—*Syn.* invent, make, form, plan, design, plot.
control, *v.*—*Syn.* restrain, hold, rule, govern, direct, guide, check, coerce. *Ant.* let go, abandon, give up, resign, relinquish, leave, quit.
controversy—*Syn.* argument, dispute, quarrel, bickering, wrangling. *Ant.* peace, restraint, patience, accord.
convenient—*Syn.* ready, handy, suited. *Ant.* unsuitable, of-the-way, unavailable, inconvenient.
conventional—*Syn.* customary, usual, ordinary. *Ant.* unconventional, informal, strange, irregular, unusual.
convert, *v.*—*Syn.* turn (from), change, transform, transmute, transfigure, modify. *Ant.* endure, maintain, remain, persist, hold.
convey—*Syn.* carry, move, transport, transmit, give, bear. *Ant.* hold, keep, retain.
cool—*Syn.* frigid, shivery, fresh, indifferent, unfeeling, apathetic, distant, irresponsive, cold. *Ant.* hot, warm, glowing, torrid, sultry, kind, feeling.
cooperate—*Syn.* assist, help, plan, work together, relieve, befriend, succor, second, approve, promote. *Ant.* hinder, obstruct, impede, prevent.
corpulent—*Syn.* fat, obese, stout, swollen. *Ant.* thin, lean, delicate, weak.
correct—*Syn.* chastise, beat, punish, castigate, reform, improve, amend, rectify. *Ant.* pamper, indulge, cherish, soften, spoil, wrong, incorrect.
corrupt, *a.*—*Syn.* base, low, mean, contemptible, debased, impure, infected, rotten, tainted, unsound. *Ant.* clean, pure, wholesome, sound, pure, decent, honorable.
corrupt, *v.*—*Syn.* debase, vitiate, falsify, degrade, taint, contaminate, tarnish, stain, defile, pollute, spoil. *Ant.* ennoble, elevate, improve, better, raise, cleanse, refine.
corruption—*Syn.* putridity, rotten, putrefaction, decay, meanness, depravity, wickedness. *Ant.* clean, purity, virtue, upright, innocence, integrity, honesty.
counsel, *n.*—*Syn.* advice, suggestion, recommendation, warning, instruction, admonition, guidance, lawyer, barrister, adviser.
courage—*Syn.* bravery, valor, boldness, intrepidity, fearlessness, firmness, fortitude, gallantry. *Ant.* cowardice, dastardliness, poltroonery, timidity, pusillanimity, weakness.
courteous—*Syn.* polite, obliging, mannerly, urbane, affable, agreeable, conciliating, attentive. *Ant.* impolite, discourteous, rude, rough, unmannerly, overbearing, uncivil.
covetousness—*Syn.* avarice, cupidity. *Ant.* beneficence, liberality, benevolence.
crime—*Syn.* sin, outrage, misdeed. *Ant.* virtue, goodness, innocence, honor.
criminal—*Syn.* vile, vicious, wicked, sinful, immoral, unlawful, wrong, illegal, felonious. *Ant.* honest, honorable, moral, unstained, faultless, immaculate, stainless, sinless, innocuous, lawful, right.
criterion—*Syn.* test, standard, rule, proof, touchstone, fact, law, principle. *Ant.* guess, conjecture, fancy, supposition, probability, chance, haphazard.
crooked—*Syn.* bent, curved, curving, winding, bowed, deformed, deceitful, criminal. *Ant.* straight, right, upright, unbent, direct, honest, respectable.
cruel—*Syn.* barbarous, brutal, inhuman, savage, ferocious, merciless, pitiless, tyrannical. *Ant.* kind, considerate, feeling, merciful, prudent, thoughtful, unselfish.
culture—*Syn.* education, learning, scholarship, manners, refinement, breeding. *Ant.* ignorance, denseness, illiteracy.
cursory—*Syn.* hasty, superficial, slight, desultory, careless. *Ant.* thorough, complete, perfect.
custom—*Syn.* fashion, habit, manner, practice, usage, wont. *Ant.* irregularity, deviation, divergence, difference.

D

dainty—*Syn.* delicate, particular, choice, refined, pure, elegant, exquisite, soft, tender, pleasing. *Ant.* bitter, tasteless, clumsy, unpleasant, coarse, harsh.
damage—*Syn.* harm, injury, detriment, loss, hurt. *Ant.* benefit, advantage, emolument, reward, recompense, award, boon, profit, favor, improve.
danger—*Syn.* peril, jeopardy, hazard, risk, chance. *Ant.* safety, security, certainty, confidence.
daring—*Syn.* bold, brave, adventurous, courageous, fearless, intrepid. *Ant.* modest, shy, timid, afraid, cowardly.
dark—*Syn.* obscure, dismal, murky, shadowy, somber, black, dusky, mysterious. *Ant.* light, clear, vivid, bright, visible, lucid, apparent, distinct, luminous, shining, radiant.
daunt—*Syn.* intimidate, discourage, dishearten, frighten, scare. *Ant.* encourage, assist, animate, incite, urge, impel, promote.
dead—*Syn.* deceased, defunct, lifeless, inanimate, extinct, gone, departed. *Ant.* alive, living, existent, existing, being, continuing, subsisting, enduring, animate.
deadly—*Syn.* fatal, mortal, enervating, debilitating. *Ant.* invigorating, stimulating, energizing, preservative.
dear—*Syn.* costly, expensive, valuable, scarce, high-priced, precious, beloved, cherished. *Ant.* cheap, inexpensive, low-priced, less, unimportant.
death—*Syn.* decease, demise, dissolution, extinction, departure, release. *Ant.* life, existence, being.
decay—*Syn.* decline, collapse, downfall, putrefaction, decomposition, rot. *Ant.* growth, development, vigor, health, force, flourish, progress.
deceit—*Syn.* deception, duplicity, trickery, cunning, guile, treachery, artifice. *Ant.* truth, honesty.
deceive—*Syn.* delude, gull, cheat, mislead, trick, fool, defraud, bamboozle, guile, entrap. *Ant.* advise, assist, assure, truthful, frank, candid, straightforward.
deception—*Syn.* falsehood, fabrication, trickery, deceit, fraud, guile. *Ant.* candor, honesty, sincerity, veracity.
decide—*Syn.* determine, settle, adjudicate, resolve, regulate.*Ant.* put off, hesitate, wait, postpone, procrastinate.
decipher—*Syn.* read, spell, interpret, solve, translate, reveal. *Ant.* misinterpret, mix, vacillate, confuse, snare, distort.
decision—*Syn.* determination, conclusion, resolution, outcome, firmness. *Ant.* vacillation, procrastination, delay, postponement.
declamation—*Syn.* oratory, elocution, harangue, effusion, debate.
declaration—*Syn.* avowal, statement, profession, manifestation, presentation. *Ant.* denial, concealment, suppression.
decrease—*Syn.* abate, lessen, diminish, decline, curtail, reduce, narrow, minimize. *Ant.* increase, enlarge, add, extend, develop, widen, expand.
decree, *v.*—*Syn.* decide, direct, order, ordain, enjoin, determine, dictate, command, sentence, judge, adjust, settle.
dedicate—*Syn.* devote, consecrate, offer, set, apportion, ascribe.
deed—*Syn.* act, action, commission, achievement, accomplishment, exploit, feat, performance.
deem—*Syn.* judge, estimate, consider, think, suppose.
deep—*Syn.* down, far, profound, beneath, below, low, astute, subterranean, abstruse, learned, experienced, artful, contriving, penetrating. *Ant.* shallow, superficial, inexperienced, unintelligent.
deface—*Syn.* disfigure, deform, blemish, mar, mark, injure, spoil, erase, obliterate. *Ant.* beautify, adorn, embellish, deck.
default—*Syn.* lapse, failure, forfeit, absence, omission, neglect. *Ant.* perfection, advantage, accuracy, vigilance, watchfulness, observance.
defeat, *v.*—*Syn.* overcome, vanquish, conquer, rout, beat, subdue, frustrate, overthrow, annihilate. *Ant.* yield, submit, succumb, accede, surrender.
defect—*Syn.* imperfection, flaw, fault, blemish, spot, stain, deficiency, weakness. *Ant.* betterment, enhancement, perfection, support, faultlessness, excellence.
defend—*Syn.* protect, justify, save, insure, shield, shelter, safeguard, secure. *Ant.* abandon, leave, quit, abdicate, relinquish, vacate.
defense—*Syn.* vindication, plea, excuse, apology, bulwark, rampart, shield, protection. *Ant.* desertion, capitulation, surrender, abandonment.
defer—*Syn.* delay, postpone, prolong, suspend. *Ant.* expedite, accelerate, stimulate, forward, advance, hurry.
deficient—*Syn.* inadequate, incomplete, scanty, wanting, short. *Ant.* adequate, sufficient, enough, ample, full, satisfactory.
defile—*Syn.* pollute, corrupt, sully, stain, contaminate, spoil. *Ant.* clean, cleanse, wash, disinfect, hallow, purify, sanctify.
define—*Syn.* fix, settle, determine, limit, describe, ascertain. *Ant.* mix, muddle, confuse, tangle, twist, distort.
definite—*Syn.* fixed, determined, exact, limited, precise, certain, positive. *Ant.* indefinite, uncertain, unknown, undefined, vague, confused, uncertain.
deformed—*Syn.* maformed, crippled, disjointed, disfigured, distorted, misshapen. *Ant.* beautiful, handsome, shapely, graceful, well-formed.
defray—*Syn.* meet, liquidate, pay, discharge. *Ant.* repudiate, refuse, disavow, abjure, disclaim.
degradation—*Syn.* baseness, disgrace, dishonor, debasement, dismissal. *Ant.* honor, exaltation, praise.
degree—*Syn.* grade, extent, measure, mark, space, step. *Ant.* space, mass, size.
dejection—*Syn.* depression, despondency, melancholy, sadness. *Ant.* joy, cheer, delight, gaiety, exhilaration.
delay, *v.*—*Syn.* defer, postpone, procrastinate, prolong, protract, retard, hesitate, halt, hinder. *Ant.* forward, advance, speed, hasten, accelerate, expedite.
delegate—*Syn.* representative, legate, deputy, envoy, commissioner, ambassador.
deliberate, *v.*—*Syn.* think, ponder consider, meditate, debate, examine. *Ant.* reject, discard, repudiate, scoff.
deliberate, *a.*—*Syn.* careful, cautious, intentional, considered, pondered, weighed, judged, reasoned, wary, prudent, slow. *Ant.* incautious, sudden, rash, careless.
delicacy—*Syn.* daintiness, refinement, tact, softness, consideration, lightness. *Ant.* indelicacy, boorishness, roughness, rudeness, coarseness, fierceness.
delicate—*Syn.* dainty, fastidious, gentle, refined, tender. *Ant.* rough, rude, coarse, vulgar, mean, contemptible.
delicious—*Syn.* sweet, palatable, pleasing, delightful, tasteful. *Ant.* bitter, distasteful, unsavory, nauseous.
delight—*Syn.* enjoyment, pleasure, happiness, transport, ecstasy, gladness, rapture, bliss, joy. *Ant.* sorrow, pain, distress, dismay, misery, sadness, despair, melancholy.
deliver—*Syn.* liberate, free, rescue, pronounce, give, hand over. *Ant.* hold, retain, confine.
delusion—*Syn.* hallucination, illusion, fallacy, deception, apparition, specter. *Ant.* reality, actuality, certainty, fact, truth, substance.
demand—*Syn.* aks, request, seek, require, want, beg. *Ant.* tender, present, offer, give, proffer.
demolish—*Syn.* ruin, raze, destroy, level, wreck, devastate. *Ant.* build, repair, construct, create.
demonstrate—*Syn.* prove, show, exhibit, illustrate, display, present. *Ant.* hide, conceal, cover, screen, veil, cloak, puzzle, perplex, complicate, bewilder, confuse.
denial—*Syn.* disavowal, renunciation, contradiction, dissent, rejec-

tion. *Ant.* admission, acknowledgement, confession, declaration.
denounce—*Syn.* condemn, charge, blame, indict, censure, reprimand. *Ant.* praise, laud, commend.
deny—*Syn.* contradict, disavow, disclaim, oppose, refuse, repudiate, renounce. *Ant.* acknowledge, confess, concede, avow, admit, attest, accede.
depart—*Syn.* leave, quit, decamp, retire, go withdraw, vanish. *Ant.* remain, stay, tarry, abide.
depict—*Syn.* delineate, portray, describe, draw, picture, illustrate, represent.
deplore—*Syn.* bemoan, lament, mourn, grieve, complain, fret, regret. *Ant.* rejoice, delight, cheer.
depreciate—*Syn.* underrate, lower, decry, detract, disparage. *Ant.* boost, raise, praise, commend, approve, laud.
depress—*Syn.* lower, abase, degrade, deject, dispirit, debase, humuliate, slur. *Ant.* praise, comfort, cheer, encourage, inspirit, urge, stimulate, impel.
depression—*Syn.* oppression, misery, gloom, poverty, sorrow, unhappiness, dejection, melancholy. *Ant.* happiness, cheer, contentment, satisfaction, comfort.
deprive—*Syn.* strip, despoil, divest. *Ant.* give, add, help, assist, restore, return, replace, renew, repair.
depute—*Syn.* appoint, commission, name, delegate, accredit, authorize, intrust, assign, constitute. *Ant.* reject, eject, refuse, exclude, repudiate.
deride—*Syn.* ridicule, mock, taunt, scoff, scorn, slur, gibe, banter, fool, trick, bamboozle *(slang)*, humbug, delude, deceive, laugh (at), mimic, jeer, flout, insult. *Ant.* encourage, advise, guide, cheer, inspirit, stimulate, incite, animate, inspire, comfort.
derision—*Syn.* scorn, contempt, condemnation, disrespect, slur, insult, contumely. *Ant.* flattery, adulation, servility, submission.
derivation—*Syn.* origin, source, beginning, cause, root, nucleus, spring. *Ant.* result, resultant, issue, effect, outcome.
descent—*Syn.* declivity, slope, fall, extraction, origin, pedigree, ancestry, generation, assault, attack, decline. *Ant.* ascent, climb, rising, ascension, upgrade, lift.
describe—*Syn.* delineate, portray, explain, illustrate, depict, relate, narrate, represent. *Ant.* misrepresent, caricature, lie, deceive, misstate.
desecrate—*Syn.* profane, secularize, misuse, abuse, pollute, violate, defile, deprave, taint, debase. *Ant.* sanctify, purify, consecrate, hallow.
desert, *v.*—*Syn.* forsake, abandon, leave, quit, abdicate. *Ant.* remain, stay, continue, wait, abide, dwell, tarry.
design—*Syn.* delineation, drawing, object, contrivance, plan, intention.
desirable—*Syn.* good, acceptable, profitable, valuable, proper, judicious, beneficial, advisable, expedient. *Ant.* undesirable, bad, evil, harmful, detrimental.
desire—*Syn.* longing, yearning, wish, craving, affection. *Ant.* repugnance, repulsion, hatred, dislike, distaste, abhorrence.
desist—*Syn.* cease, stop, discontinue, drop, quit, relinquish. *Ant.* continue, endure, wait, hold, retain, remain, carry on.
desolate—*Syn.* abandoned, deserted, forsaken, lonely, solitary, forlorn, waste, uninhabited, bare, dismal. *Ant.* pleasant, happy, genial, lovely, enjoyable, inhabited, crowded, populous.
despair—*Syn.* hopelessness, desperation, discouragement, despondency, depression. *Ant.* hope, courage, confidence, expectation, faith. encouragement, assurance, cheer.
despatch—*Syn.* send, transmit, speed, hasten, expedite.
desperate—*Syn.* wild, reckless, bold, audacious, rash, despairing, hopeless. *Ant.* calm, cool, collected, hopeful, confident, contented.
despicable—*Syn.* low, mean, base, cowardly, contemptible, vile, worthless, pitiful, scurrilous, shameless. *Ant.* high, worthy, decent, upright, honorable.
despise—*Syn.* condemn, scorn, disdain, contemn, spurn, detest, abhor, loathe. *Ant.* love, cherish, praise, applaud, admire.
destiny—*Syn.* fate, decree, lot, fortune, condition, chance.
destitution—*Syn.* indigence, poverty, want, privation. *Ant.* riches, wealth, luxury, plenty, abundance, affluence.
destroy—*Syn.* ruin, demolish, exterminate, consume, raze, devastate, kill, slay. *Ant.* construct, add, build, replace, adorn, ornament, renew, repair, refresh, revive, invigorate.
destruction—*Syn.* desolation, devastation, waste, extinction, eradication, extermination, demolition. *Ant.* restoration, replacement, reestablishment, reparation, restitution.
desultory—*Syn.* rambling, discursive, irregular, superficial, unsettled. *Ant.* steady, fixed, stable, constant.
detach—*Syn.* separate, withdraw, disengage, disconnect, sever. *Ant.* unite, bind, join, connect, combine, adhere, merge, couple, link, attach.
detail, *v.*—*Syn.* report, narrate, particularize, tell. *Ant.* conceal, hide, keep silent, cover, withhold.
detain—*Syn.* hold, keep, restrain, stop. *Ant.* free, liberate.
detect—*Syn.* discover, find, uncover, determine. *Ant.* miss, omit.
deter—*Syn.* warn, stop, dissuade, terrify, discourage, restrain. *Ant.* encourage, persuade, embolden, incite, influence, favor.
determined—*Syn.* decided, firm, resolute, steady, unwavering. *Ant.* undecided, vacillating, wavering, uncertain.
detest—*Syn.* hate, loathe, abhor. *Ant.* like, love, admire, respect.
detract—*Syn.* defame, derogate, vilify, slander, deprecate. *Ant.* laud, praise, commend, applaud, extol.
detraction—*Syn.* slander, defamation, calumny, aspersion, depreciation, derogation. *Ant.* praise, admiration, respect, commendation.
detriment—*Syn.* loss, harm, injury, deterioration, impairment. *Ant.* advantage, gain, profit, benefit, help, favor.
devastate—*Syn.* ravage, sack, pillage, ruin, demolish, wreck. *Ant.* replenish, restore, renew, build.
develop—*Syn.* unfold, enlarge, exhibit, unravel. *Ant.* curtail, shorten, abbreviate, conceal, lessen, compress, confine.
deviate—*Syn.* deflect, digress, swerve, wander, stray, turn aside. *Ant.* keep on, keep to the right, go ahead, persevere, continue, stick to it *(colloq.)*, stick it out *(colloq.)*.
device—*Syn.* artifice, contrivance, emblem, motto.
devoid—*Syn.* void, wanting, empty, bare, lacking. *Ant.* full, complete, furnished, equipped, sufficient.
devote—*Syn.* dedicate, consign, assign, apply, appropriate, allot. *Ant.* waste, squander, misuse, alienate.
devour—*Syn.* consume, waste, destroy, gorge, raven, swallow (up), munch, chew, gulp, bolt, prey upon.
devout—*Syn.* holy, pious, religious, reverent, godly, righteous, devotional. *Ant.* irreligious, irreverent, ungodly, sinful, unholy.
dictate—*Syn.* prompt, suggest, order, command, direct, instruct, prescribe, deliver, tell, speak. *Ant.* beg, ask, implore, crave.
dictorial—*Syn.* imperative, imperious, domineering, tyrannical, overbearing, haughty. *Ant.* submissive, bashful, retiring, passive, docile, yielding, unobtrusive.
diction—*Syn.* style, expression, wording, vocabulary, phrase, verbiage, language.
die—*Syn.* expire, cease, decease, perish, decay, wither, vanish, lose, pass away. *Ant.* begin, live, exist, endure, last, remain, survive.
diet—*Syn.* food, fare, sustenance, victuals, nutriment, nourishment, nutrition.
difference—*Syn.* separation, disagreement, dissent, discord, estrangement, variety, disparity, unlikeness. *Ant.* agreement, similarity, concurrence, accord, accordance, harmony, amity, concord.
different—*Syn.* various, diverse, unlike, separate, distinct, discordant. *Ant.* similar, alike, resembling, common, same.
difficult—*Syn.* hard, involved, perplexing, obscure, arduous, laborious, unmanageable, unyielding, puzzling, complex, complicated. *Ant.* easy, facile, simple, yielding, light, lightsome, unconstrained, free, calm, plain, slight, trivial.
diffuse, *v.*—*Syn.* spread, expand, scatter, sow, disperse, permeate, disseminate. *Ant.* confine, narrow, limit, control, restrict, prevent.
dignify—*Syn.* exalt, elevate, prefer, honor, reverence, advance, promote, adorn, decorate, ennoble, proclaim, boost, extol, invest, aggrandize, magnify, glorify. *Ant.* degrade, shame, disgrace, despise, detract, slander, scorn, insult, humble, humiliate, demean, lower, dishonor.
dilate—*Syn.* stretch, widen, broaden, expand, swell, extend, enlarge, open, extend, discuss, debate. *Ant.* shorten, contract, compress, abridge, reduce, condense, lessen.
diligence—*Syn.* care, attention, keenness, alterness, industry, heed, intent, intensity. *Ant.* sloth, laziness, carelessness, lethargy, indifference, indolence, disregard.
diminish—*Syn.* lessen, reduce, compress, curtail, retrench, decrease, abate, degrade, shorten, abridge, epitomize, cut off, trim. *Ant.* increase, enlarge, magnify, widen, extend, expand, lengthen, amplify.
direct—*Syn.* conduct, lead, guide, order, regulate, adjust, govern, control, train, show, demonstrate, explain, teach, inform, instruct, usher, point. *Ant.* deceive, mislead, lead astray.
direction—*Syn.* aim, inclination, bearing, tendency, guidance, control, order, command, instruction.
dirty—*Syn.* unclean, soiled, polluted, mean, strained, spotted, base. *Ant.* clean, decent, unspotted, untarnished.
disability—*Syn.* unfitness, incapacity, inability, weakness, infirmity, defect. *Ant.* fitness, capacity, ability, power, capability, strength.
disadvantage—*Syn.* loss, detriment, injury, hurt, hindrance, harm. *Ant.* advantage, gain, benefit, profit, emolument, help.
disagree—*Syn.* differ, dissent, dispute, wrangle, oppose. *Ant.* agree, concur, consent, acquiesce.
disaster—*Syn.* calamity, misfortune, misadventure, catastrophe, adversity. *Ant.* fortune, advantage, happiness.
discern—*Syn.* perceive, observe, recognize, discriminate, rate, see, distinguish, discover. *Ant.* overlook, neglect, slight.
discipline—*Syn.* order, method, training, rule, instruction, drill. *Ant.* confusion, chaos, disorder, disturbance, irregularity.
disclose—*Syn.* unfold, reveal, tell, inform, uncover, unveil, discover. *Ant.* hide, conceal, withhold, cover, mask, secrete.
discord—*Syn.* confusion, disturbance, disagreement, dissension, strife, clash. *Ant.* harmony, peace, concord, agreement, cooperation.
discover—*Syn.* disclose, invent, discern, detect, find, reveal. *Ant.* hide, mask, secrete, conceal, bury, disguise, cover, suppress, veil
discreet—*Syn.* cautious, thoughtful, prudent, wary, judicious, careful, circumspect. *Ant.* indiscreet, imprudent, reckless, foolish, unwary, rash, thoughtless, heedless, incautious.
discrepancy—*Syn.* difference, variance, disagreement. *Ant.* agreement, concurrence, harmony, union, unison.
discrimination—*Syn.* acuteness, caution, prudence, discernment, circumspection. *Ant.* rashness, temerity, haste, recklessness, imprudence.
discuss—*Syn.* argue, debate, dispute, comment, explain. *Ant.* ignore, reject, disregard.
disdain, *v.*—*Syn.* scorn, detest, loathe, despise, reject, hate. *Ant.* approve, like, love, praise, laud.
disease—*Syn.* malady, sickness, ailment, disorder, illness, infirmity. *Ant.* health, strength, vigor.
disgrace, *v.*—*Syn.* debase, degrade, defame, humiliate, dishonor, shame,, disparage. *Ant.* honor, applaud, praise, extol, elevate, laud.
disguise—*Syn.* change, mask, conceal, camouflage, screen, cloak, cover. *Ant.* bare, strip, uncover, unmask, unveil.
disgust—*Syn.* loathing, abomina-

tion, abhorrence, dislike, distaste, aversion. *Ant.* liking, admiration, approval, praise, laudation, respect, favor.

dismal—*Syn.* gloomy, sad, melancholy, dreary, dire, unhappy. *Ant.* joyful, glad, pleasant, gay, cheerful.

dismay, *v.*—*Syn.* terrify, frighten, scare. *Ant.* aid, assist, encourage, praise, laud, favor, inspirit, support.

dismiss—*Syn.* discharge, discard, decline, repel, spurn. *Ant.* retain, keep, preserve, maintain.

disorder—*Syn.* confusion, tumult, bustle, disturbance. *Ant.* order, regularity, arrangement, neatness, health, vigor.

disorderly—*Syn.* irregular, confused. *Ant.* regular, neat, orderly.

disparage—*Syn.* belittle, lower, depreciate, discredit, underrate. *Ant.* praise, acclaim, approve, applaud, compliment.

displace—*Syn.* misplace, disturb, mislay, dislodge. *Ant.* arrange, classify, order, place, put in order.

display, *v.*—*Syn.* show, arrange, spread, exhibit, expose. *Ant.* hide, conceal, cover, secrete.

dispose—*Syn.* arrange, place, order, bestow. *Ant.* disarrange, disorder, secrete, hide.

dispute—*Syn.* argument, debate, controversy, quarrel, disagreement, contention, discord. *Ant.* agreement, harmony, unison, concord.

dissent—*Syn.* disagree, differ, vary, dispute, disclaim. *Ant.* agree, coincide, concur, approve, indorse, confirm.

distant—*Syn.* remote, far, removed, separate, indifferent, haughty, shy, indirect. *Ant.* near, adjacent, convenient, close, next, affectionate, solicitous, kind, sympathetic, helpful.

distinct—*Syn.* clear, plain, obvious, well-marked, disunited. *Ant.* obscure, abstruse, mixed.

distinguished—*Syn.* eminent, illustrious, famous, renowned, celebrated, prominent, noted. *Ant.* obscure, humble, unknown, unassuming, unobtrusive, ordinary.

distract—*Syn.* perplex, bewilder, puzzle, disorder, dazzle, confound. *Ant.* mollify, please, calm, reassure, ameliorate, moderate.

distress—*Syn.* suffering, pain, agony, grief, trouble, adversity, sorrow. *Ant.* pleasure, satisfaction, joy, gaiety, festivity, revelry.

disturb—*Syn.* annoy, trouble, vex, confuse, derange, agitate, arouse, disarrange, disorder. *Ant.* pacify, quiet, soothe, mollify, placate, conciliate, still, allay, compose, tranquilize.

disuse—*Syn.* discontinuance, abolition, discontinuance, abrogation. *Ant.* use, continuance, usage.

divide—*Syn.* part, separate, distribute, sever, disunite, disconnect. *Ant.* join, unite, attach, connect, combine, annex, link, bind.

division—*Syn.* separation, detachment, partition, section, compartment, difference, discord. *Ant.* union, unity, accord, agreement, uniformity.

divulge—*Syn.* tell, inform, describe, relate, disclose, impart, show, uncover, unveil. *Ant.* secrete, cover, cloak, hide, conceal, mask.

do—*Syn.* execute, perform, accomplish, make, transact, complete, effect, commit, realize, act. *Ant.* neglect, avoid, miss, miscarry, mar, spoil, tarry, defer.

docile—*Syn.* meek, mild, gentle, pliant, submissive, tame, amendable. *Ant.* stubborn, unyielding, resolute, determined, dogged, obstinate, intractable, tough, headstrong.

doctrine—*Syn.* belief, dogma, tenet, principle, teaching, religion, creed, faith, persuasion. *Ant.* schism, unbelief, error, disbelief, infidelity, incredulity, skepticism.

doleful—*Syn.* sad, sorrowful, sorry, woebegone, rueful, dismal, piteous, woeful, cheerless, mournful, pathetic, pitiable, wretched, miserable, abject, disconsolate, forlorn. *Ant.* cheerful, jolly, joyous, sprightly, gay, mirthful, jovial, merry, lively, sportive, happy, sunny, buoyant, enlivening, blithe, bright, entertaining, amusing.

dominant—*Syn.* controlling, predominant, commanding, governing, ruling, prevailing, authoritative. *Ant.* obscure, meek, lowly, unassuming, backward, reserved, nonaggressive, reluctant.

donation—*Syn.* grant, gratuity, endowment, gift, benefit, bequest, boon, charity, provision.

doom—*Syn.* sentence, verdict, judgement, fate, lot, destiny, fortune, finish, end.

doubt, *n.*—*Syn.* distrust, disbelief, skepticism, unbelief, suspicion, uncertainty, scruple, misgiving, hesitancy. *Ant.* faith, belief, confidence, fidelity, trust, credence, conviction, assurance, certainty.

draw—*Syn.* pull, haul, drag, attract, inhale, sketch, describe, convey, lure, tow, allure, pull, induce, trail. *Ant.* repel, repulse, alienate, reject, abandon.

dread—*Syn.* fear, horror, terror, alarm, dismay, awe, fright, panic, anxiety, timidity, misgiving. *Ant.* bravery, courage, calmness, confidence, presumption, effrontery, valor.

dream—*Syn.* fantasy, illusion, imagination, vision, delusion. *Ant.* certainty, fact, reality, actuality, existence.

dress—*Syn.* clothes, attire, apparel, garments, costume, garb, raiment. *Ant.* nudity, nakedness, undress, disarray.

drift—*Syn.* tendency, effort, direction, end, purpose, object, scope, aim. *Ant.* aimlessness, motionlessness, inertia, sluggishness, passiveness.

drive—*Syn.* urge, propel, compel, push, ride, thrust, incite, force, instigate, press. *Ant.* stop, halt, hinder, discourage, retard, curb.

droll—*Syn.* laughable, comic, funny, whimsical, amusing, entertaining, diverting, pleasing, witty, merry. *Ant.* heavy, serious, ponderous, weighty, dreary, tedious, stolid, slow, sluggish, sleepy, tiresome, uninteresting, irksome.

drown—*Syn.* inundate, swamp, immerse, submerge, engulf, overwhelm, perish, plunge. *Ant.* rescue, save, raise, float, recover, deliver, extricate.

dry—*Syn.* arid, parched, lifeless, dull, tedious, uninteresting, meagre, dull, tedious, uninteresting. *Ant.* wet, damp, soaking, saturated, muddy.

dull—*Syn.* stupid, stolid, obtuse, lifeless, senseless, heavy, insipid, dismal. *Ant.* lively, quick, sharp, witty, brisk, spirited, smart, brainy, intelligent.

duplicate—*Syn.* likeness, facsimile, copy, replica, transcript, reproduction, representation, resemblance. *Ant.* original, phototype.

durable—*Syn.* lasting, permanent, abiding, continuing, constant, changeless, enduring, remaining. *Ant.* passing, transitory, evanescent, vanishing, fleeting, impermanent, perishable, ephemeral, temporary, brief, short.

duty—*Syn.* office, function, responsiblity, accountability, business, obligation. *Ant.* irresponsibility.

dwell—*Syn.* stay, inhabit, abide, linger, remain, lodge, live, reside. *Ant.* move, remove, discontinue, abandon, leave, quit.

E

eager—*Syn.* earnest, enthusiastic, anxious, keen, fervent, ardent, intent, hot, impetuous. *Ant.* diffident, retiring, apathetic, cool, heedless, uninterested, dispassionate, stony, unmindful.

earn—*Syn.* gain, acquire, obtain, win, merit, attain, get. *Ant.* lose, waste, fail, miss, spend.

earnest—*Syn.* ardent, serious, grave, solemn, sincere, eager, urgent, warm, decided, firm, resolute, steady, obstinate, immovable. *Ant.* trifling, frivolous, light, unheeding, careless, heedless, inattentive, negligent, incautious, inconsiderate, thoughtless, unconcerned, unmindful, unsteady, regardless, slack, hesitant.

ease, *n.*—*Syn.* comfort, rest, quietness, quietude, repose, tranquillity, restfulness, easiness, calmness, solace, knack, readiness. *Ant.* worry, sorrow, grief, disquiet, turmoil.

easy—*Syn.* pleasant, facile, indulgent, gentle, smooth, unconcerned, pliant. *Ant.* intricate, complex, involved, troublesome, severe entangled.

eccentric—*Syn.* odd, strange, abnormal, particular, anomalous, unusual, crochety, cranky. *Ant.* regular, plain, orderly, methodical, formal, usual, natural, common, conventional, uniform.

economical—*Syn.* saving, sparing, careful, frugal, provident, stingy, mean, close, penurious, chary, watchful. *Ant.* liberal, generous, wasteful, squandering, careless, bounteous, beneficent, free, munificent, improvident, thoughtless, lavish, prodigal.

ecstasy—*Syn.* joy, overjoy, delight, rapture, rejoicing, exultation, gratification, cheer, glee, fun. *Ant.* worry, trouble, sorrow, doldrums, despair, pessimism, misery, calamity, unhappiness.

edge—*Syn.* boundary, brim, margin, rim, ring, periphery, keenness. *Ant.* surface, flat, level, area, space, interior, plain, plane, dullness.

edict—*Syn.* decree, proclamation, order, law, manifesto, announcement, ordinance, mandate.

education—*Syn.* schooling, training, culture, learning, study, information, instruction, scholarship. *Ant.* ignorance, illiteracy, stupidity, stagnation.

efface—*Syn.* obliterate, erase, cancel, annul, destroy. *Ant.* keep, retain, confirm, indorse, sanction, strengthen, approve, renew.

effect, *n.*—*Syn.* consequence, issue, meaning, outcome, finish, consummation, conclusion, determination. *Ant.* cause, beginning, commencement, foundation, spring.

effect, *v.*—*Syn.* accomplish, operate, finish, conclude, perform, consummate. *Ant.* fail, neglect, abandon, cease, disappoint, desert, omit, quit, leave, overlook, give up.

effective—*Syn.* efficient, serviceable, useful, efficacious, productive, capable. *Ant.* inoperative, inefficient, useless, inadequate, incapable, non-productive.

efficient—*Syn.* competent, fitting, suitable, suited, effective, efficacious, capable, skillful, clever. *Ant.* inadequate, unsuitable, incapable, unqualified, unfit, ineffectual, dull, unable, deficient.

egotism—*Syn.* egoism, conceit, self-conceit, arrogance, insolence, overconfidence, ostentation, boastfulness. *Ant.* humility, mildness, modesty, diffidence, shyness, restraint, deference.

egotistic—*Syn.* egoistic, vain, boastful, inflated, self-centered. *Ant.* retiring, reserved, meek, modest.

eject—*Syn.* banish, dismiss, discharge, oust, dislodge, remove, evict, exile, discard. *Ant.* take in, accept, establish, confirm, sanction, fix, settle, authorize, allow, countenance, appoint.

elaborate, *a.*—*Syn.* gaudy, showy, garnished, decorated, ostentatious, imposing, ornamented, embellished, polished, refined, beautified. *Ant.* plain, common, ordinary, general, usual, unrefined, normal, regular.

elation—*Syn.* enthusiasm, delight, exaltation, joy, gratification, satisfaction. *Ant.* depression, gloom, sadness, despair, melancholy.

elegant—*Syn.* polished, refined, graceful, pleasing, well-formed, handsome. *Ant.* crude, awkward, obnoxious, coarse, unrefined, ungraceful, displeasing, disagreeable.

elementary—*Syn.* primary, rudimental, simple, easy, unmixed, undeveloped, not difficult. *Ant.* difficult, complicated, involved, troublesome, abstruse, intricate.

elevate—*Syn.* raise, hoist, heighten, magnify, dignify, honor, respect, revere, esteem. *Ant.* lower, deprecate, denounce.

eliminate—*Syn.* expel, dislodge, banish, oust, cancel, discharge, remove. *Ant.* replace, restore, keep, retain, hold, approve, accept, add.

eloquence—*Syn.* oration, expression, ability, diction, speech, voice, address, fluency. *Ant.* dullness, silence, stammering.

elucidate—*Syn.* interpret, expound, clarify, illuminate. *Ant.* obscure, darken, confuse.

elude—*Syn.* dodge, evade, baffle, parry, fence, frustrate, mock, equivocate, escape. *Ant.* seek, entice, inveigle.

emancipate—*Syn.* free, liberate, deliver, release, discharge. *Ant.* suppress, imprison, hold, restrain, bind, repress, coerce, enslave.

embarrass—*Syn.* annoy, trouble, puzzle, disconcert, hamper, confuse, complicate, worry, confound, mystify, bother. *Ant.* please, mollify, help, assist, encourage.

embezzle—*Syn.* steal, forge, pilfer, appropriate, purloin, rob, swindle. *Ant.* reimburse, compensate.

emblem—*Syn.* symbol, figure, image, token, sign, memento, type, representation, souvenir, keepsake, medal, miniature, motto, design.

embolden—*Syn.* animate, urge, stimulate, instigate, nerve, strengthen, rouse, arouse, force, importune, invigorate. *Ant.* weaken, depress, deject, unnerve, dispirit.

embrace—*Syn.* encircle, comprehend, accept, contain, subscribe to, seize, cling to. *Ant.* neglect, ignore, lose, shun, slight.

emergency—*Syn.* crisis, necessity, exigency, urgency, dilemma, puzzle, perplexity, difficulty, importunity, tension, distress. *Ant.* commonness, normalcy, stability, routine, conventionality.

emigrate—*Syn.* migrate, leave, quit, abandon, depart, move. *Ant.* remain, stay, abide, reside.

eminent—*Syn.* distinguished, well-known, prominent, noted, renowned. *Ant.* obscure, unknown, modest, diffident, lowly, unpretentious, paltry, insignificant.

emissary—*Syn.* agent, scout, mediator, representative, envoy, legate, ambassador, diplomat.

emit—*Syn.* discharge, vent, open, utter, report, issue forth, draw out, express. *Ant.* retain, stifle, withhold, conceal, restrain.

emotion—*Syn.* commotion, excitement, disturbance, feeling, disquiet, uneasiness, tumult, turmoil. *Ant.* quiet, quietude, rest, tranquility, restraint, calm, peace.

emphatic—*Syn.* strong, determined, forceful, forcible, positive, important, energetic, effective, cogent, powerful, irresistible. *Ant.* weak, vacillating, wavering, uncertain, timid.

employ—*Syn.* engage, hire, use, occupy, procure, contract. *Ant.* remove, banish, abandon, fire (*colloq.*).

empower—*Syn.* grant, authorize, permit, sanction, license.

empty—*Syn.* bare, vacant, vacated, void, devoid, destitute, barren. *Ant.* full, filled, replete, occupied, complete.

enchant—*Syn.* charm, fascinate, bewitch, captivate, enthral, enrapture, ravish, attract. *Ant.* repel, disgust, revolt, offend, displease, anger, provoke, dissatisfy, disappoint.

encompass—*Syn.* gird, beset, inclose, surround, include, envelop.

encounter—*Syn.* assault, engagement, battle, action, meeting, assailment, invasion, inroad, clash, collision, impact. *Ant.* peace, amity, agreement, concord, truce, conformity, harmony, union.

encourage—*Syn.* sanction, animate, cheer, incite, advise, instigate, enliven, inspire, spur. *Ant.* dampen, depress, dishearten, deject, dissuade, deter, deride, distract, lower, abase, denounce.

encroach—*Syn.* infringe, trespass, invade, intrude. *Ant.* shun, avoid, evade, elude.

encumbrance—*Syn.* burden, hinderance, drawback, drag, clog, impediment, load, obstacle, difficulty. *Ant.* advantage, help, assistance, incentive, spur, goad, aid, vantage, succor, stimulus, stimulant.

end, *v.*—*Syn.* stop, finish, close, quit, terminate, break off, cease, desist, conclude. *Ant.* begin, start, commence, originate, institute, initiate, introduce, establish.

endanger—*Syn.* peril, imperil, expose, hazard, risk, jeopardize, venture. *Ant.* guard, protect, watch, cover, hide, fend.

endeavor—*Syn.* attempt, exert, undertake, struggle, labor, work, aspire. *Ant.* idle, rest, cease, quit, shun, defer, delay.

endowment—*Syn.* benefit, gift, bequest, donation, grant. *Ant.* loss, damage, drawback.

endurance—*Syn.* sufferance, submission, forebearance, continuation, duration, trial, tribulation, stamina. *Ant.* surrender, breakdown, faltering, failing, despair.

endure—*Syn.* suffer, tolerate, allow, permit, support, undergo, submit. *Ant.* faint, falter, resign, give up, fail, succumb, yield, surrender, break.

enemy—*Syn.* foe, rival, antagonist, detractor. *Ant.* friend, benefactor, ally, adherent.

energetic—*Syn.* effective, powerful, vigorous, determined, strong, potent. *Ant.* weak, vacillating, unsteady, wavering, inactive, sluggish, indolent, listless.

energy—*Syn.* vim, vigor, power, effectiveness. *Ant.* weakness, vacillation, hesitancy, idleness, tiredness, weariness, apathy, inactivity, fatigue, sluggishness, vapid.

enervate—*Syn.* debilitate, weaken, enfeeble, impair, reduce, sap. *Ant.* strengthen, vigorate, energize, enthuse, enliven.

enforce—*Syn.* urge, compel, incite, exert, drive, press, impel. *Ant.* neglect, abandon, omit, dismiss.

engage—*Syn.* employ, invite, allure, hire, retain, attack, use, commission, appoint, delegate, empower. *Ant.* dismiss, discharge, oust, eject, discard, shun, expel.

engulf—*Syn.* imbibe, submerge, drown, bury, overwhelm, sink, swamp, deluge, inundate.

enjoin—*Syn.* order, direct, admonish, instruct, advise, counsel, forbid, halt. *Ant.* prevent, prohibit, preclude, inhibit, forbid, disallow.

enjoyment—*Syn.* satisfaction, sensuality, indulgence, delight, happiness, comfort, gladness. *Ant.* woe, misery, grief, calamity, strife, unhappiness, misfortune, suffering, melancholy, discomfort, uneasiness.

enlarge—*Syn.* extend, swell, broaden, expand, magnify, spread, lengthen, heighten, distend. *Ant.* diminish, reduce, lower, curtail, abridge, abbreviate.

enlighten—*Syn.* instruct, teach, tell, impart, educate, acquaint, apprise, disclose, advise, indoctrinate. *Ant.* becloud, confuse, delude, obscure, dim, disconcert, confound.

enlist—*Syn.* enter, register, enroll, embody, engage, retain, procure, obtain, get. *Ant.* dissuade, shun, avoid, discourage.

enmity—*Syn.* malice, rancor, spite, animosity, hostility, antagonism, opposition, dislike, antipathy, aversion. *Ant.* friendship, kindness, concord, sympathy, harmony, alliance, intimacy, companionship, comity, peace, love.

enormous—*Syn.* gigantic, colossal, huge, vast, immense, amazing, extraordinary, marvelous, miraculous, astonishing, ponderous, great, mammoth, stupendous, wonderful, wondrous. *Ant.* small, little, insignificant, microscopic, inconsiderable, light, trivial, petty, paltry, slight, trifling, dwarfish, imponderable, unimportant, inconsequential, slender, diminutive, infinitesimal, minute, Lilliputian, delicate, thin.

enough, *a.*—*Syn.* sufficient, plenty, abundant, adequate, full, plenteous, copious, ample, complete. *Ant.* scarce, lacking, wanting, scant, deficient, bare, insufficient, inadequate.

enrage—*Syn.* anger, goad, tempt, infuriate, madden, exasperate, incense, inflame, agitate, irritate, provoke, chafe, craze. *Ant.* soften, mollify, soothe, calm, pacify, appease, conciliate, reconcile, assuage, compose, mitigate, ameliorate, moderate.

enrapture—*Syn.* enchant, charm, allure, fascinate, bewitch, captivate, enthral, enthuse, entrance, ravish, delight, enamour, please. *Ant.* repel, repulse, disgust, shock, annoy, anger, agitate, irritate, weary, tire, displease, offend, vex, pique, provoke.

enroll—*Syn.* register, enlist, inscribe, subscribe, enter, fill out, sign, mark, affix. *Ant.* discard, reject, abrogate, repudiate, pass over, omit, neglect, protest, cancel, dismiss.

enterprise—*Syn.* undertaking, venture, work, endeavor, energy, scheme, risk, hazard, business, action, activity. *Ant.* idleness, inactivity, inaction, sloth, slothfulness, indolence, passiveness.

entertain—*Syn.* amuse, cheer, please, interest, enliven, delight, divert, beguile, recreate, disport, gratify, occupy, charm, rouse, enthuse. *Ant.* weary, tire, disgust, bore, annoy, disturb, sadden, harass, distress, perplex, trouble.

enthusiasm—*Syn.* fervor, ardor, joy, excitement, emotion, eagerness, exhileration, mirth, merriment, gaiety. *Ant.* weariness, indifference, apathy, wariness.

entrance—*Syn.* gate, door, doorway, portal, opening, access, admission. *Ant.* exit, withdrawal, expulsion.

entrap—*Syn.* catch, decoy, lure, entice, implicate. *Ant.* warn, advise, admonish, counsel, guide, assist, release, clear, liberate.

entreat—*Syn.* implore, ask, importune, petition, request, crave. *Ant.* demand, command, take, force, compel.

envious—*Syn.* jealous, suspicious, resentful, covetous. *Ant.* kind, charitable.

epitome—*Syn.* brief, abridgement, synopsis, precis, digest, contraction, condensation. *Ant.* enlargement, expansion, augmentation, increment.

equal—*Syn.* even, like, alike, same, uniform, fair, just, equitable. *Ant.* unequal, unfair.

equivocal—*Syn.* ambiguous, uncertain, indefinite, indeterminate, puzzling, doubtful, obscure, vague, involved, hazy, wavering. *Ant.* clear, plain, obvious, distinct, lucid.

eradicate—*Syn.* exterminate, destroy, uproot, abolish, disperse, extinguish, remove. *Ant.* plant, settle, secure.

error—*Syn.* mistake, fault, oversight, wrong, slip, transgression. *Ant.* correctness, certainty, truth, exactness, accuracy.

especially—*Syn.* chiefly, principally, definitely, truly. *Ant.* usually, ordinarily, normally.

essay—*Syn.* tract, effort, trial, paper, composition, thesis, article, comment.

establish—*Syn.* confirm, verify, found, endow, institute, confirm, ratify, prove, demonstrate, substantiate, constitute. *Ant.* topple, ruin, destroy, raze, tumble, defeat, wreck, disprove, break up, unsettle.

esteem, *v.*—*Syn.* appreciate, respect, revere, treasure, regard, rate, admire. *Ant.* slight, ridicule, spurn, disdain.

estimate—*Syn.* appraise, appreciate, esteem, prize, value, measure, count, number.

eternal—*Syn.* unending, perpetual, endless, boundless, immortal, continual, timeless, incessant, constant, enduring. *Ant.* finite, ending, temporary, short, ceasing, inconstant, mutable, fluctuating, brief, fleeting, momentary.

evade—*Syn.* prevaricate, lie, dodge, shun, shuffle, avoid, elude, trick, shift, conceal, veil. *Ant.* acknowledge, declare, face, confront, illustrate, verify, confirm.

even—*Syn.* equal, uniform, flat, regular, unbroken. *Ant.* rough, jagged, ridged, rugged, irregular.

event—*Syn.* fact, case, result, issue, outcome, consequence, circumstance, occurrence, end.

evident—*Syn.* clear, open, obvious, distinct, visible, discernible, conspicuous, unmistakable, apparent. *Ant.* obscure, hidden, concealed, invisible, unseen.

evil—*Syn.* harm, mischief, sin, wickedness, depravity, corruption, crime. *Ant.* virtue, honor, decency, respect, esteem, renown.

exact—*Syn.* right, correct, proper, true, reliable, careful, precise, timely, appropriate, specific. *Ant.* wrong, false, untrue, unreliable, inaccurate, careless.

exalt—*Syn.* dignify, raise, heighten, promote, extol, magnify, glorify, praise, advance, laud, applaud. *Ant.* degrade, denounce, condemn, abase, dishonor, disgrace, depose, lower, disdain.

examination—*Syn.* investigation, inquiry, search, scrutiny, inspection.

example—*Syn.* pattern, type, specimen, standard, warning, prototype, original, copy.

exceed—*Syn.* excel, outdo, overdo, transcend, outstrip. *Ant.* lag, dally, dawdle, fall behind.

exceptional—*Syn.* extraordinary, scarce, unusual, remarkable, incomparable, unprecedented. *Ant.*

common, ordinary, customary, normal, expected, general.
excess—*Syn.* profusion, abundance, luxuriance, surplus, plenty. *Ant.* lack, want, necessity, insufficiency, dearth, inadequacy.
excite—*Syn.* provoke, arouse, agitate, inflame, kindle, anger, stimulate, induce, enrage, exasperate, tease, annoy, infuriate, goad, taunt. *Ant.* soothe, soften, lull, compose, repress, assuage, appease, subdue, calm, mollify.
excursion—*Syn.* jaunt, tour, trip, outing, expedition, journey, voyage.
execute—*Syn.* perform, do, carry out, accomplish, effect, complete, achieve, administer, finish, gain. *Ant.* fail, omit, ignore, overlook, forget, miss, disregard, leave, relinquish, quit, forego.
exempt, *v.*—*Syn.* liberate, release, discharge, excuse, exonerate, let off. *Ant.* hold, confine, keep, enforce.
exercise—*Syn.* exertion, drill, training, use, performance, act, activity, operation. *Ant.* inactivity, relaxation, idleness, inaction.
exhausted—*Syn.* tired, wearied, worn, spent, consumed, drained, empty. *Ant.* fresh, keen, ready, strong, refreshed, invigorated.
exigency—*Syn.* necessity, distress, difficulty, crisis. *Ant.* normalcy, regularity.
expense—*Syn.* cost, price, expenditure, outlay, charge. *Ant.* profit, return, receipt, proceeds, income, gain, acquisition.
experiment—*Syn.* test, verification, examination, exercise.
explain—*Syn.* interpret, illustrate, teach, translate, unfold. *Ant.* puzzle, complicate, tangle, confuse, confound, darken, cloud, befuddle.
explicit—*Syn.* definite, clear, intelligible, comprehensible, evident, precise, obvious. *Ant.* indefinite, doubtful, hazy, mixed, confused, puzzling, vague, uncertain, obscure, dubious.
express—*Syn.* declare, signify, utter, tell, set forth, designate, denote, represent, send. —*Syn.* withhold, retain, back, check, repress.
extemporaneous—*Syn.* offhand, unpremeditated, improvised, impromptu. *Ant.* elaborated, premeditated, studied, prepared.
extend—*Syn.* reach, lengthen, enlarge, protract, amplify, augment, expand. *Ant.* contract, narrow, compress, decrease, lessen, reduce.
exterminate—*Syn.* destroy, banish, expel, uproot, remove, wipe out. *Ant.* preserve, protect, foster, cherish, nurture, save, maintain.
extravagant—*Syn.* lavish, wasteful, liberal, immoderate, excessive, extreme. *Ant.* miserly, niggardly, mean, stingy, close, perunious.
extreme—*Syn.* last, final, terminal, ultimate, remote, far. *Ant.* medium, limited, calm, quiet, steady, ordinary, near.
extricate—*Syn.* free, deliver, liberate, unbind, unchain, disentangle, evolve, release, unfasten. *Ant.* tie, bind, confine, imprison, restrict, limit, restrain, shackle.
exult—*Syn.* rejoice, vaunt, brag. *Ant.* bewail, sorrow, deplore, lament.

fable—*Syn.* tale, yarn, parable, allegory, myth, fiction. *Ant.* reality, truth, fact, certainty.
fabricate—*Syn.* make, construct, manufacture, produce, build, put together. *Ant.* ruin, destroy, wreck, raze.
fabulous—*Syn.* legendary, mythical, wonderful, amazing. *Ant.* historical, proven, true, common.
face, *v.*—*Syn.* meet, oppose, resist, dare, venture, challenge. *Ant.* fear, shrink, slink, withdraw, retire, refuse.
facetious—*Syn.* jocular, funny, humorous. *Ant.* solemn, melancholy, sad, stolid, formal.
facile—*Syn.* ready, dexterous, skillful, quick, artful, clever, adroit. *Ant.* difficult, laborious, clumsy, awkward, slow, plodding, arduous.
facility—*Syn.* readiness, quickness, dexterity, ease, proficiency. *Ant.* hardness, difficulty, slowness, ineptitude.
facsimile—*Syn.* copy, likeness, reproduction, resemblance. *Ant.* difference, distinction, dissimilarity.
factor—*Syn.* steward, representative, substitute, delegate, proxy.

fail—*Syn.* miss, omit, decline, desert, disappoint, abandon, neglect, drop. *Ant.* win, gain, deliver, attain.
faint—*Syn.* timid, faltering, powerless, worn, listless, exhausted. *Ant.* brave, courageous, bold, dashing, unafraid, strong, fearless, vigorous, sturdy.
fair—*Syn.* sunny, dry, pleasant, mild, frank, honest, candid, just, reasonable, honorable, civil, upright. *Ant.* wet, cloudy, rainy, showery, dark, threatening, rough, unjust, dishonest, partial, unfair, dishonorable, unfavorable, repellent.
fairy—*Syn.* sprite, elf, goblin, hobgoblin, spirit, enchantress.
faith—*Syn.* belief, truth, confidence, credence, tenets, credit, doctrine, trust, fidelity. *Ant.* misgiving, infidelity, disbelief, distrust, skepticism, doubt.
faithful—*Syn.* constant, attached, dependable, honest, straight, honorable, trustworthy, firm, devoted. *Ant.* capricious, fickle, unreliable, untrue, untrustworthy, false, wavering, perfidious, treacherous, unable, vacillating, whimsical.
fall—*Syn.* sink, descend, drop, totter, lower, settle, plunge, lessen, diminish. *Ant.* rise, surmount, climb, scale, tower, soar, strengthen, attain.
fallacy—*Syn.* delusion, sophism, sophistry, illusion, error, mistake. *Ant.* truth, truism, sureness, fact, certainty, surety.
false—*Syn.* lying, fallacious, fabricated, counterfeit, sham, unreal, deceptive. *Ant.* true, correct, right, established, known, pure, real.
falter—*Syn.* hesitate, doubt, weaken, demur, waver, shrink, fluctuate, pause, delay. *Ant.* continue, persist, pursue, insist, endure, remain, press, impel.
fame—*Syn.* celebrity, reputation, honor, report, notoriety, distinction, laurels. *Ant.* infamy, discredit, dishonor, shame, disgrace, blemish.
familiar—*Syn.* intimate, unceremonious, affable, easy, unreserved, courteous, accessible, approachable. *Ant.* reserved, restrained, distant, stiff, constrained, formal.
famous—*Syn.* well-known, notorious, illustrious, eminent, noted, distinguished. *Ant.* unknown, humble, retired, hidden, degraded.
fanatical—*Syn.* bigoted, narrow-minded, unreasonable, stubborn. *Ant.* broad, liberal, unprejudiced, tolerant.
fanciful—*Syn.* capricious, fantastic, odd, queer, freakish, changeable, unsteady, inconstant, imaginative, visionary, unreal, romantic, variable. *Ant.* steady, constant, serious, grave, earnest, undeviating, equable, steadfast, determined, invariable, sure, literal, calculated, solid.
fantastic—*Syn.* fanciful, whimsical, capricious, odd, imaginary, uncommon. *Ant.* common, ordinary, customary, usual, normal, conventional.
fantasy—*Syn.* vision, image, imagination, ideality, unreality, idea, view, conceit. *Ant.* reality, actuality, existence, substance, substantiality.
farewell—*Syn.* adieu, dismissal, furlough, valediction, departure, parting.
fascinate—*Syn.* charm, enchant, captivate, beguile, attract, entice, delight, ravish. *Ant.* repel, weary, worry, agitate, anger, horrify, frighten, daunt.
fast—*Syn.* quick, rapid, fleet, swift, expeditious, speedy, accelerated, nimble, active, agile, alert, brisk. *Ant.* slow, sluggish, tardy, inactive, heavy.
fat—*Syn.* fleshy, beefy, portly, stout, obese, swollen. *Ant.* lean, thin, slender, lithe, sinewy, slim, slight.
fatal—*Syn.* mortal, destructive, murderous. *Ant.* enlivening, vivifying, healthy, healthful, invigorating.
fate—*Syn.* destiny, lot, fortune, luck, end, finish, chance, predetermination.
fatigue—*Syn.* weariness, exhaustion, languor, debilitation, weakness. *Ant.* vigor, briskness, liveliness, vim, sprightliness, vivacity.
fault—*Syn.* flaw, imperfection, misdeed, delinquency, slip, defect, weakness, omission, error. *Ant.* advantage, help, gain, benefit, good, favor.
favorable—*Syn.* advantageous, helpful, friendly, kindly, conducive, convenient, beneficial. *Ant.* unfavorable, disadvantageous, derogatory.
fear—*Syn.* fright, affright, horror, panic, dread, scare, tremor, awe, apprehension, anxiety. *Ant.* bold, brave, endurance, heroism, valor, intrepidity, fearlessness.
fearless—*Syn.* bold, brave, courageous, gallant, intrepid, undaunted, dauntless. *Ant.* timid, retiring, cowardly, timorous, fearful, afraid.
feast—*Syn.* banquet, entertainment, festivity, festival, treat, repast. *Ant.* want, privation, famine, poverty, destitution, fast, hunger, scarcity, lack, dearth.
feat—*Syn.* act, effort, deed, performance, exploit, exercise, achievement. *Ant.* inaction, abstinence, passiveness.
feeble—*Syn.* weak, puny, delicate, frail, debilitated, faint, forceless, enervated, weakened, languid, exhausted, impaired. *Ant.* strong, vigorous, forceful, powerful, lusty, robust, firm, hardy, solid, hale, hearty.
feeling—*Syn.* sense, susceptibility, emotion, perception, excitement, sensitiveness, tenderness, opinion, sentiment. *Ant.* insensibility, apathy, indifference, stupidity, unfeeling, impassiveness, lethargy, stoicism, unconcern.
felicity—*Syn.* bliss, rapture, ecstacy, joy, gladness, cheer, pleasure, jollity, frolic. *Ant.* misery, sadness, dejection, melancholy, grief, misfortune, gloom, depression.
felonious—*Syn.* malicious, underhand, vile, despicable, heinous, harmful, hurtful, injurious, vicious, destructive. *Ant.* good, generous, praiseworthy, commendable, kind, decent, helpful, beneficent, meritorious.
feminine—*Syn.* womanly, female, effeminate, soft, tender, delicate. *Ant.* masculine, manly, male, strong.
ferocious—*Syn.* fierce, wild, barbarous, untamed, brutal, vehement, violent, bloodthirsty, brutish, frightful. *Ant.* mild, meek, gentle, tame, tender, peaceful, harmless, innocent, inoffensive, delicate.
fertile—*Syn.* fruitful, prolific, productive, yielding, producing, rich, luxuriant, abundant, plentiful, ample. *Ant.* sterile, barren, unproductive, fruitless, destitute, unprofitable, useless.
feud—*Syn.* quarrel, row, strife, enmity, hostility, controversy, brawl, fray, riot, fracas, vendetta, altercation, argument, disagreement. *Ant.* peace, fraternity, brotherhood, friendliness, harmony.
fickle—*Syn.* uncertain, unreliable, vacillating, unstable, inconstant, mutable, wavering, irresolute, unsteady, volatile. *Ant.* steady, constant, settled, unchanging, resolute, determined, fixed, firm, unvarying, stable, unalterable, sure.
fiction—*Syn.* invention, myth, fable, creation, story, novel, fabrication. *Ant.* history, fact, reality, truth.
fidelity—*Syn.* conscientiousness, trustworthiness, fealty, integrity, loyalty earnestness. *Ant.* unfaithfulness, traitorous, treachery, chicanery, trickery, falsehood.
fierce—*Syn.* furious, ferocious, fiery, wild, enraged, savage, untrained, passionate, angry. *Ant.* mild, gentle, quiet, docile, soft, tame, harmless, tender.
fiery—*Syn.* fierce, vehement, spirited, fervid, irascible, angry, violent, furious, ardent, excited, intense. *Ant.* dull, sluggish, subdued, tiresome, flat, slow, prosy, commonplace.
fill—*Syn.* pack, stuff, pour, feed, swell, satisfy, pervade, occupy, cover, engage, use. *Ant.* empty, exhaust, void, drain, dry, remove, expend, waste, leave, vacate.
filth—*Syn.* dirt, contamination, pollution, foulness, impurity. *Ant.*

cleanliness, purity, cleanness.

find—*Syn.* meet, confront, experience, detect, discover, recover, attain, discern, see. *Ant.* lose, miss, fail, mislay, forfeit, ruin, drop, abandon.

fine, *a.*—*Syn.* beautiful, attractive, showy, dainty, choice, rare, delicate, excellent, polished, refined, slender, minute, thin, suitable, keen, nice, admirable, exquisite, clarified, sharp, clear, small, smooth, elegant, handsome, subtle, pure, sensitive, slight, tenuous, splendid, grand, imposing, gorgeous. *Ant.* coarse, clumsy, heavy, awkward, stout, thick, rude, blunt, rough, gross, indelicate, uncouth, immodest, vulgar, unrefined, brutal, brutish, beastly, bluff, impolite, indecorous, unbecoming, indecent, impudent, shameless, barbarous, uncivil, clownish, ignorant, churlish, rustic, insolent, illiterate, surly, impertinent, saucy, unpolished.

fine, *n.*—*Syn.* penalty, forfeiture, confiscation, damage, loss, punishment. *Ant.* reward, recompense, remuneration, indemnity, reimbursement, amends.

fire—*Syn.* blaze, conflagration, flame, burning, fuel, warmth. heat. *Ant.* cold, chill, bleakness.

firm—*Syn.* solid, strong, enduring, steady, unyielding, unfaltering, resolute, rugged, sturdy, robust, constant. *Ant.* weak, yielding, unsettled, loose, defective, untied, unstable.

fit—*Syn.* suitable, adapted, proper, apt, adequate, expedient, competent, suited, decent, fitted, pertinent, proper. *Ant.* unfit, unsuited, unseemly, amiss, ill-fitting.

fix—*Syn.* determine, establish, limit, fasten, bind, attach, plant, secure, apply, set, root, establish. *Ant.* change, unsettle, weaken, unlock, unbolt, loose, loosen, shake, disturb, unfix, unlatch, detach, disarrange, displace, free, set free.

flat—*Syn.* dull, tasteless, unpleasing, prostrate, fallen, horizontal, level, positive, low. *Ant.* sharp, effervescing, keen, spirited, lively, raised, elevated, uneven, rugged, hilly, mountainious.

flatter—*Syn.* praise, laud, extol, blandish, caress, gratify, satisfy, please. *Ant.* condemn, denounce, mock, despise, scorn.

fleeting—*Syn.* transient, transitory, brief, ephemeral, short, passing, temporary, momentary. *Ant.* long, enduring, lasting, constant, continual, eternal, endless.

flexible—*Syn.* pliant, supple, yielding, limber, lithe, bending, docile, tractable. *Ant.* stiff, unbending, unyielding, rigid, resistant, obstinate.

flimsy—*Syn.* gauzy, thin, transparent, trifling, slight, weak, unsubstantial, feeble. *Ant.* thick, solid, heavy, serious, strong, firm, substantial, tough, unbreakable, tenacious.

flock—*Syn.* herd, litter, brood, drove, pack, bevy, collection, company, throng, gathering, congregation.

flourish—*Syn.* prosper, increase, grow, accumulate, triumph, overcome, conquer, wave, twirl, shake. *Ant.* decay, diminish, weaken, descend, sink, decrease, tumble, collapse, deteriorate, wither.

flow—*Syn.* stream, issue, course, run, float, move, pass, circulate. *Ant.* stop, stagnate, check, cease, obstruct, cork.

fluctuate—*Syn.* vacillate, hesitate, digress, deflect, wander, undulate, veer, alter, stay, stick, abide, remain, delay, postpone, decide.

fluent—*Syn.* liquid, moving, voluble, smooth, easy, glib, apt, expert, prepared. *Ant.* hesitant, hesitating, stuttering, slow, unprepared, dilatory, sluggish, motionless.

foe—*Syn.* antagonist, adversary, opponent, combatant, competitor. *Ant.* friend, helper, assistant, associate, companion, comrade.

folk—*Syn.* people, persons, individuals, group, crowd, congregation, community, members, association.

follow—*Syn.* pursue, chase, accompany, imitate, copy, ensue, use, go after, attend, observe, heed, mimic, mock. *Ant.* discard, reject, scorn, ignore, shun, disregard, elude, slight, abjure.

follower—*Syn.* retainer, henchman, attendant, partisan, disciple, adherent, successor, protege. *Ant.* enemy, antagonist, adversary.

folly—*Syn.* weakness, foolishness, absurdity. *Ant.* wisdom, knowledge, sapience, prudence, understanding, judgement, cunning.

fond—*Syn.* affectionate, kind, devoted, ardent. *Ant.* cold, reserved, unattached, scornful, indifferent, cool, restrained, unconcerned.

foolish—*Syn.* simple, brainless, preposterous, ridiculous, fatuous, thick-headed. *Ant.* wise, astute, keen, careful, prudent, judicious, sagacious, well-advised, discerning, circumspect, considerate.

fop—*Syn.* coxcomb, idler, loafer, lounger, trifler, pretender, impostor. *Ant.* gentleman, hero, scholar, philosopher, savant.

forbear—*Syn.* pause, spare, desist, avoid, delay, cease, bear, endure, stay. *Ant.* act, do, perform, accomplish, persevere, continue.

forbid *Syn.* prohibit, debar, restrain, interdict, hinder, obstruct, bar, deny, exclude. *Ant.* sanction, encourage, commend, recommend, approve, command, abet, permit.

force, *v.*—*Syn.* coerce, compel, drive, make, impel, constrain, press, rush, instigate, incite. *Ant.* restrain, hinder, impede, block, obstruct, prevent, stop, check, suppress, retard, thwart.

forebode—*Syn.* betoken, foretell, prognosticate, surmise, predict, forewarn.

forecast, *v.*—*Syn.* predict, prophesy, foretell, divine, soothsay. *Ant.* recall, call up, remember, recollect, look back.

forego—*Syn.* quit, relinquish, waive, renounce, resign, leave, pass by. *Ant.* hold, keep, retain, preserve, maintain.

foreign—*Syn.* alien, strange, outside, extraneous, outside, far, distant, irrelevant, unaccustomed. *Ant.* native, indigenous, similar, familiar, aboriginal, known.

forerunner—*Syn.* herald, harbinger, precursor, predecessor, sign, warning. *Ant.* successor, descendant, offspring, follower, disciple.

foresight—*Syn.* premeditation, foreknowledge, prognostication, prudence, prevision. *Ant.* ignorance, wastefulness, foolishness, thoughtlessness.

forever, *adj.*—*Syn.* everlasting, continual, unending, ceaseless, endless, eternal, enduring, immortal, perpetual. *Ant.* temporary, brief, short, transitory, momentary, transient, fleeting, fading, perishable.

forever*adv.*—*Syn.* perpetual, everlasting, continual, endless, constant, unceasing, unremitting. *Ant.* temporary, briefly, transitorily, fleeting.

forge—*Syn.* falsify, counterfeit, fabricate, frame, force, drive, impel, make, fashion, produce, reproduce.

forgive—*Syn.* remit, absolve, acquit, excuse, cancel, release, clear, exonerate. *Ant.* withhold, retain, accuse, charge, arraign, blame.

forlorn—*Syn.* forsaken, forgotten, misereable, alone, solitary, deprived, deserted, abject, desolate, lost, dejected, bereaved. *Ant.* glad, merry, cheerful, joyous, gay, happy, gratified, satisfied, comfortable.

form, *v.*—*Syn.* shape, fashion, construct, devise, plan, design, contrive, produce, invent, arrange, plot, compose, erect, build. *Ant.* ruin, wreck, disarrange, scatter, tear down, overthrow, devastate, raze, upset, undo.

formal—*Syn.* ceremonial, precise, exact, punctilious, orderly, official, imposing, solemn, decorous. *Ant.* common, ordinary, usual, customary, habitual, regular, conventional, general, accustomed.

former—*Syn.* foregoing, before, prior. *Ant.* latter, after, succeeding, following, consequent.

formidable—*Syn.* dangerous, impregnable, invincible, awe-inspiring, impressive, awful, fearful. *Ant.* harmless, helpless, feeble, weak, powerless, insignificant.

forsake—*Syn.* desert, leave, relinquish, fail, renounce, abdicate, evacuate, disown. *Ant.* remain, stay, continue, persevere, assist, comfort, hold, maintain, claim.

fortification—*Syn.* fort, fortress, breastwork, escarpment, defense, citadel, stronghold, parapet, protection.

fortitude—*Syn.* courage, strength, firmness, intrepidity, fearlessness, courage, bravery, daring, dauntlessness, valor, forbearance. *Ant.* weakness, cowardice, fear, panic, timidity, fright, trepidation, dismay.

fortune—*Syn.* chance, fate, luck, destiny, lot, riches, wealth, inheritance.

foster—*Syn.* cherish, nurture, nourish, tend, indulge, favor, please, comfort, care for. *Ant.* neglect, ignore, spurn, slight, shun, disdain, reject, abandon.

foul—*Syn.* filthy, unclean, defiled, tainted, polluted, offensive, rotten, corrupt, contaminated, soiled, tarnished, fotid, coarse, vulgar, noxious, unfair, dishonest. *Ant.* purified, untainted, unsullied, unblemished, innocent, speckless, lovely, becoming, agreeable.

foundation—*Syn.* base, root, origin, bottom, underpinning, endowment, institution, rudiments, support. *Ant.* top, crown, apex, roof, dome, tower, covering, summit, pinnacle.

foxy—*Syn.* cunning, sly, tricky, experienced, crafty, knowing, shrewd, sagacious, artful, shifty, wary. *Ant.* foolish, rash, impetuous, heavy, heedless, careless, undiscerning.

fragile—*Syn.* frail, weak, breakable, infirm. *Ant.* lusty, robust, tough, unbreakable, resistant, enduring.

fragments—*Syn.* scraps, leavings, remains, residue, remainder. *Ant.* all, total, aggregate, entire, gross.

frame—*Syn.* fashion, make, fabricate, invent, plan, shape, adjust, contrive. *Ant.* wreck, scatter, ruin, demolish, raze.

franchise—*Syn.* right, suffrage, liberty, privilege, voice, choice. *Ant.* bondage, slavery, serfdom, servitude, oppression.

frank—*Syn.* sincere, familiar, open, ingenuous, plain. *Ant.* secretive, deceptive, insincere, hypocritical, deceitful, disingenuous, tricky.

frantic—*Syn.* raging, frenzied, violent, agitated, delirious, angry. *Ant.* quiet, subdued, meek, mild, docile, tractable, easy, gentle, kind, cool, collected, dispassionate.

fraud—*Syn.* deceit, cheat, artifice, chicanery, swindle, treason, trick, dishonesty, cheating. *Ant.* integrity truth, good, faith, justice, probity, sincerity, equity, right.

free, *v.*—*Syn.* liberate, discharge, unfetter, unbind, release, set free, deliver, rescue, emancipate, acquit, absolve, clear, extricate, exonerate, forgive. *Ant.* bind, incarcerate, confine, restrict, bound, limit, check, curb, prevent, repress, suppress, chain, secure, shackle.

freedom—*Syn.* liberty, openness, outspokenness, license, liberality, exemption, privilege, right, immunity, familiarity. *Ant.* slavery, imprisonment, confinement, submission, captivity, restriction, hindrance.

frequently—*Syn.* often, regularly, usually. *Ant.* rarely, seldom, infrequently.

fret—*Syn.* chafe, gnaw, corrode, agitate, anger, annoy. *Ant.* calm, comfort, soften, please, placate, smooth, heal.

friend—*Syn.* associate, companion, acquaintance, familiar, ally, chum *(colloq.)*, messmate, comrade, pal *(slang)*, buddy *(slang)*, side-kick *(slang)*, mate, accomplice, adherent, partner, coadjutor, assistant, confidant. *Ant.* enemy, adversary, opponent, backbiter, calumniator, slanderer, vilifier, foe, foeman, antagonist, competitor, rival, defamer, detractor.

friendship—*Syn.* friendliness, companionship, brotherhood, fraternity, attachment, fellowship. *Ant.* hatred, rancor, dislike, antipathy, aversion, ill will, abhorrence, loathing.

frighten—*Syn.* daunt, intimidate, alarm, shock. *Ant.* assure, encourage, strengthen.

frightful—*Syn.* calamitous, shocking, terrible, awful, horrid, direful, appalling, detestable. *Ant.* appealing, captivating, agreeable, delightful, admirable, amiable.

frivolous—*Syn.* petty, trifling, unimportant, worthless, inconsequential, paltry. *Ant.* important, witty, solemn, weighty, formal, thoughtful, significant, essential, pertinent.

frugality—*Syn.* economy, conservation, providence, thrift, stinginess, avarice. *Ant.* waste, lavishness, spending, extravagance, liberality, indulgence, excess, superfluity, squandering.

fruitful—*Syn.* fertile, rich, luxuriant, yielding, ample, bountiful, exuberant. *Ant.* waste, unproductive, empty, unprofitable, unyielding, bare, impotent, ineffective, spent, depleted.

frustrate—*Syn.* nullify, baffle, confound, disconcert, bar, thwart, hinder, counteract, prevent. *Ant.* help, assist, encourage, cooperate, succor, aid, befriend, countenance, stimulate, incite.

fulfill—*Syn.* perform, execute, do, achieve, consumate, terminate, realize, discharge, attain. *Ant.* fail, omit, disappoint, miss, cease, resign, stop, abandon, forsake, relinquish.

furious—*Syn.* vehement, angry, rolling, impetuous, frantic, raging, mad, desperate, dangerous, wild, ferocious, delirious, frenzied, rabid, infuriated, excited, reckless, fuming. *Ant.* cool, collected, peaceful, mild, gentle, gratified, pacific, unruffled, placid, undisturbed, affable, gracious, indulgent.

futile—*Syn.* vain, ineffective, ineffectual, inefficient, fruitless, unavailing, abortive, empty, worthless, resultless, unsatisfying, bootless, valueless. *Ant.* effective, satisfactory, efficient, fruitful, advantageous, profitable, yielding, gainful, beneficial, useful, helpful.

G

gain, *n.*—*Syn.* profit, advantage, benefit, winnings, interest, achievement, increase, improvement. *Ant.* loss, disadvantage, deprivation, defeat, detriment, damage.

gallant—*Syn.* brave, intrepid, heroic, fearless, courteous, chivalrous, valiant, valorous, puissant, undaunted, strong, mighty, forcible, daring, civil, polite, dauntless. *Ant.* coward, timid, fearful, craven, sneaking, dastardly, base, mean, contemptible, discourteous, unpolished, rough, vulgar, ungracious.

galling—*Syn.* irritating, vexing, annoying, provoking, troublesome, distressing, tantalizing. *Ant.* consoling, mollifying, softening, allaying, appeasing.

game, *a.*—*Syn.* brave, bold, daring, enduring, gallant, courageous, cocky, fearless, plucky. *Ant.* cowardly, shrinking, craven, timid.

gang—*Syn.* horde, troop, crew, crowd, tribe, clan, company, association, fraternity, group, sect.

gap—*Syn.* cavity, cleft, crevice, rift, chink, break, opening, passage, space, vacuity, crack, aperture, fissure, hole, rent, orifice. *Ant.* inclosure, fence, wall, rail, bolt, barrier, guard.

garnish—*Syn.* embellish, furnish, supply, ornament, bedeck, grace, trim. *Ant.* spoil, deface, disfigure, impair, mar, injure, destroy, raze, obliterate, ruin, harm.

garrulous—*Syn.* talkative, loquacious, chattering, verbose, babbling. *Ant.* silent, reserved, quiet, still, reticent.

gather—*Syn.* accumulate, amass, assemble, meet, aggregate, congregate, pick, cull, convene, hoard, pile, store, garner. *Ant.* spread, dispel, dissipate, distribute, dispense, share, assign, diffuse, separate.

gaudy—*Syn.* tawdry, glittering, bespangled, adorned, ornamented, fine, garish, alluring, dazzling, sparkling, scintillating, glistening, glamorous, glossy. *Ant.* dull, lustreless, solemn, heavy, tarnished, gloomy, depressing, dismal, dusky, obscure, colorless, faded, withered.

gaunt—*Syn.* skinny, meagre, spare, slender, empty, bony, shriveled, shrunk, hungry. *Ant.* fat, obese, robust, fleshy, corpulent, gross, portly, well-fed, lusty, vigorous, hale, well-developed.

gay—*Syn.* lively, sportive, jovial, showy, cheerful, joyous, happy, bright, buoyant, jocular, witty. *Ant.* dull, listless, discouraged, morose, sulky, dogged, sullen, solemn, moody, melancholy, languid, petulant, gloomy, grim, angry, depressed, crushed, dejected.

general—*Syn.* common, universal, comprehensive, inclusive, public, prevalent, usual, customary, normal, frequent, habitual, usual, conventional, regular. *Ant.* particular, definite, limited, rare, circumscribed, unusual, unknown, exceptional, unlike, alone, single, solitary.

generally—*Syn.* usually, mainly, commonly, ordinarily, principally. *Ant.* particularly, rarely, seldom, infrequently.

generate—*Syn.* form, bear, furnish, bring forth, yield, breed, engender, create. *Ant.* destroy, demolish, abolish, extinguish, obliterate, annihilate, suppress, overthrow, shatter, undo.

generation—*Syn.* race, stock, reproduction, creation, progeny, era, span, period. *Ant.* destruction, wreck, extinction, demolition, abolition, dissolution, obliteration, breakdown.

generous—*Syn.* beneficent, liberal, munificent, open-handed, free, freehanded, magnanimous, unselfish. *Ant.* miserly, closefisted, parsimonious, stingy, penurious, beggarly, avaricious, mean, sordid, covetous, grasping, greedy, ignoble.

genial—*Syn.* kind, warmhearted, pleasant, cheering, merry, revivifying, inspiring, affable, polite, fraternal, cheerful, jolly, joyful. *Ant.* dull, moody, gloomy, dismal, sour, morose, sulky, dogged, sullen, solemn, austere, irritable, testy, surly, depressing, rude, uncongenial, splenetic, fretful, pensive.

genius—*Syn.* talent, intellect, brains, gift, faculty, wisdom, gumption, longheadedness, astuteness, sagacity. *Ant.* idiocy, folly, silliness, incapacity, moroseness, hebetude, stupidity, foolishness, brainlessness, incompetence, futility.

genteel—*Syn.* polite, cultured, pleasing, graceful, elegant, mannerly, courteous, elegant, kind, bland. *Ant.* rough, gruff, gross, coarse, thick, dense, stupid, dull, doleful, dolesome, boorish, sour, surly, sulky, sullen, severe, stern, harsh, rugged, dogged, stubborn, clownish, rustic, rude, ill-bred, ill-mannered, grouchy, grumpy, harsh, morose, censorious, captious, snappish, snarling, growling, disagreeable, forbidding, odious, repulsive, repugnant, repelling.

gentle—*Syn.* bland, peaceful, meek, soothing, calm, easy, tender, pleasant. —*Syn.* rough, boorish, uncultured, uncouth, coarse, harsh, rude, wild, unpolished, vulgar, gross, uncivil, ungracious.

genuine—*Syn.* real, veritable, proven, tested, unmixed, authentic, actual, unquestioned, right, exact, sincere, factual, unquestionable. *Ant.* false, deceptive, unreal, unacceptable, illegitimate, adulterated, mixed.

germ—*Syn.* origin, source, beginning, bud, embryo, sprout, sprig, offshoot, root.

gesture—*Syn.* action, motion, movement, carriage, pose, manner, demeanor.

get—*Syn.* receive, procure, earn, attain, acquire, secure, win, beget. *Ant.* leave, quit, relinquish, surrender.

ghastly—*Syn.* grim, shocking, ghostlike, weird, unnatural, terrible, grisly, frightful, dreadful. *Ant.* pleasing, pleasant, agreeable, beautiful, fine, lovely, attractive, compelling, healthy, rosy, vigorous, strong.

gibe—*Syn.* sneer, jeer, taunt, mimic, ape, ridicule, harass, fool, tantalize, tease, twit, irritate. *Ant.* praise, encourage, laud, eulogize, applaud, commend, forward, urge, sanction, admire, advance.

giddy—*Syn.* light, light-hearted, unsteady, doddering, shaky, uncertain, dizzy, silly. *Ant.* solemn, serious, reliable, firm, constant, calm, cool, level-headed, sedate, careful.

gift—*Syn.* presentation, largess, grant, gratuity, boon, present, endowment, bequest, legacy, bequeathment, favor, bestowal. *Ant.* loss, privation, deprivation, forfeiture, damage, injury, penalty, disinheritance.

gigantic—*Syn.* huge, immense, enormous, prodigious, vast, great, mammoth, massive. *Ant.* small, little, minute, diminutive, slight, inconsiderable, abbreviated.

give—*Syn.* bestow, yield, deliver, furnish, supply, cede, deliver. *Ant.* take, deprive, divest, remove, keep, retain.

glad—*Syn.* cheerful, gratified, joyous, delighted, happy, pleasing, gay, blithesome, jolly, lively, sprightly, vivacious. *Ant.* sad, sorrowful, gloomy, dull, mournful, cast down, grieved, discouraged.

glare—*Syn.* glisten, scintillate, glitter, shine, flash, glimmer, gleam, glow.

glaring—*Syn.* staring, piercing, penetrating, obvious, outstanding, gazing.

glassy—*Syn.* vitreous, smooth, polished, transparent, glossy, translucent. *Ant.* opaque, dull, lustreless, dim, obscure, dusky, dark.

glee—*Syn.* joviality, merriment, mirth, hilarity, gaiety, joy, exhilaration. *Ant.* dullness, gloom, sadness, sorrow, misery, melancholy.

gloom—*Syn.* darkness, duskiness, obscurity, sadness, depression, dejection, dullness, misfortune. *Ant.* rejoicing, fun, frivolity, mirth, joy, delight, happiness.

glorify—*Syn.* magnify, extol, celebrate, praise, worship, honor, revere, esteem, applaud, elevate. *Ant.* debase, lower, dishonor, disrespect, despise, condemn, depress, disgrace, humiliate, shame, disparage.

glorious—*Syn.* famous, renowned, distinguished, illustrous, splendid, wonderful, marvelous, brilliant. *Ant.* infamous, disgraceful, shameful, shameless, ignominious.

glory—*Syn.* honor, renown, grandeur, celebrity, brightness, brillancy, blaze. *Ant.* disgrace, dishonor, abasement, degradation, humiliation, debasement, depression, shame, infamy, opacity, gloom, obscurity.

glossy—*Syn.* shining, reflecting, lustrous, polished, smooth. *Ant.* dull, lustreless, clouded, dimmed, stained, unpolished.

glut—*Syn.* fill, stuff, cram, satiate, surfeit, feast, satisfy, consume, raven. *Ant.* abstain, fast, restrain, reduce, curb, moderate.

go—*Syn.* move, pass, proceed, step, walk, disappear, travel, run, leave, recede, relinquish. *Ant.* come, become, begin, approach, appear, arrive.

God—*Syn.* Lord, Ruler, Creator, Almighty, Omnipotence, Providence, Author, Divinity, Supreme Being, Deity.

good, *a.*—*Syn.* righteous, upright, virtuous, honest, true, just, moral, chaste, pure, fine. *Ant.* bad, evil, wicked, vile, sinful, depraved, impure, corrupt, unsound, dishonorable.

gorgeous—*Syn.* grand, magnificent, stately, surpassing, glorious, great, majestic, imposing, brilliant, dazzling. *Ant.* plain, simple, unpretentious, dull, common, modest.

govern—*Syn.* rule, direct, control, manage, moderate, guide, curb, influence, reign, sway, restrain, conduct, regulate. *Ant.* obey, submit, yield, comply, assent, accede.

graceful—*Syn.* becoming, comely, beautiful, neat, fit, suitable, fitting, charming. *Ant.* awkward, uncouth, ungraceful, undignified, vulgar, rude, careless, negligent, unrefined.

gracious—*Syn.* kind, kindly, beneficent, nice, munificent, courteous. *Ant.* rough, rude, dominating, harsh, unkind, ungracious.

gradual—*Syn.* creeping, progressive, continuous, unintermittent, gradational, regular. *Ant.* sudden, unexpected, precipitate, intermittent, hasty.

grand—*Syn.* dignified, lofty, elevated, exalted, splendid, sublime, great, illustrious, elegant. *Ant.* shabby, mean, inferior, beggarly, low, ragged, tattered, unimposing, ordinary.

grant, *n.*—*Syn.* gift, reward, present, stipend, benefaction, gratuity, endowment, bequest. *Ant.* loss, deprivation, deduction.

grasp—*Syn.* clutch, seize, retain, grip, capture, comprehend, understand, discern, recognize, deduce. *Ant.* lose, slip, let go, miss, free, liberate, extricate, misconstrue, misunderstand.

grateful—*Syn.* thankful, appreciative, beholden, obliged, accepatable, gratifying, delicious. *Ant.* thankless, unmindful, forgetful, heedless.

gratification—*Syn.* satisfaction, delight, reward, comfort, happiness,

content, compensation. *Ant.* denial, sacrifice, abstinence, humiliation, disappointmont.
gratify—*Syn.* indulge, humor, satisfy, please, placate, grant. *Ant.* displease, deprive, provoke.
grave, *n.*—*Syn.* tomb, sepulchre, vault, pit, hollow, burial, place, crypt, mausoleum, catacomb.
great—*Syn.* large, huge, gigantic, vast, noble, grand, extensive, bulky, extended, wide, strong, eminent, famous, illustrious, famed, renowned, honorable.
greedy—*Syn.* avaricious, grasping, rapacious, gluttonous, voracious, devouring, miserly, close-fisted, grudging, stingy, covetous. *Ant.* liberal, charitable, philanthropic, profuse, lavish, spendthrift, extravagant.
grief—*Syn.* sadness, affliction, regret, woe, melancholy, misfortune, adversity, calamity, trouble, hardship, worry, anguish. *Ant.* joy, gladness, rejoicing, happiness, ecstasy, delight, gratification, satisfaction, pleasure.
grim—*Syn.* sullen, stern, austere, severe, sour, harsh. *Ant.* pleasant, mild, bland, blithe, merry, gay, jovial, cheerful.
grind—*Syn.* crush, harass, tire, worry, annoy, afflict, dominate, inflict, overwhelm, grate. *Ant.* lighten, relieve, succor, help, assist, comfort, alleviate, allay, soften, lessen, soothe, mollify, gladden.
grisly—*Syn.* horrible, terrible, disgusting, repugnant, abominable. *Ant.* pleasing, attractive, compelling, nice, handsome, beautiful, alluring.
gross—*Syn.* indelicate, rough, vulgar, corrupt, impure, dense, bulky, enormous, corpulent, large, ponderous, rude, low, vulgar. *Ant.* fine, delicate, dainty, refined, comely, fair, slender, thin, graceful, handsome.
ground—*Syn.* land, estate, property, section, quarter, part, surface, region, territory, locality, habitat, basis.
group—*Syn.* collection, order, class, assemblage, bunch, crowd, audience, company, throng.
grovel—*Syn.* fawn, sneak, stoop, kneel, crouch, cower, snivel, beseech, implore. *Ant.* command, order, control, govern, direct, rule, lead, master, scorn, disdain, deride.
grow—*Syn.* expand, swell, enlarge, augment, stretch, spread, develop, extend. *Ant.* decrease, diminish, lessen, abate, reduce, lower, fade, decline.
growl—*Syn.* snarl, complain, murmur, mutter, bemoan, groan, rumble, speak harshly.
grudge—*Syn.* malice, hatred, aversion, animosity, enmity, ill-will, malevolence, antipathy. *Ant.* goodwill, benevolence, friendliness, kindness, tenderness, kindheartedness, affection, love, affinity.
guarantee—*Syn.* certify, testify, aver, vouch, attest, assure, indorse, insure, obligate, confirm, affirm, allege. *Ant.* deny, disown, ignore, deprecate, disapprove, condemn, censure, disclaim, oppose, reject, disavow, renounce.
guard—*Syn.* watch, protect, guide, secure, defend, safeguard, keep, preserve, shield, supervise. *Ant.* neglect, forsake, abandon, disregard, desert, leave, quit, relinquish.
guide—*Syn.* lead, direct, control, regulate, persuade, induce, order, contrive, manage, educate.
guile—*Syn.* craft, cunning, artifice, duplicity, deceit, trickery, dishonesty. *Ant.* honesty, openness, candor, fair-dealing, frankness, sincerity, integrity.

H

habit—*Syn.* practice, tendency, fashion, form, manner, routine, addiction, use; method, covering, dress, raiment. *Ant.* irregularity, disuse, rarity, infrequency, uncoventionality, unpunctuality.
hack, *v.*—*Syn.* cut, chop, mangle, tear, split, break, lacerate, botch, notch, chip, drudge, toil.
Hades—*Syn.* hell, underworld, inferno, infernal regions. *Ant.* heaven, paradise.
haggard—*Syn.* gaunt, fretted, worried, wrinkled, lean, meagre, thin, emaciated, wasted, tired, exhausted, weak, debilitated. *Ant.* strong, robust, healthy, blooming, exuberant, lively, active.
hail—*Syn.* call, address, salute, greet, compliment, approach, welcome, honor, acclaim, applaud. *Ant.* ignore, neglect, disregard, slight, scorn, avoid, elude.
hall—*Syn.* entrance, vestibule, passage, castle, room, auditorium, meeting-place, headquarters, public building.
halt—*Syn.* stop, check, linger, limp, falter, stammer, demur, doubt, pause, cease, rest, suspend, intermit, discontinue. *Ant.* go, proceed, advance, continue, walk, run, progress, move, endure, pursue.
hamper—*Syn.* impede, thwart, embarrass, perplex, confuse, annoy, disconcert, prevent, retard, check, hinder, prevent, restrain. *Ant.* facilitate, help, assist, encourage, succor, favor, comfort, relieve, support, forward, promote.
handsome—*Syn.* beautiful, graceful, lovely, pretty, elegant, shapely, agreeable, large, ample. *Ant.* ungraceful, offensive, revolting, mean, poor, miserly, small, insignificant.
handy—*Syn.* convenient, useful, helpful, ready, skilled, resourceful, apt, dexterous. *Ant.* unhandy, clumsy, unskilled, untrained, awkward, inexpert, fumbling.
haphazard—*Syn.* accidental, chancy, risky, sudden, careless, random. *Ant.* considered, premeditated, deliberate, intentional, determined, planned, intended.
hapless—*Syn.* unfortunate, miserable, unlucky, ill-fated. *Ant.* fortunate, lucky, favored, fortuitous, happy, satisfied.
happen—*Syn.* bechance, occur, chance, fall, supervene, arrive, ensue, result, eventuate.
happily—*Syn.* fortunately, gracefully, luckily, successfully, felicitously. *Ant.* unfortunately, unluckily, unsuccessfully, disastrously.
happiness—*Syn.* bliss, beautitude, blessedness, aptness, joy, contentment, satisfaction, delight, exulta tion. *Ant.* misery, misfortune, unhappiness, grief, sorrow, melancholy, gloom, despair, calamity.
happy—*Syn.* joyous, joyful, merry, mirthful, glad, delighted, delightful, cheerful, contented, satisfied, felicitous, blithe, jolly, blissful, jovial, gratified, pleasing. *Ant.* sad, unhappy, moody, morose, sour, discontented, disappointed, unfortunate, gloomy, dejected, despairing, tormented, disconsolate, cheerless, hopeless, forsaken, distressed.
harass—*Syn.* annoy, vex, irritate, plague, tantalize, taunt, provoke, worry, molest, pester, rouse, inflame, enrage, incense, defame, arouse, infuriate. *Ant.* cheer, appease, encourage, assist, advise, befriend, comfort, incite, revive, refresh, strengthen, sustain, relieve.
hard—*Syn.* compact, solid, unyielding, resisting, strong, substantial, stable, compressed, close, dense, pressed, rocky, rigid. *Ant.* soft, yielding, light, pliant, susceptible, muddy.
hardship—*Syn.* burden, privation, affliction, oppression, adversity, misfortune, disaster, distress, trouble, tribulation. *Ant.* benefit, good, profit, gain, utility, vantage, emolument, blessing, boon, benefit, improvement, sustenance.
hardy—*Syn.* enduring, tenacious, unyielding, intrepid, brave, robust, vigorous, dauntless, daring, spirited, valorous. *Ant.* weak, yielding, soft, tender, timid, debilitated, impaired, apprehensive, timid, shrinking, submissive.
harm—*Syn.* wrong, damage, hurt, detriment, evil, deterioration, loss, deprivation. *Ant.* good, benefit, advantage, advancement, interest, blessing, profit.
harmless—*Syn.* innocuous, inoffensive, innocent, blameless, simple, unblemished, spotless. *Ant.* harmful, injurious, noxious, bad, malicious, sinful.
harmonious—*Syn.* agreeable, accordant, corresponding, suitable, fit, adapted, melodious, tuneful, similar, like. *Ant.* discordant, disagreeable, unlike, opposed, unsuitable, dissonant, clashing, jangling, incompatible.
harmony—*Syn.* concord, agreement, unison, accord, union, unanimity, congruity, unity, uniformity, melody, consistency, concert, conformity, music, tune. *Ant.* discord, jangle, disagreement, dissonance, discordance, inconsistency, difference, incongruity, disunion, wavering, variation, deviation, alternation, conflict, contention.
harsh—*Syn.* rough, rigorous, severe, austere, stern, gruff, hard, cruel, sharp, cutting, keen, acrimonious, bitter, ungracious, brutal, ill-tempered, jarring, rigid, strict, unrelenting, merciless, selfish, surly, sour, snarling, rude, overbearing. *Ant.* gentle, mild, easy, unselfish, meek, placid, even, kind, moderate, peaceful, quiet, unassuming, bashful, merciful, patient, calm, humble, soft, tender, yielding, sympathetic, feeling, agreeable, pleasant, congenial, consoling, encouraging.
harvest—*Syn.* product, result, profit, product, yield, crop, growth, intake, amount, reaping.
hastle—*Syn.* hurry, speed, nimbleness, rapidity, celerity, swiftness, quickness, urgency, rush, activity. *Ant.* tardiness, lagging, loitering, delay, lateness, stay, inaction, leisure, ease, rest, collapse.
hasten—*Syn.* accelerate, speed, expedite, hurry, run, sprint, dash, scamper. *Ant.* delay, postpone, loiter,, linger, defer, prolong, lag, drawl, saunter, plod, trudge, drag, dawdle, limp, totter, stagger.
hasty—*Syn.* hurried, rash, eager, quick, speedy, precipitate, rushing, sudden, foolhardy, thoughtless, heedless, impulsive, careless, reckless, incautious. *Ant.* thoughtful, patient, slow, deliberate, careful, considerate, intentional, wary, discreet, contemplative, calculating, observing, calm, cool.
hate—*Syn.* abhor, abominate, loathe, detest, dislike, despise, denounce. *Ant.* love, regard, like, approve, praise, value, admire, esteem, adore, respect, revere.
hateful—*Syn.* odious, detestable, repugnant, revolting, repulsive, disagreeable, obnoxious. *Ant.* lovable, amiable, attractive, estimable, agreeable, engaging, pleasing, satisfying, enchanting, chaste, incorrupt.
hatred—*Syn.* enmity, rancor, antipathy, abhorrence, aversion, dislike, hostility, loathing, spite, malice, grudge, resentment, acrimony, bitterness, repugnance, animosity. *Ant.* love, kindness, friendship, fondness, regard, admiration, devotion, enchantment, affection, reverence.
haughtiness—*Syn.* arrogance, disdain, pride, presumption, vanity, conceit, pretension, affectation, egotism, insolence, swagger, ostentation. *Ant.* modesty, timidity, unobtrusiveness, diffidence, meekness, mildness, gentility, graciousness, shyness, subserviency, deference.
haughty—*Syn.* arrogant, disdainful, supercilious, proud, imperious, pompous, bumptious, affected, prim. *Ant.* lowly, humble, unassuming, bashful, backward, submissive, timid, afraid, unobtrusive, unpretentious, unpretending, ashamed, browbeaten, crushed.
hazard—*Syn.* risk, venture, chance, danger, peril, casualty, adventure, pssibility, gamble, uncertainty, presumption. *Ant.* certainty, assurance, fact, reality, determination, decision, confidence, conviction, reliance, security, actuality, realization, protection.
hazy—*Syn.* cloudy, foggy, murky, misty, nebulous, filmy, gauzy, vaporous, smoky, thick, dim, obscure, uncertain, wavering. *Ant.* clear, transparent, bright, luminous, light, vivid, distinct, lucid, brilliant, radiant.
head—*Syn.* summit, top, crown, peak, crest, acme, apex, culmination, pinnacle, guide, leader, ruler, chief, boss, foreman, master, overseer, source, beginning, intellect, mind, brain, faculty, reason, understanding, mentality, intelligence, reasoning, instinct, capacity. *Ant.* base, bottom, foot, foundation, sub-

structure, ground, basis, level, support, rest, follower, disciple, pupil, attendant, imitator, incapacity.
healthy—*Syn.* sound, salubrious, robust, strong, wholesome, hale, vigorous, virile, well, hearty, unimpaired, lusty, invigorating, prophylactic, bracing, nutritious, sanative, sanitary, sanatory, healing, hygeian, hygienic. *Ant.* unhealthy, bad, corrupt, rotten, septic, deadly, weak, worn, emaciated, sick, unsound, ill, fragile, frail, fainting, exhausted, disposed, infirm, ailing, disordered.
heap, *n.*—*Syn.* pile, accumulation, mass, quantity, load, collection, aggregation, abundance, profusion, plenty, lump, sum, whole. *Ant.* modicum, minimum, molecule, speck, dot, iota, fragment, chip, piece, trifle, morsel, mite, bit.
heap, *v.*—*Syn.* pile, aggregate, accumulate, amass, collect, gather, increase, hoard, add, augment, enlarge, swell, expand. *Ant.* lessen, abate, diminish, reduce, decrease, curtail, minimize, lower, dwindle, shrivel, shrink, constrict, contract, compress.
hearty—*Syn.* cordial, warm, sincere, cheery, cheerful, vivacious, gay, healthy, animated, jovial, jolly, friendly, ardent, genial, fervid, glowing, enthusiastic. *Ant.* insincere, false, dissembling, deceitful, hypocritical, deceptive, smug, mealy, unctuous, simpering, affected, simulating, pretending, feigned, spurious, counterfeit, sham, mock, perfidious.
heat—*Syn.* warmth, calidity, fire, flame, blaze, furnace, ardor, passion, excitement, temperature, fever, intensity, fervor, zeal, agitation, emotion, flush, glow. *Ant.* cold, frost, chilliness, frigidity, apathy, unconcern, stoicism, lethargy, repression.
heavy—*Syn.* weighty, ponderous, burdensome, massive, cumbersome, bulky, large. *Ant.* light, slight, trivial, inconsequental, trifling.
heed—*Syn.* attention, devotion, watch, observation, notice, application, consideration, concern, solicitude, caution, regard. *Ant.* carelessness, neglect, disregard, unconcern, difference, apathy.
heighten—*Syn.* enhance, emphasize, intensify, strengthen, increase, augment, amplify, magnify, raise, elevate, acclaim. *Ant.* lower, weaken, lessen, deprecate, depreciate, reduce, abate, underrate, traduce.
heinous—*Syn.* atrocious, flagrant, awful, terrible, infamous, wicked, nefarious, immoral, bad, evil, vile, outrageous, infernal, corrupt, dissolute, disgraceful, disreputable, loathsome, degrading, notorious, abominable, abhorrent, detestable, foul. *Ant.* virtuous, moral, good, righteous, deserving, worthy, fine, laudable, excellent, commendable, admirable, exemplary, ideal, ethical, pure, exalted, approved, acceptable, proper, honorable, elevated, dignified, upright.
help—*Syn.* assist, aid, succor, relieve, support, uphold, sustain, encourage, advise, abet, foster, cooperate, nurture, maintain, prop, favor, benefit. *Ant.* oppose, hinder, obstruct, impede, check, retard, annoy, bother, clog, arrest, stop, contravene, thwart, frustrate, hamper.
heretic—*Syn.* dissenter, nonconformist, secularist, deserter, nonjuror, apostate, renegade, traitor.
heroic—*Syn.* fearless, intrepid, valiant, brave, courageous, gallant, daring, bold, valorous, spirited, resolute, firm, hardy, plucky. *Ant.* cowardly, timid, fearful, mean, base, dastardly, shy.
hesitate—*Syn.* falter, pause, stammer, waver, fluctuate, vacillate, question, ponder, defer, delay, wait, demur, shrink, dodge, shirk. *Ant.* try, persevere, continue, decide, resolve.
heterogeneous—*Syn.* unlike, mixed, variant, discordant, dissimilar, conglomerate, various, different, promiscuous. *Ant.* alike, homogeneous, like, same, uniform, similar, identical, conforming, unchanging.
hide—*Syn.* conceal, secrete, mask, protect, disguise, screen, cover, bury, cloak, veil, suppress, shield, shade, shelter. *Ant.* expose, exhibit, show, display, offer, present, open, disclose, reveal, divulge, unveil, impart, advertise, avow, unmask, tell, manifest, publish, promulgate.
hideous—*Syn.* ghastly, frightful, horrible, terrible, awful, revolting, fierce, abominable, abhorrent, shocking, terrifying, repulsive, forbidding, repellent, monstrous, loathsome, odious, detestable. *Ant.* beautiful, lovely, attractive, handsome, appealing, pleasing, satisfying, nice, exquisite, fine, alluring, charming, grand, agreeable, delightful, enticing, lovable.
high—*Syn.* lofty, tall, elevated, raised, eminent, exalted, haughty, proud, arrogant, ostentatious, conceited. *Ant.* low, short, stunted, depressed, deep, inferior, weak, mean, contemptible, despicable, degraded, worthless, dishonorable, ignoble.
hinder—*Syn.* impede, obstruct, prevent, check, retard, block, thwart, bar, embarrass, oppose, encumber, inhibit, stop, repress, interrupt, arrest, delay, restrain, curb, resist, prolong, foil, deter, postpone. *Ant.* help, assist, aid, encourage, facilitate, further, advance, promote, urge, expedite, speed, hurry, drive, hasten, impel, stimulate, instigate, forward, incite, cheer.
hint, *n.*—*Syn.* suggestion, intimation, innuendo, inkling, whisper, insinuation, reference, advice, information, communication, notice, observation. *Ant.* repression, concealment, secrecy, latency, obscurity, mystery, silence.
hint, *v.*—*Syn.* allude, refer, suggest, insinuate, intimate, imply, notify, tell, warn, acquaint, remind, mention, impart. *Ant.* conceal, cover, disguise, camouflage, stifle, reserve, withhold, ignore.
history—*Syn.* chronicle, account, narrative, record, register, archives, memoir, memorial, biography, events, facts. *Ant.* legend, romance, myth, novel, invention, imagery, figment, fabrication, fable, allegory, parable, fiction.
hold—*Syn.* retain, keep, own, occupy, maintain, detain, continue, sustain, regard, think, restrain, confine, contain, persevere, resist, affirm. *Ant.* lose, drop, suspend, adjourn, relinquish, cede, convey, bestow, present, confer, free, renounce, leave, quit, desert.
holiness—*Syn.* sanctity, piety, sacredness, godliness, devotion, veneration, consecration, sanctification, grace, reverence, humility. *Ant.* wickedness, sin, blasphemy, hypocrisy, cant, irreverence, profanity.
hollow—*Syn.* concave, empty, vacant, depressed, insincere, unsound, unsubstantial, artificial, transparent, false, unfilled. *Ant.* full, solid, convex, raised, material, stable, strong, substantial, dependable, sincere, truthful, earnest, faithful, honest.
holy—*Syn.* devout, pious, religious, saintly, divine, blessed, consecrated, hallowed, devoted, sacred, pure, immaculate, unstained, righteous, virtuous, godly, devout, reverent, sanctified. *Ant.* sinful, vicious, evil, contaminated, obscene, immoral, lascivious, profane, blasphemous, sacrilegious, infernal, satanic, unholy, nefarious, irreverent, unsanctified, cursed.
home—*Syn.* house, abode, residence, dwelling, domicile, apartment, habitation, haven, rest, grave, birthplace, country, habitat.
homely—*Syn.* plain, rough, rude, awkward, coarse, ungainly, unadorned, common, ordinary, thick, blunt. *Ant.* beautiful, handsome, refined, polished, suave, polite, nice, attractive, stately, dignified, graceful, agreeable.
honest—*Syn.* frank, open, truthful, sincere, upright, straightforward, candid, reliable, true, honorable, just, equitable, fair, incorrupt, scrupulous, reputable. *Ant.* dishonest, dishonorable, unjust, unfair, crooked, tricky, deceptive, deceitful, fraudulent, perfidious, misleading, elusive, false, untrustworthy, lying, disingenuous.
honesty—*Syn.* integrity, probity, honor, rectitude, integrity, confidence, faithfulness, fairness, justice, sincerity. *Ant.* dishonesty, cheating, trickery, false pretense, chicanery, fraud, deceit, artifice, deception, theft, larceny.
honor—*Syn.* respect, reverence, esteem, admiration, dignity, reputation, renown, adultation, praise, reguard, trust, faith, reliance, glory. *Ant.* dishonor, disgrace, degradation, derision, shame, ignominy, reproach, blemish, censure, abasement, contempt, denunciation, infamy, humiliation, corruption.
hope—*Syn.* confidence, expectation, trust, desire, anticipation, prospect, aspiration, optimism, presumption, reliance, assumption. *Ant.* despair, dejection, pessimism, discouragement, disappointment, fear.
hopeless—*Syn.* despairing, desperate, reckless, rash, lost, abandoned, gone, dejected, undone, ruined, irredeemable, irrevocable. *Ant.* hopeful, encouraging, reassuring, sanguine, dauntless, promising, probable, plucky, daring, expectant.
horizontal—*Syn.* level, flat, even, plane, plain, parallel, straight, linear. *Ant.* rugged, uneven, irregular, broken, hilly, lumpy, slanting, sloping, rolling, inclined.
hot—*Syn.* ardent, buring, fiery, flaming, incandescent, blazing, glowing, heated, passionate, excited, eager. *Ant.* cold, frigid, freezing, chilling, bleak, raw, biting, stiff, distant, rigid, affected, insensitive, cool.
however—*Syn.* nevertheless, notwithstanding, yet, still, though, although, but, in spite of, as if.
humane—*Syn.* kind, benevolent, sympathetic, merciful, compassionate, human, forgiving, gracious, charitable, benignant, gentle, clement, benign, indulgent, lenient. *Ant.* barbarous, atrocious, savage, pitiless, inhuman, cruel, uncouth, ferocious, wild, fierce.
humble, *a.*—*Syn.* lowly, mild, docile, unassuming, submissive, unpretentious, simple, bashful, modest, retiring, restrained, unobtrusive, reserved, shy, timid, yielding. *Ant.* proud, arrogant, ostentatious, boastful, overbearing, presumptuous, pretentious, conceited, vain, assuming.
humble, *v.*—*Syn.* humiliate, chasten, lower, depress, degrade, shame, reduce. *Ant.* raise, elevate, praise, laud, applaud, commend, promote.
humor, *n.*—*Syn.* wit, disposition, banter, chaff, jesting, jocularity, comicality, jest, joke, quip. *Ant.* dullness, heaviness, taciturnity, obtuseness, sullenness, melancholy.
humor, *v.*—*Syn.* indulge, pamper, coddle, appease, placate, spoil, fondle, caress. *Ant.* provoke, taunt, irritate, annoy, twit, chafe, nettle, exasperate, enrage.
hunt, *n.*—*Syn.* search, chase, quest, investigation, probe, seeking, inquiry.
hunt, *v.*—*Syn.* seek, chase, follow, pursue, search, inquire, expel, banish, dismiss.
hurt, *n.*—*Syn.* injury, damage, harm, bruise, blow, stroke, wrong, impairment, bane, misfortune, infliction, grief, suffering, pain, dolor, discomfort. *Ant.* pleasure, delight, joy, comfort, ease, relief, content, solace, consolation, balm.
hurt, *v.*—*Syn.* wound, injure, damage, harm, bruise, impair, abuse, tarnish, mar. *Ant.* heal, cure, benefit, restore, remedy, reward, assist, succor, aid, comfort, assuage, alleviate, soothe.
hurtful—*Syn.* harmful, injurious, bad, noxious, destructive, deleterious, distressing, weakening. *Ant.* beneficial, good, healthy, stimulating, energizing, wholesome, salutary, salubrious, healing, helpful, invigorating.
husbandry—*Syn.* agriculture, tillage, culture, cultivation, crop production, farming, gardening horticulture, agronomy, cattle-raising, stock-feeding, frugality, thrift, good management. *Ant.* waste, destruction, bad management, mismanagement, loss, squandering, misuse.
hustle—*Syn.* hurry, rush, run, haste, expedite, accelerate, bustle. *Ant.* trifle, procrastinate, loaf, idle, dissipate, loll.
hypocrisy—*Syn.* deception, sanctimony, dissimulation, pretense, counterfeit, affectation, cant. *Ant.* honesty, truth, candor, sincerity, frankness, ingenuousness, clearness, impartiality, fairness, integrity, rectitude.

hypocrite—*Syn.* impostor, pretender, deceiver, cheat, adventurer, rogue, charlatan, quack, fraud. *Ant.* the antonymns of this term occur in substantive phrases in which personal nouns are preceded by such qualifying adjectives as *honest, true, sincere, just, reliable, reputable, fair, honest* official.
hypocritical—*Syn.* dishonest, deceptive, deluding, deceiving, pretending, assuming, pretentious, false. *Ant.* honest, truthful, reliable, reputable, just, fair, trustworthy, dependable, ingenuous, open, sincere, candid, earnest.
hypothesis—*Syn.* theory, supposition, surmise, speculation, system, conjecture, assumption, presumption, thesis, proposal. *Ant.* evidence, fact, proof, certainty, conviction, discovery, confirmation, assurance, affirmation, consequence, inference.
hypothetic—*Syn.* supposed, imaginary, postulated, conditional, conjectural, assumed, indeterminate, problematical, speculative, indefinite. *Ant.* proved, proven, demonstrated, confirmed, affirmed, approved, factual, literal, exact, genuine, actual, authentic, indisputable, certain, reliable, undoubted.

I

ideal—*Syn.* imaginary, visionary, unreal, intellectual, subjective, psychological, exemplary, consummate, fitting, perfect. *Ant.* actual, real, material, common, commonplace, ordinary, imperfect, undesirable.
idiocy—*Syn.* insanity, folly, foolishness, madness, senselessness, incapacity, fatuity, stupidity, paranoia, mania, lunacy, derangement. *Ant.* sense, acuteness, sharpness, wisdom, intelligence, sagacity, brilliancy, capacity, acumen, discernment, prudence.
idle—*Syn.* inactive, unused, unoccupied, waste, barren, fallow, uncultivated, shiftless, sluggish, indolent, listless, inert, futile, vain, useless, unimportant. *Ant.* busy, industrious, diligent, employed, working, active, occupied, cultivated, untiring, indefatigable.
ignoble—*Syn.* mean, base, dishonorable, contemptible, reproachful, shameful, worthless, abject, immodest, indecent, ribald, coarse. *Ant.* noble, high, stately, dignified, august, generous, grand, decent, ennobled, decorous, respectable, admirable, gracious, kind.
ignominious—*Syn.* shameful, scandalous, disgraceful, infamous, heinous, wicked, offensive, abusive, hateful, low, mean, base, cowardly, flagrant, abhorrent, disgusting, dishonorable, disreputable, debasing, ribald, outrageous. *Ant.* reputable, stately, dignified, gracious, creditable, worthy, noble, fine, laudable, commendatory, popular, estimable, distinguished, good, exemplary, honorable, admirable, respectable, virtuous, magnificent.
ignominy—*Syn.* shame, disgrace, scandal, infamy, reproach, contempt, dishonor, abasement, degradation, humiliation, defamation, dislike. *Ant.* honor, respect, fame, glory, renown, reputation, dignity, respectability, admiration, regard, esteem.
ignorance—*Syn.* illiteracy, darkness, incapacity. *Ant.* knowledge, enlightenment, learning, education, information, culture, attainment, understanding.
ignorant—*Syn.* uneducated, stupid, dense, obtuse, unlearned, illiterate, shallow. *Ant.* enlightened, learned, scholarly, cultured, cultivated, educated, trained, informed, wise, sage, literate, lettered, erudite.
ill, *a.*—*Syn.* sick, unwell, indisposed, ailing, impaired, evil, wicked. *Ant.* well, fine, cheery, healthy, robust, hale, hearty, vigorous, good, pleasing.
ill, *n.*—*Syn.* evil, wicked, misfortune, harm, mischief, danger, accident, calamity, pain, trouble, misery, distress. *Ant.* good, luck, fortune, privilege, advantage, benefit, boon, gain, achievement, favor.
illegal—*Syn.* unlawful, illicit, contraband, prohibited, banned, outlawed, illegitimate, irregular. *Ant.* legal, permitted, sanctioned, confirmed, allowed, lawful, judicial, authorized, approved.
illusion—*Syn.* fantasy, phantom, image, dream, vision, apparition. *Ant.* reality, fact, actuality, occurrence, happening, certainty, event, episode.
illustrious—*Syn.* celebrated, eminent, famous, renowned, distinguished, acclaimed, great, superior, superlative. *Ant.* lowly, mean, obscure, humble, poor, unpretentious, unassuming, meek, ignoble, depraved.
image—*Syn.* representation, appearance, form, show, conception, portrait, photograph, copy, imitation, resemblance, facsimile, depictment, reproduction, illustration.
imaginary—*Syn.* ideal, illusory, unreal, fancied, visionary, hypothetical, assumed, conceived, whimsical, dreamy. *Ant.* real, true, factual, genuine, substantial, physical, material, existing, proven, tangible, evident, definite.
imagination—*Syn.* fancy, conception, fantasy, idea, notion, impression, concept, conceit, reflection, supposition, contemplation. *Ant.* reality, actuality, existence, substance, being.
imagine—*Syn.* conceive, fancy, apprehend, think, presume, suppose, guess, visualize. *Ant.* sleep, doze, drowse.
imbecile—*Syn.* senile, simple, childish, fatuous. *Ant.* sane, wise, sagacious, rational, sound, intelligent.
imitate—*Syn.* copy, mimic, mock, counterfeit, duplicate, reproduce, simulate. *Ant.* vary, alter, change, modify, diverge, disagree, conflict, oppose, dispute.
immaculate—*Syn.* untainted, unsullied, spotless, pure, virgin, clean, untarnished, innocent, stainless. *Ant.* defiled, unclean, tarnished, spotted, impure, corrupt, stained, foul, defamed, infamous.
immediately—*Syn.* instantly, forthwith, directly, presently, straightaway. *Ant.* after a while, in the future, tomorrow, next week, when convenient, shortly.
immense—*Syn.* colossal, huge, great, large, bulky, vast, enormous, titanic, mighty, gigantic. *Ant.* small, little, insignificant, petty, trifling, puny, diminutive, trivial, light, minute, paltry.
immerse—*Syn.* submerge, sink, dip, overwhelm, involve, engage, deeply. *Ant.* raise up, take up, uncover, release, recover, regain, restore, retrieve.
imminent—*Syn.* impending, menacing, overhanging, approaching, near, coming, brewing. *Ant.* distant, afar, receding, retrograding, retiring, retreating, withdrawing, departing, unlikely, doubtful, unexpected.
immunity—*Syn.* exemption, privilege, prerogative, release. *Ant.* condemnation, proscription, blame, censure, interdiction, exclusion.
impair—*Syn.* injure, diminish, decrease, deteriorate, weaken, corrupt, defile, degrade, vitiate, pollute, damage, harm, hurt, blemish, deface, blight, corrode, mar. *Ant.* improve, better, restore, renew, revive, heal, mend, repair, cure, rally, renovate, rectify, redeem, reclaim, remedy, redress, refresh, reestablish, rejuvenate.
impart—*Syn.* reveal, divulge, disclose, bestow, afford, inform, tell, enlighten, notify, signify, mention, communicate, intimate, acquaint, advise, instruct. *Ant.* conceal, secrete, hide, deny, keep, hold, suppress, stifle, veil, withhold.
impartial—*Syn.* fair, just, equitable, unbiased, right, equal, evenhanded, unprejudiced. *Ant.* biased, prejudiced, unjust, unfair,, unequal, unreasonable, inequable.
impassioned—*Syn.* glowing, burning, fiery, vehement, intense, warm, thrilling, stirring, exciting, raging, fuming, flaming, hysterical. *Ant.* cool, collected, calm, undisturbed, placid, composed, quiet, patient, reserved, modest, retiring, staid, steady, restrained, stoical, tranquil, forbearing.
impatient—*Syn.* eager, restless, fretful, irascible, mercurial, chafing, hurried, turbulent, nervous, agitated. *Ant.* patient, calm, cool, peaceful, tranquil, serene, collected, resigned, chastened, tolerant.
impeach—*Syn.* accuse, charge, arraign, censure, blame, indict, discredit, berate, brand. *Ant.* defend, protect, approve, support, uphold, vindicate, honor, appreciate.
impede—*Syn.* hinder, retard, obstruct, prevent, offset, check, delay, hamper, oppose, stop, block, bar, encumber, neutralize, resist, restrain. *Ant.* help, assist, facilitate, abet, support, encourage, stimulate, instigate, back, forward, advance, second, endorse, serve, sustain.
impediment—*Syn.* obstruction, hindrance, barrier, bar, encumbrance, restriction, restraint, block, prohibition, inhibition, blockade. *Ant.* aid, assistance, help, support, benefit, succor, relief, advantage, concurrence, consent, indorsement, recommendation, commendation.
impel—*Syn.* incite, induce, animate, actuate, drive, force, move, urge, prod, start. *Ant.* recoil, react, revulse, rebound, reverberate, balk, repulse.
imperative—*Syn.* commanding, urgent, irresistible, dictatorial, compulsory, obligatory, mandatory, dominant, inexorable, peremptory, absolute, preponderant, paramount, decretive, decretory, jussive, necessary, requisite, essential, indispensable, exigent, pressing. *Ant.* voluntary, optional, discretional, free, discretionary, unconstrained, spontaneous, original, willing, intentional, deliberate, purposed, unrestrained, premeditated, designed, contemplated.
imperfection—*Syn.* fault, blemish, stain, defect, failing, drawback, weakness, vice, deficiency, frailty, incompleteness, immaturity, infirmity, transgression, depravity, sin, sinfulness, wrong, viciousness. *Ant.* advantage, perfection, completeness, goodness, improvement, blessing, favor, popularity, esteem, admiration, loyalty, confidence, respect.
imperil—*Syn.* endanger, hazard, jeopardize, peril, expose, risk, chance, venture. *Ant.* safeguard, protect, care for, guard, watch, preserve, defend, shield, secure.
imperious—*Syn.* authoritative dictatorial, stern, commanding, overbearing, tyrranical, lordly, domineering, imperative, insolent, arrogant, presumptuous, self-assertive, swaggering, bullying, saucy, nervy, *Ant.* obsequious, subservient, cringing, fawing, crouching, sycophantic, truckling, toadying, servile, groveling, mealymouthed, mean, sneaking, base, abased, pliant, soapy, oily, dough-faced *(colloq.)* parasitical, abject, slavish, beggarly.
impertinent—*Syn.* saucy, impudent, insolent, rude, officious, meddling, intrusive, contumelious, irrelevant, forward, bold, brazen, underbred, insulting, audacious, abusive, contemptuous, gross, coarse, vulgar. *Ant.* polite, suave, flattering, appeasing, mollifying, meek, humble, gentle, refined, courteous, civil, obliging, condescending, conciliating, respectful, polished, affable, urbane, submissive, mild, bland, pleasant, complaisant, pleasing, well-mannered.
impetuous—*Syn.* boisterous, vehement, violent, headstrong, rash, hasty, impulsive, fiery, obstinate, intractable. *Ant.* calm, steady, careful, considerate, mild, hesitant, composed, unobtrusive.
impious—*Syn.* blasphemous, irreligious, irreverent, reprobate, unregenerate, hypocritical, unholy. *Ant.* inspired, pious, devout, holy, spiritual, religious.
implicate—*Syn.* involve, incriminate, charge, impute, stigmatize, impeach, blame, imply, cite. *Ant.* defend, assist, absolve, condone, support, sanction, approve, ratify.
important—*Syn.* significant, weighty, grave, material, considerable, relevant, dignified, essential, serious, substantial, prominent, determining, powerful, foremost, principal. *Ant.* slight, trivial, paltry, petty, unimportant, subordinate, non-essential, shallow, weak,

mean, inconsiderable, meagre, insignificant, inane.

imposing—*Syn.* impressive, striking, grand, august, sublime, towering, superlative, commanding, paramount, leading, foremost, illustrious, eminent. *Ant.* small, meagre, unimportant, petty, paltry, insignificant, absurd, subordinate, ordinary, commonplace, light, trivial, shabby, worthless, despicable, contemptible, weak, tawdry, gimcrack, trumpery, cheap, trashy, scurvy, beggarly,useless, negligible, inconsiderable, feeble, foolish.

impotent—*Syn.* weak, feeble, powerless, unable, enfeebled, nerveless, useless, disabled, infirm, incapacitated, frail, puny, delicate, enervated, debilitated, exhausted, sterile, incapable, inefficient, ineffectual, barren. *Ant.* strong, potent, powerful, mighty, forcible, robust, efficient, effectual, virile, puissant, efficacious, energetic, vigorous, manly, productive, fertile, sturdy, lusty, capable, able, masterful, masterly, dominating, active.

impressive—*Syn.* forcible, affecting, moving, stirring, exciting, deep, profound, soul-stirring, thrilling, penetrating, absorbing, notable, remarkable, prominent, momentous, vital, commanding, imposing, grave, serious, solemn. *Ant.* light, trivial, trifling, petty, paltry, unimpressive, unimportant, shallow, inconsequential, common, ordinary, regular, normal, insignificant, slight, frivolous, inane, commonplace, uninteresting, cheap.

imprison—*Syn.* immure, incarcerate, confine, restrain, lock up, impound, circumscribe, keep, hold, detain, inclose, limit, pen, constrain, debar. *Ant.* free, liberate, release, discharge, let go, loose, loosen, unchain, dismiss, unbind, acquit, extricate, reprieve, disenthrall, unbar, deliver, set free.

improve—*Syn.* mend, amend, better, reform, rectify, apply, ameliorate, apply, use, employ, emend, advance, revise, correct, refine, purify. *Ant.* deteriorate, degrade, impair, vitiate, damage, injure, corrode, ravage, blight, wither, decay, fade, degenerate, decline, droop, sink, weaken.

improvident—*Syn.* careless, incautious, prodigal, imprudent, wasteful, reckless, spendthrift, extravagant, lavish, unthrifty, thriftless, dissipated, profuse, squandering. *Ant.* parsimonious, niggardly, miserly, thrifty, penurious, stingy, close-fisted, close, tight-fisted, tight, grudging, gripping, sordid, mercenary, avaricious, greedy.

impudence—*Syn.* assurance, impertinence, confidence, insolence, rudeness, boldness, effrontery, sauciness, presumption, incivility, pertness, forwardness, officiousness, intrusiveness, brazenness, assumption, cheek *(slang)*, audacity, nerve *(slang)*, overbearance, blustering. *Ant.* humility, humbleness, fawning, sycophancy, toadeating, flunkeyism, subserviency, timeserving, truckling, knuckling, cringing, crawling, coyness, bashfulness, diffidence, submissiveness, lowliness, modesty, meekness, abasement, servility, obsequiousness, abjectness, slavishness.

impudent—*Syn.* saucy, brazen, bold, impertinent, audacious, forward, rude, insolent, immodest, shameless, uncivil, caustic, sarcastic, presumptuous, pert, officious, arrogant, self-assertive, haughty, supercilious, flippant, blustering, swaggering, hectoring, domineering, fresh *(slang)*. *Ant.* retiring, modest, humble, backward, coy, bashful, mealy-mouthed, groveling, sycophantic, cringing, servile, slavish, abject, parasitical, lowly, fearful, timid, self-effacing, apprehensive, cowardly, crouching, crawling, fawning, afraid, soapy *(slang)*, lily-livered *(slang)*.

impute—*Syn.* count, reckon, attribute, ascribe, charge, estimate, blame, assign, allege, reproach, stigmatize, implicate, denounce, indict, brand, inculpate, call to account. *Ant.* defend, advocate, extenuate, palliate, bolster up, excuse, justify, exculpate, clear, exonerate, vindicate, support, countenance, indorse, stand up for.

incentive—*Syn.* motive, inducement, impulse, spur, goad, reason, ground, magnet, enticement, allurement, consideration, stimulus, whip, bribe, lure, decoy, temptation, bait, charm, spell, stimulation. *Ant.* discouragement, dissuasion, scruple, monition, warning, dehortation, reluctance, curb, restraint, admonition, expostulation.

incite—*Syn.* excite, instigate, stimulate, urge, encourage, impel, provoke, inspirit, rouse, arouse, animate, actuate, encourage, spur, goad, exhort, force, persuade, influence, sway, coax, wheedle, induce, prick, taunt, egg on. *Ant.* deter, hold back, dishearten, dissuade, admonish, check, discourage, remonstrate, expostulate, warn, restrain, damp, dampen, depress, dispirit, frustrate, stop, prevent.

inclination—*Syn.* leaning, slope, disposition, tendency, bent, bias, affection, attachment, wish, desire, liking, fancy, allurement, hobby, fascination, attraction, proneness, aptness, predilection, propensity, animus, partiality, penchant. *Ant.* unconcern, indifference, neutrality, nonchalance, apathy, inappetence, supineness, coldness, inattention, impotence, insouciance, heedlessness.

incommode—*Syn.* annoy, plague, molest, disturb, inconvenience, trouble, vex, disarrange, inhibit, disquiet, tease, worry, bother, pester, bore, harass, harry, badger, heckle, bait. *Ant.* please, satisfy, gratify, induldge, humor, flatter, enliven, amuse, regale, comfort, refresh, gladden, delight, charm, captivate, fascinate, attract, benefit, exhilerate.

incompetent—*Syn.* unskillful, inexpert, bungling, unable, incapable, inadequate, unfit, inefficient, insuffient, ineffectual, unhandy, maladroit, unqualified, disqualified, stupid, floundering, stumblilng, ignorant, unskilled, inept, unsuitable, benighted. *Ant.* skillful, dexterous, expert, proficient, competent, deft, adroit, clever, talented, capable, knowing, masterly, skilled, erudite, informed, able, experienced, practical, efficient, effectual, qualified, trained, apt, handy, adept.

incongruous—*Syn.* inconsistent, inappropriate, absurd, incompatible, inharmonious, disagreeing, unsuitable, inapposite, contrary, repugnant, mismated, irreconcilable, mismatched, incoherent, discordant, discrepant, ill-matched, incommensurable, contradictory, conflicting, different, heterogeneous, divergent, disparate, inconformable, unconformable, modified, diversified, differential, variform. *Ant.* accordant, suitable, matched, harmonious, consistent, agreeing, compatible, identical, coinciding, homogeneous, uniform, homologous, same, self-same, connatural, consonant, invariable, unvarying, unchanging, undeviating, analogous, cognate, corresponding, allied, congeneric, apposite.

increase, *n.*—*Syn.* augmentation, addition, accession, enlargement, extension, increment, accretion, growth, development, inflation, gain, multiplication, expansion, turgescence, amplification, dilation, spread, intumescence, distension. *Ant.* decrease, contraction, shrinkage, decrement, compression, deflation, attenuation, diminution, lessening, reduction, decimation, decrescence, atrophy, abridgement, deterioration, abstraction, subtraction, curtailment, abbreviation.

increase, *v.*—*Syn.* augment, extend, enlarge, dilate, expand, amplify, raise, enhance, magnify, grow, develop, lengthen, broaden, double, triple, quadruple, etc., produce, spread, inflate, widen, swell, accresce, bourgeon, bud, germinate, fructify, tumefy, distend, protuberate, reinforce, add, supplement. *Ant.* diminish, lessen, contract, shrink, wither, fade, atrophy, dwindle, shrivel, narrow, decrease, compress, deflate, condense, squeeze, pucker, reduce, abridge, curtail, subtract, deduct, abstract, consume, subside, decay, crumble, erode, wear away, fall off.

incumbent—*Syn.* pressing, urgent, obligatory, binding, devolving, coercive, necessary, imperative, stringent, behooving, peremptory, unavoidable, persistent, inescapable. *Ant.* free, immune, exempt, released, unencumbered, excusable, irresponsible, unaccountable, unamenable, liberated, privileged, absolved, clear, cleared.

indefinite—*Syn.* vague, uncertain, unsettled, loose, lax, indeterminate, indistinct, undefined, unlimited, inexact, inconclusive, ambiguous, equivocal, confused, undefinable, obscure, oracular. *Ant.* clear, definite, exact, apparent, certain, indubitable, indisputable, conclusive, unquestionable, evident, sure, reliable, infallible, assured, positive, absolute, decided, ascertained, known.

indicate—*Syn.* show, disclose, mark, tell, point out, designate, denote, reveal, manifest, testify, evidence, determine, differentiate, specify, imply, signify, connote. *Ant.* confuse, disconcert, discompose, perplex, bewilder, moider, lead astray, fluster, flurry, humbug, distract, derange, confound, embarrass.

indifference—*Syn.* apathy, carelessness, listlessness, insensibility, nonchalance, insouciance, inattention, coldness, unconcern, phlegm, impassibleness, impassibility, impassiveness, impassivity, hebetude, supineness, callousness, neutrality, stoniness, insusceptability. *Ant.* feeling, warmth, sympathy, sensitiveness, enthusiasm, tender-heartedness, compassion, softness, sentimentality, desire, inclination, attention, heed, carefulness, vivacity, tenderness, vivaciousness, impressiblity, passion, liveliness, cordiality, sincerity, zeal, application, assiduity.

indigence—*Syn.* poverty, want, need, hunger, privation, starvation, penury, destitution, misery, insufficiency, dearth, scarcity, want, famine, stint, scantiness, pauperism, distress, necessity, mendicancy, beggary. *Ant.* plenty, plenitude, fullness, repletion, wealth, opulence, affluence, fortune, independence, money, capital, resources, property, substance, competence, riches, luxury, abundance, sufficiency.

indignation—*Syn.* anger, wrath, ire, resentment, scorn, fury, displeasure, umbrage, rage, passion, animosity, exasperation, pique, huff, temper, irascibility, spleen, sulks, tantrums, acrimony, virulence, bitterness, agitation, excitement. *Ant.* calmness, coolness, benignity, quiet, gentleness, modesty, humility, patience, forbearance, imperturbability, toleration, sang-froid *[Fr.]*, tranquility, dispassion, restraint, equanimity, self-possession, self-control, self-restraint, hebetation, poise, passiveness.

indignity—*Syn.* affront, disrespect, dishonor, reproach, ignominy, discourtesy, disparagement, mockery, slight, taunt. *Ant.* esteem, praise, honor, consideration, respect, veneration, approbation, homage, regard.

indispensable—*Syn.* essential, necessary, requisite, needful, fundamental, basic, expedient, required, prerequisite. *Ant.* unnecessary, superfluous, supernumerary, useless, redundant, needless.

indisputable—*Syn.* undeniable, incontestable, indubitable, irrefutable, unquestionable, incontrovertible, positive, certain, sure, assured, definite, unequivocal. *Ant.* doubtful, uncertain, dubious, questionable, indeterminate, equivocal, undefined, untrustworthy, controvertible, disputable, indefinite, ambiguous, undetermined.

indistinct—*Syn.* vague, uncertain, confused, indefinite, indistinguishable, ambiguous, dim, ill-defined, blurred, misty, nebulous. *Ant.* clear, distinct, plain, visible, conspicuous, perceptible, definite, obvious, luminous, explicit, intelligible, positive, apparent, evident.

indolent—*Syn.* lazy, idle, sluggish, slack, inert, torpid, dull, lethargic, soporific, languid, listless. *Ant.* active, quick, keen, eager, vivacious, lively, prompt, anxious, laboring, bustling, spry, alert, indefatigable, busy, earnest, energetic, diligent, persevering.

indorse—*Syn.* ratify, confirm, sanction, approve, subscribe, accept, guarantee, praise, recommend, uphold, support. *Ant.* condemn, depreciate, disparage, denounce, re-

prove, reprimand, admonish, stigmatize, rebuke, protest, deprecate, objurgate, reprove.
indulge—*Syn.* cherish, fondle, gratify, please, pamper, humor, favor, placate, concede, satisfy, nourish, nurture, sustain. *Ant.* torment, torture, annoy, trouble, disquiet, molest, plague, bother, pester, displease.
industrious—*Syn.* diligent, busy, active, laborious, occupied, zealous, indefatigable, laboring, businesslike. *Ant.* inactive, idle, indolent, slothful, sluggish, lethargic, slack, remiss, inert, languid, laggard, dilatory, listless, lackadaisical.
industry—*Syn.* activity, diligence, labor, persistence, effort, attention, application, pursuit, enterprise, business, undertaking. *Ant.* idleness, indolence, sluggishness, inertness, inconstancy, dawdling, languor, lethargy, torpor, shirking.
inevitable—*Syn.* unavoidable, certain, necessary, irresistible, imminent, inescapable. *Ant.* uncertain, unlikely, doubtful, vague, indeterminate, questionable, indefinite.
infamous—*Syn.* heinous, disgraceful, abhorrent, shameful, ignominious, disreputable, despicable, opprobrious, shocking, notorious, profligate, foul, base, vile, perfidious, scandalous, malevolent, flagrant, foul, evil. *Ant.* virtuous, good, pure, worthy, meritorious, righteous, immaculate, unblemished, moral, incorruptible, fine, perfect, admirable, exemplary, true, constant, honest, clean, conscientious, honorable, trustworthy, dignified, reputable, respectable, beloved.
inference—*Syn.* conclusion, assumption, judgement, corollary, result, sequence, reason, upshot. *Ant.* prejudgement, anticipation, foreknowledge, foregone, conclusion.
infernal—*Syn.* diabolical, malicious, satanic, demoniacal, horrible, incarnate, Mephistophelian, wicked. *Ant.* heavenly, angelic, divine, pure, celestial, hallowed, consecrated, predestined.
infinite—*Syn.* unlimited, boundless, immeasurable, interminable, unbounded, countless, immense, innumerable, incalculable, endless. *Ant.* limited, definite, particular, circumscribed, numbered, measurable, finite, confined, transitory, narrow, brief, fleeting, transient, fixed, determinate.
infirm—*Syn.* weak, feeble, decrepit, tottering, invalid, sickly, enervated, exhausted, frail, languid, spent, wasted. *Ant.* strong, robust, vigorous, sturdy, potent, energetic, forceful, healthy, hearty, sound, virile.
inflame—*Syn.* anger, irritate, enrage, chafe, incense, nettle, aggravate, embitter, exasperate, arouse, excite, stir, provoke, incite, taunt, harass, heckle, infuriate, goad. *Ant.* soothe, mollify, pacify, calm, assuage, appease, alleviate, allay, quell, soften, restrain, mitigate, placate, tranquilize.
influence, *n.*—*Syn.* control, sway, authority, weight, supremacy, superiority, patronage, reputation, character, ascendancy, importance, prestige. *Ant.* uselessness, subordination, inefficacy, inferiority, servility, meanness, weakness, inefficiency, incapacity.
influence, *v.*—*Syn.* sway, control, prejudice, modify, bias, act upon, direct, regulate, rule, actuate, dominate, predominate. *Ant.* lack power, be of no importance, produce no effect.
infringe—*Syn.* transgress, violate, trespass, invade, encroach, intrude, repudiate. *Ant.* observe, obey, comply with, perform, redeem, discharge, satisfy, acquiesce, concur, resist, repulse, submit.
ingenious—*Syn.* clever, resourceful, inventive, productive, imaginative, keen, talented, apt, deft, proficient, capable, endowed, adroit, sagacious. *Ant.* unskilled, bungling, inapt, incompetent, unable, awkward, dull, fumbling, maladroit, unfit, unqualified, unhandy, green, immature.
ingenuous—*Syn.* open, frank, fair, undisguised, candid, unequivocal, honest, sincere, plain, generous, natural, simple, unsophisticated, naive, guileless, unsuspicious, unreserved, straightforward, blunt. *Ant.* sly, subtle, crafty, shifty, wily, intriguing, designing, underhand, shrewd, politic, deceptive, Machiavellian, deceitful, stealthy.
inhabit—*Syn.* dwell, occupy, sojourn, stay, remain, abide, lodge. *Ant.* withdraw, retreat, retire, vacate, exit, desert, abandon.
inherent—*Syn.* innate, latent, natural, inseparable, internal, intrinsic, ingrained, subjective, indispensable. *Ant.* superficial, incidental, supplemental, ulterior, transient, subsidiary, fortuitous, accidental.
inhibit—*Syn.* hinder, check, repress, suppress, curb, prohibit, interdict, restrict, impede, block, obstruct, prevent, interfere, oppose, discourage, proscribe, forbid, bar, disallow, suspend, stop, abrogate, nullify, rescind, annul. *Ant.* permit, warrant, authorize, approve, accord, allow, grant, charter, license, consent, assent, free, aid, help, sustain, adopt, commend.
inhuman—*Syn.* cruel, savage, barbarous, ruthless, malevolent, brutal, truculent, harsh, devilish. *Ant.* humane, sympathetic, indulgent, tender, compassionate, considerate, obliging, gracious, kindly, amiable, affectionate, fraternal, charitable, philanthropic, beneficient, cordial, accommodating, complacent, comforting.
iniquitous—*Syn.* nefarious, vicious, unjust, unfair, lawless, immoral, profligate, shameful, degrading, infamous, satanic. *Ant.* good, virtuous, pure, innocent, moral, upright, honest, decent, worthy, creditable, admirable, excellent, kind, harmless, equitable, honorable.
injurious—*Syn.* hurtful, harmful, pernicious, mischievous, detrimental, destructive, disadvantageous. *Ant.* beneficial, helpful, wholesome, salubrious, useful, inoffensive, healing, constructive, favorable.
injury—*Syn.* hurt, harm, damage, detriment, injustice, disadvantage, outrage, prejudice, blemish, loss, mischief, evil. *Ant.* good, benefit, emolument, help, advantage, profit, gain, utility, assistance, succor.
injustice—*Syn.* wrong, grievance, iniquity, violation, injury, partiality. *Ant.* justice, right, privilege, equity, fairness, propriety, honesty, rectitude, integrity, equality, impartiality, righteousness.
innocent—*Syn.* good, guiltless, pure, virtuous, immaculate, noxious, harmless, inoffensive, righteous, clear, exemplary, clean, innocuous, simple, plain, unaffected, open, honest, straightforward, candid. *Ant.* guilty, culpable, bad, immoral, impure, intemperate, artful, cunning, evasive.
innocuous—*Syn.* harmless, inoffensive, beneficial, salutary, salubrious, safe, wholesome, healthy, bracing, invigorating, stimulating, refreshing, reviving, restorative, advantageous, helpful. *Ant.* noxious, deleterious, bad, injurious, maleficient, impairing, detrimental, deteriorating, blighting, deadly, baneful, tainted, toxemic, luetic, noisome, unwholesome, damaging, prejudicial, destructive, pernicious, morbiferous, harmful.
inordinate—*Syn.* excessive, undue, intemperate, unlimited, profuse, lavish, overwhelming, profuse, prodigal. *Ant.* moderate, meager, insufficient, scanty, sparse, exhausted, depleted, short.
inquire—*Syn.* ask, solicit, search, question, examine, analyze, probe, ransack, look, pry, hunt, explore. *Ant.* answer, respond, retort, reply, shun, shelve, delay, procrastinate.
inquiry—*Syn.* quest, search, investigation, interrogation, research, question, inquisition, survey, analysis, inspection. *Ant.* neglect, indisposition, disregard, procrastination, insouciance, inattention.
inquisitive—*Syn.* searching, inquiring, intrusive, curious, meddling, peering, intruding, aggressive. *Ant.* bashful, inattentive, abstracted, indifferent, neglectful, negligent.
insane—*Syn.* mad, deranged, demented, frenzied, frenetic, unsound, crazy, daft, fanatical, possessed, wild, muddled, idiotic, unsettled, paranoiac, raging. *Ant.* sane, sound, lucid, normal, whole, rational, sober, steady, regular, calm, cool, level, ordinary, unruffled, practical, solid, correct, intelligent, sedate, settled.
insanity—*Syn.* frenzy, mania, delirium, derangement, lunacy, madness, aberration, alienation. *Ant.* clearness, lucidity, common sense, sanity, rationality, normalcy, sobriety, steadiness, regularity, saneness, reasonableness, discernment, judgement, sagacity.
insidious—*Syn.* cunning, designing, intriguing, deceitful, wily, treacherous, sly, deceptive, crafty. *Ant.* open, frank, candid, sincere, unsophisticated, plain, honorable, unreserved.
insight—*Syn.* judgement, introspection, penetration, cleverness, acumen, shrewdness, inspection, keenness, intuition, perception, comprehension. *Ant.* ignorance, unconsciousness, shallowness, incapacity, illiteracy, perplexity, confusion, doubt, lack of judgement.
insinuate—*Syn.* suggest, intimate, hint, introduce, infuse, signify, connote, imply, purport, denote, allude, communicate, disclose, indicate. *Ant.* conceal, hide, mask, camouflage, veil, cloud, cloak, screen, evade, suppress, cover, stifle, shade, muffle, shroud.
insipid—*Syn.* tasteless, flat, dull, stale, vapid, inanimate, unsavory, slow, uninteresting. *Ant.* tasty, piquant, pungent, tart, savory, flavored, spiced, delicious, luscious, interesting, lively, quick, enterprising.
insolent—*Syn.* impudent, impertinent, offensive, rude, overbearing, arrogant, bold, contemptuous, defiant, haughty, imperious, brazen, blustering, audacious. *Ant.* fawning, sponging, abject, servile, cringing, groveling, sneaking, mean, abased, cowardly.
insolvent—*Syn.* bankrupt, ruined, impoverished, indigent, penniless, indebted, destitute, impecunious, reduced. *Ant.* solvent, affluent, independent, wealthy, substantial, rich, warm, comfortable.
insouciant—*Syn.* careless, heedless, reckless, unconcerned, carefree, indifferent, abstracted, giddy. *Ant.* careful, cautious, watchful, attentive, observant, serious, prudent, preoccupied, circumspect, vigilant, cognizant, deliberate, wary, discreet.
inspiration—*Syn.* acumen, subtlety, perspicacity, sagacity, comprehension, imagination, invention, impulse, predilection, emotion, manifestation. *Ant.* foolishness, dullness, incapacity, inability, insensibility, apathy, callousness, unconcern, indifference, inertness.
instance—*Syn.* precedent, example, type, point, illustration, occurrence, pattern, specimen, sample. *Ant.* exception, breach, rarity, abnormality, irregularity, aberration.
instigate—*Syn.* incite, urge, stimulate, encourage, persuade, influence, sway, arouse, induce, entice, tempt, encourage, prompt, exhort. *Ant.* dissuade, discourage, expostulate, warn, deter, dampen, deprecate, admonish, avert, prevent, constrain, restrain, suppress, repress, overwhelm, stifle, smother.
instill—*Syn.* infuse, diffuse, suffuse, transfuse, combine, inject, infiltrate, blend, interject, introduce, inculcate, indoctrinate. *Ant.* eliminate, remove, extract, draw, eradicate, expel, dislodge, exclude, discard, shed, void.
instruct—*Syn.* teach, inform, guide, direct, initiate, enlighten, educate, train, advise, tutor, coach, tell, convey, impart, promulgate, proclaim, expound. *Ant.* misrepresent, pervert, abandon, forget, withhold, withdraw, dispute, impugn, repudiate, refuse, deny.
insufferable—*Syn.* unbearable, intolerable, grievous, shocking, appalling, dreadful, excruciating, harrowing. *Ant.* pleasant, agreeable, delightful, refreshing, comfortable, delicious, soothing, healing, easing, emollient, enjoyable, satisfying, ameliorating, salubrious, salutary, invigorating.
insult—*Syn.* indignity, outrage, affront, abuse, insolence, contempt, disdain, impudence, disrespect, bitterness, derision, taunt. *Ant.* respect, regard, reverence, tribute, admiration, fealty, deference, courtesy, humility, cordiality, politeness, gentility, amenity, esteem, benevolence, kindness, sympathy.
integrity—*Syn.* honesty, moral, honor, righteousness, probity, rec-

titude, trustworthiness, loyalty, merit, fidelity. *Ant.* dishonesty, pretension, sham, corruption, turpitude, infidelity, unfairness, disgrace, shame.

intellectual—*Syn.* mental, learned, accomplished, ideal, meditative, thoughtful, studious, thinking, keen, sharp, acute. *Ant.* dull, stupid, inane, foolish, vacuous, unintellectual, irrational.

intelligible—*Syn.* comprehensible, clear, obvious, distinct, perceptible, lucid, unequivocal, vivid, expressive, definite, positive. *Ant.* unintelligible, perplexing, difficult, abstruse, muddled, obscure, incomprehensible, unknowable.

intemperate—*Syn.* drunk, unrestrained, excessive, inordinate, dissipated, inebriated, intoxicated. *Ant.* sober, temperate, teetotal, abstemious, steady, moderate, nonindulgent.

intensity—*Syn.* ardor, energy, tension, concentration, force, strain, rush, pressure, vigor, ferment. *Ant.* inactivity, inaction, inertness, flatness, apathy, indolence.

intentional—*Syn.* intended, designed, deliberate, premeditated, studied, contemplated, meant, projected, calculated. *Ant.* chancy, accidental, speculative, tentative, fortuitous, unpremeditated, random, aimless, indiscriminate, haphazard, casual, incidental, occasional.

intercourse—*Syn.* communication, connection, commerce, correspondence, intimacy, familiarity. *Ant.* unfriendliness, enmity, hatred, animosity, estrangement, malice, alienation, aversion, isolation, solitude.

interest, *n.*—*Syn.* profit, share, portion, advantage, benefit, gain, concern, attention, stake, right, title, claim, premium. *Ant.* unconcern, apathy, indifference, loss, default.

interest, *v.*—*Syn.* entertain, amuse, enliven, please, divert, delight, gratify. *Ant.* bore, weary, tire, annoy, disturb, disgust, bother, worry.

interpose—*Syn.* interfere, intervene, intercede, meddle, mediate, arbitrate, intrude, interpolate, intercept, interrupt, interject. *Ant.* withhold, withdraw, refuse, ignore, disregard, overlook, shun.

interpret—*Syn.* translate, elucidate, clear, unravel, unfold, explain, construe, render, define, describe, paraphrase. *Ant.* misinterpret, misconstrue, misapply, distort, travesty, confuse, tangle, pervert, falsify, parody, subvert.

intimidate—*Syn.* frighten, daunt, threaten, browbeat, dismay, dictate, coerce, menace. *Ant.* encourage, hearten, inspire, console, mollify, soften, gratify, stimulate, stir up, instigate.

intolerable—*Syn.* insufferable, unbearable, shocking, appalling, horrifying. *Ant.* consoling, soothing, allaying, assuaging, healing, satisfying, delightful, charming.

intrepid—*Syn.* brave, fearless, bold, courageous, unafraid, undaunted, firm, valiant, daring, heroic, aweless, lionhearted, unflinching, self-reliant. *Ant.* afraid, timid, shrinking, cowardly, craven, cringing, diffident, nervous, shaky, frightened, scared, trembling, hesitant.

intricate—*Syn.* complex, tangled, twisted, involved, convoluted, difficult, mixed, raveled, knotted, complicated. *Ant.* tidy, methodical, arranged, orderly, systematic, regulated, orderly, trim, proper, clear, uniform, normal.

intrigue—*Syn.* plot, scheme, complication, conspiracy, ruse, plan, craftiness, trickery, machination. *Ant.* innocence, honesty, sincerity, simplicity, candor, bluntness.

intrinsic—*Syn.* real, genuine, honest, fundamental, natural, innate, essential, ingrained, congenital, syngenic. *Ant.* extrinsic, objective, without, extraneous, incidental, casual, occasional, contingent, foreign, external.

invasion—*Syn.* attack, incursion, inroad, foray, aggression, raid. *Ant.* defense, protection, safeguard, fortification, escarpment, rampart, bulwark, stronghold.

invective—*Syn.* censure, condemnation, denouncement, accusation, reproach, sarcasm, satire, abuse, disparagement, depreciation, remonstrance, disapproval. *Ant.* approbation, approval, sanction, admiration, commendation, praise, acclamation, applause.

invent—*Syn.* devise, discover, fashion, form, fabricate, design, plan, frame, contrive, outline, sketch, draft, project, scheme, carry out, lie, falsify, misrepresent, imagine, simulate, deceive, humbug, mystify, misstate, equivocate, conjure up, visualize, romance, fancy, conceive.

investigation—*Syn.* inquiry, examination, search, research, scrutiny, inquisition, review, interrogation, cross-examination, discussion, catechism, catechesis, exploitation, quest, pursuit.

invidious—*Syn.* odious, hateful, envious, malignant, provoking, galling, heartbreaking, vexatious, troublesome, irksome, irritating, wearisome, provoking, painful, annoying, obnoxious. *Ant.* pleasant, pleasurable, delightful, gratifying, satisfying, consoling, soothing, comforting, cordial, refreshing, delectable, attractive, benevolent, charitable.

invigorate—*Syn.* strengthen, animate, energize, vitalize, brace, nerve, fortify, harden, refresh, vivify, stimulate, pep up *(slang)*, nerve, embolden. *Ant.* weaken, enervate, enfeeble, unnerve, sap, debilitate, impair, attenuate, paralyze, waste, injure, cripple, reduce, devitalize.

invincible—*Syn.* unconquerable, insuperable, resistless, impregnable, insurmountable, irresistible, indomitable, incontestable, mighty, overpowering, all-powerful, all-sufficient, sovereign. *Ant.* weak, puny, deficient, defective, frail, fragile, flimsy, effeminate, faint, enervated, unnerved, crippled, languishing, languid, sickly, feeble, wasted, emaciated, spent.

involve—*Syn.* entangle, implicate, imply, embarrass, compromise, overwhelm, contain, include, connect with, signify, denote, betoken, mean. *Ant.* separate, disconnect, explicate, remove, distinguish, disentangle, free, unravel, clear, extricate, disengage, untwist.

irony—*Syn.* sarcasm, satire, burlesque, ridicule, mockery, raillery, skit, quip, twit, banter, parody, travesty, derision, persiflage, buffoonery, scoffing, jeering, gibe, sneer, taunt. *Ant.* respect, veneration, attention, homage, courtesy, deference, obsequiousness, admiration, consideration, obeisance, submission, approbation, approval.

irrational—*Syn.* foolish, demented, ridiculous, absurd, silly, imbecile, fatuous, stupid, feeble-minded, brutish, illogical, queer, evasive, odd, strange, unreasonable, loony *(slang)*, crazed, crazy, perverted, weak-minded, paralogical, paralogistic, daft, nutty *(slang)*, unsound, vacuous. *Ant.* rational, logical, sound, steady, reliable, intellectual, reasoning, judicial, throughtful, reflective, meditative, studious, cultured, accomplished, talented, sane, wise, sober, sober-minded, lucid, self-possessed, normal, commonsense, ordinary.

irreligious—*Syn.* impious, wicked, ungodly, profane, sacrilegious, desecrating, irreverent, blasphemous, unholy, unregenerate, reprobate, hardened, perverted. *Ant.* pious, godly, saintly, devout, devoted, reverend, prayerful, spiritual, pietistic, pietistical, consecrated, regenerated, sacred, solemn.

irrepressible—*Syn.* insuppressible, unrepressible, free, uncontrollable, irresistible, unconfined, excitable, unconstrained, independent, unshackled, unfettered, unrestricted, absolute, ebullient, high-strung, tumultuous, effervescing. *Ant.* passive, calm, placid, quiet, flat, dull, cold-blooded, grave, serious, melancholy, solemn, imperturbable, cool, collected, composed, meek, patient, tolerant, submissive, resigned.

irresolute—*Syn.* wavering, doubting, undecided, shaky, undetermined, vacillating, fickle, uncertain, fluctuating, unsettled, lukewarm, hesitant, hesitating, shilly-shally, drifting, unstable, half-hearted, volatile. *Ant.* resolute, firm, determined, resolved, decided, definite, purposed, unvarying, courageous, indomitable.

irresponsible—*Syn.* arbitrary, irresolute, unstable, undecided, hesitating, fluctuating, unsettled, faltering, wavering, infirm of purpose, unreliable, excusable, vacillating, weak, foolish, devil-may-care, not accountable, exempt, capricious, frothy, light, light-minded, feeble-minded, giddy, flighty, harum-scarum, rash, thoughtless. *Ant.* responsible, accountable, steady, firm, reliable, trustworthy, answerable, amenable, liable, unexempt, susceptive, subject, open to, dependent on, resolute, determined, strong-willed, self-reliant, earnest.

irritable—*Syn.* sensitive, susceptible, irascible, excitable, thin-skinned, fretful, fidgety, ill-tempered, touchy, testy, huffy, querulous, captious, peevish, petulant, fractious, snappy, waspish, cantankerous, hasty. *Ant.* pleasant, agreeable, suave, gentle, mild, calm, cool, passive, composed, enduring, good-tempered, tranquil, dispassionate, patient, tolerant, submissive, serene, impertubable, self-possessed, forbearing.

irritate—*Syn.* provoke, exasperate, exacerbate, excite, foment, sting, pique, agitate, ruffle, embitter, fluster, flurry, disturb, annoy, madden, infuriate, inflame, aggravate, anger, enrage, vex, harass, worry, perplex, nettle, chafe, irk, plague. *Ant.* soothe, calm, mollify, comfort, console, ease, alleviate, mitigate, palliate, assuage, salve, allay, ameliorate, moderate, soften, appease, placate, pacify, conciliate, please.

issue, *n.*—*Syn.* result, consequence, effect, aftermath, denouement, event, eventuality, occurrence, incident, circumstance, casualty, contingency, termination, conclusion, upshot, resultant, finish, culmination, product, publication, progeny, offspring, fruits, family, brood, seed, children, emanation, outpouring, effusion, exudation, egression.

issue, *v.*—*Syn.* flow, emanate, exude, proceed, emerge, rise, spring, break out, begin, arise, start, eventuate, ensue, result, originate, publish, promulgate, spread, bring out, get out, go forth, send out, express, utter, circulate paper money or coin, publish, distribute, send out, deliver.

J

jealous—*Syn.* envious, covetous, suspicious, dubious. *Ant.* honorable, righteous, trusting, faithful, incorrupt, clean, faithful, honest.

journey—*Syn.* trip, voyage, travel, transit, tour, expedition, excursion.

jovial—*Syn.* merry, gay, happy, joyous, frolicsome, cheerful, hilarious, sparkling. *Ant.* sad, solemn, serious, morose, morbid, sorrowful.

joy—*Syn.* gladness, exultation, rapture, delight, happiness, glee. *Ant.* grief, sorrow, trouble, worry, unhappiness, despair.

jubilant—*Syn.* gay, rejoicing, celebrating, joyous, triumphant, cheerful, delighted. *Ant.* downcast, gloomy, sorrowful, sad, disappointed, despondent, unhappy.

judge—*Syn.* referee, umpire, adjudicator, master.

judgement—*Syn.* discrimination, penetration, decision, sagacity, understanding, reason. *Ant.* thoughtlessness, vacuity, misjudgement, misconception.

judicious—*Syn.* discerning, wise, thoughtful, just, prudent, sensible, sagacious. *Ant.* foolish, silly, fatuous, driveling, senseless, irrational, nonsensical, inept.

just—*Syn.* honest, impartial, upright, precise, right, reasonable, equitable, evenhanded, righteous, legitimate. *Ant.* wrong, unjust, unfair, unequal, unreasonable.

justice—*Syn.* fairness, impartiality, equity, integrity, faith, right, law. *Ant.* injustice, wrong, unfairness, dishonesty, perfidy, inequity.

justify—*Syn.* warrant, maintain, excuse, defend, exculpate, clear, exonerate, acquit. *Ant.* accuse, incriminate, impute, charge, tax, blame, censure, reproach, denounce, brand, impeach, indict, arraign, stigmatize, slur, implicate, condemn.

juvenile—*Syn.* young, youthful, childish, tender, undeveloped, adolescent, growing. *Ant.* old, antiquated.

K

keen—*Syn.* eager, penetrating, acute, piercing, poignant, energetic, vivid, witty, quick. *Ant.* dull, thick, lazy, obtuse, insipid, tardy, dawdling, careless.
keep—*Syn.* hold, preserve, maintain, save, supply, confine, conserve, carry, sustain, withhold, observe, protect, uphold, continue, secure. *Ant.* relinquish, give up, renounce, abandon, surrender, forsake, desert, discard, depart, quit, spend, exhaust, disperse, vacate.
kill—*Syn.* murder, destroy, massacre, slaughter, immolate, dispatch, stifle, choke, suffocate, smother, execute. *Ant.* preserve, guard, safeguard, protect, watch, defend, uphold, save, free.
kind, *a.*—*Syn.* benevolent, good, affectionate, loving, caring, beneficient, generous, charitable, kindly, cordial, humane, friendly, sympathetic, considerate. *Ant.* malignant, harsh, cruel, inhuman, bitter, invidious, merciless, caustic, unkind.
kindred—*Syn.* relation, relationship, affinity, race, genus, species, variety, tribe, clan, breed, progeny.
knot—*Syn.* bond, tie, connection, bunch, collection, gathering, group.
knowledge—*Syn.* information, erudition, skill, understanding, scholarship, comprehension, wisdom, experience, acquaintance, conscience. *Ant.* ignorance, darkness, stupidity, incomprehension, illiteracy, obscurity, mystery, misunderstanding.

labor—*Syn.* work, undertaking, effort, travail, task, employment, achievement, operation, transaction, striving, industry. *Ant.* idleness, sloth, inertia, inactivity, dawdling, inaction, relaxation, loafing, loitering, ease, unemployment.
laborious—*Syn.* arduous, hard, difficult, stiff, heavy, pressing, hardworking, wearing, plodding, troublesome, strenuous, tough. *Ant.* easy, facile, trivial, smooth, petty, ordinary, common, insignificant.
lack—*Syn.* want, destitution, failure, loss, absence, deprivation, incompleteness, depletion, inadequacy, paucity, privation, poverty. *Ant.* plenty, abundance, satisfaction, sufficiency, profusion.
laconic—*Syn.* pithy, curt, brief, terse, concise, condensed, pointed, succinct. *Ant.* diffuse, rambling, dilated, profuse, wordy, loose.
lag—*Syn.* delay, tarry, retard, saunter, lounge, slacken, slow up, plod, trudge, waddle, falter, stagger, limp. *Ant.* haste, quicken, hustle, run, spurt, bound, dash, accelerate.
lame—*Syn.* crippled, defective, deformed, hesitating, faltering, impotent. *Ant.* agile, quick, active, swift, speedy.
lament—*Syn.* grieve, sorrow, weep, wail, bewail, deplore, anguish.
language—*Syn.* speech, utterance, expression, words, vocabulary, idiom, linguistics, literature.
languid—*Syn.* pensive, lethargic, flagging, feeble, dull, listless, apathetic, inactive. *Ant.* brisk, lively, animated, eager, alert.
larceny—*Syn.* theft, robbery, pillage, plunder, embezzlement, fraud. *Ant.* restoration, return, indemnification.
large—*Syn.* big, massive, immense colossal, gigantic, spacious, grand plentiful, comprehensive, abun dant, ample. *Ant.* small, insigni ficant, thin, attenuated, minute tiny, slight, paltry, mean, inconsiderable, slender, short, limited, diminutive, meagre, shrunken, withered, dwarfish.
lascivious—*Syn.* lewd, immoral, unchaste, lustful, unclean, carnal, prurient, ribald, bawdy, coarse, dissolute, obscene. *Ant.* good, pure, virtuous, uncontaminated, unsullied, unstained, chaste, unblemished, immaculate, sinless, spotless, moral, righteous, faultless.
lassitude—*Syn.* languor, weariness, tiredness, dullness, prostration, torpor, lethargy. *Ant.* vivacity, liveliness, agility, activity, vigor, animation, alertness.
last—*Syn.* latest, ultimate, final, utmost, lowest, meanest, least, extreme, conclusive. *Ant.* first, beginning, introductory, initial, primary, front, incipient.
latent—*Syn.* concealed, unknown, hidden, undeveloped, involved, imperceptible, implicit, unseen. *Ant.* apparent, perceptible, evident, manifest, exposed, clear, conspicuous, visible, public, prominent, indubitable, undisguised.
laudable—*Syn.* worthy, deserving, good, honorable, righteous, creditable, moral, obliging, excellent. *Ant.* vile, vicious, corrupt, dishonest, blameworthy, immoral, disorderly, contemptible.
laughable—*Syn.* ludicrous, ridiculous, comic,, comical, funny, droll. *Ant.* serious, solemn, impressive, fearful, depressive, sad, melancholy, sorrowful, painful, shocking, morbid.
lavish, *a.*—*Syn.* abundant, superabundant, excess, exorbitant, excessive. *Ant.* scarce, scanty, skimpy, curtailed, meagre, insufficient, wanting, sparse, deficient, inadequate.
lavish, *v.*—*Syn.* scatter, squander, gorge, deluge, flood, overload, dissipate, deplete. *Ant.* hoard, treasure up, put by, hold back, economize, skimp, conserve.
lawful—*Syn.* legitimate, allowable, righteous, legal, permitted, judicial, warranted, official. *Ant.* illegal, prohibited, unlawful, unauthorized, lawless.
lax—*Syn.* slack, remiss, flabby, undutiful, unobservant. *Ant.* tight, firm, hard, conscientious, reliable.
lazy—*Syn.* slow, idle, slack, remiss, torpid, dull, dormant, flagging, drowsy, inert. *Ant.* lively, brisk, keen, quick, prompt, spry, alert.
lead—*Syn.* guide, conduct, precede, direct, command, govern, manage, control, survey, handle, regulate, induce. *Ant.* follow, obey, conform, comply, submit, yield to.
learn—*Syn.* acquire, receive, imbibe, gain, study. *Ant.* teach, guide, disseminate.
learned—*Syn.* erudite, profound, educated, academic, well-informed. *Ant.* illiterate, uninformed, uncultured.
leave, *n.*—*Syn.* permission, liberty, allowance, consent, absence, furlough. *Ant.* retention, proscription, injunction, interdict, disallowance.
leave, *v.*—*Syn.* permit, let, allow, withdraw, depart, quit, relinquish, resign, vacate, abandon, desert. *Ant.* stay, remain, continue, rest, persist, hold, maintain, stand still, hold on.
legal—*Syn.* permissible, lawful, allowable, allowed, sanctioned, legitimate, authorized, admitted, fair. *Ant.* unfair, unlawful, illegal, illicit, disallowed, disbarred, wrong, prohibited.
lenient—*Syn.* indulgent, compassionate, merciful, tolerant. *Ant.* harsh, cruel, rough, coarse, unfeeling, severe.
let—*Syn.* permit, allow, suffer, bear, tolerate, privilege, authorize, sanction. *Ant.* prevent, hinder, hold, inhibit, oppose.
level—*Syn.* uniform, equal, flat, regular, flush. *Ant.* rough, uneven, rugged, irregular, mountainous, unequal, upright.
liable—*Syn.* responsible, answerable, bound, subject, accountable, likely, apt. *Ant.* excusable, unbound, not accountable, exempt, irresponsible.
liberal—*Syn.* generous, lavish, free, ample, munificient, unselfish, magnanimous. *Ant.* niggardly, miserly, narrow, grasping, stingy, sparing.
liberate—*Syn.* free, deliver, unchain, loose, unshackle, redeem, emancipate, rescue, dismiss, absolve, reprieve, clear. *Ant.* hold, keep, confine, shackle, bind, restrain, manacle, suppress, detain, arrest.
liberty—*Syn.* freedom, privilege, exemption, right, immunity, license, permit, allowance, discharge, acquittance. *Ant.* slavery, oppression, captivity, servitude, constraint.
life—*Syn.* existence, animation, vitality, source, origin, conduct, custom, principle, nature, endurance, duration. *Ant.* death, dissolution, departure, mortality, demise, cessation, end.
lifeless—*Syn.* dead, departed, defunct, gone, demised, sluggish, dormant, stagnant, inactive. *Ant.* alive, living, animated, spirited, vital, vigorous, active, gay.
light, *n.*—*Syn.* illumination, radiance, brightness, flame, glow, shine, gleam. *Ant.* darkness, obscurity, gloom, shade, shadow, night, heaviness.
likely—*Syn.* credible, probable, possible, feasible, apt. *Ant.* impracticable, unachievable, unattainable.
line—*Syn.* cord, thread, string, outline, sequence, span, measure, extension, rank, descent, ancestry.
linger—*Syn.* loiter, hesitate, delay, plod, falter, stagger, slouch. *Ant.* hasten, quicken, hurry, run, dash, speed, dart, scramble.
liquid—*Syn.* fluid, serous, flowing, juicy, solvent, liquefied, watery, dissolved. *Ant.* solid, dense, solidified, undissolved, coagulated.
list, *n.*—*Syn.* roll, record, schedule, index, catalog, register, inventory, account, table, syllabus, tally, file, manifest, prospectus, bulletin, directory.
list, *v.*—*Syn.* record, arrange, catalog, schedule, enter, chronicle, insert, enroll. *Ant.* cancel, erase, efface, expunge, obliterate, delete.
listen—*Syn.* attend, hear. *Ant.* ignore, shun, neglect, scorn.
listless—*Syn.* careless, forgetful, inattentive, inactive, drowsy, sleepy, heedless, spiritless, inert, leaden, dull, heavy, dreamy. *Ant.* quick, active, brisk, eager, spry, alert, acute, agile, indefatigable, ardent, attentive, diligent.
literal—*Syn.* verbal, true, accurate, precise, regular, real, actual, unerring, undisputed. *Ant.* wrong, erring, misleading, mistaken, deceiving, untrue, fallacious, unsound, distorted, figurative.
literature—*Syn.* learning, lore, education, erudition, knowledge, books, literary works, instruction, reading, culture. *Ant.* ignorance, darkness, chaos, confusion, barbarism, illiteracy, incomprehension.
little—*Syn.* small, dwarfish, minute, meagre, light, trifling, trivial, puny, tiny, stunted, undersized. *Ant.* large, bulky, huge, big, great, mighty, spacious, gigantic.
live—*Syn.* dwell, exist, reside, inhabit, subsist, endure, abide, last, be, act, do. *Ant.* die, depart, vanish, fade, disolve, disappear.
livelihood—*Syn.* maintenance, support, sustenance, substinence, living, provision, competence. *Ant.* poverty, necessity, privation, need, distress, indigence, penury, emptiness.
liveliness—*Syn.* animation, briskness, gaiety, vigor, activity, levity. *Ant.* gloom, melancholy, dejection, depression.
load, *v.*—*Syn.* burden, oppress, lade, make heavy. *Ant.* lighten, reduce, lessen.
loathe—*Syn.* abhor, detest, dislike, despise, denounce. *Ant.* like, admire, approve, revere.
lock—*Syn.* fastening, hook, catch, latch, clasp, bolt, bar, junction, conction, attachment, link, barrier, grip, tuft, curl.
lofty—*Syn.* high, elevated, proud, stately, dignified, eminent, towering, tall. *Ant.* low, depressed under, below, modest, diffident, timid, sheepish, unobtrusive, unpretentious, unassuming, reserved.
long—*Syn.* lengthy, extended, outstretched, elongated, prolonged, enduring, eternal, continued, distant, remote. *Ant.* short, shortened, abridged, abbreviated, transient, brief, concise, condensed, curt, epitomized, terse, compact.
look, *v.*—*Syn.* see, view, gaze, glance, scan, stare, behold, contemplate, watch, survey, regard, inspect, discern, perceive, glimpse.
lose—*Syn.* miss, drop, mislay, forfeit, let slip, squander, waste, fail,

falter, flounder, blunder, botch, stumble, fall short of, miscarry, be defeated, bite the dust *(slang)*. *Ant.* gain, acquire, obtain, recover, procure, win, collect, pick up, reap, get, inherit, increase, expand, extend, profit, advance, progress, forge ahead, proceed, improve, rally, mend, surmount, overcome.

loss—*Syn.* injury, damage, detriment, deprivation, forfeiture, deterioration, impairment, retrogression, decline. *Ant.* gain, profit, emolument, acquisition, advancement, assistance, help.

loud—*Syn.* noisy, uproarious, blatant, deafening, shrill, piercing, blaring, resonant, thundering. *Ant.* faint, muffled, stifled, soft, low, quiet, silent, ill-bred.

love—*Syn.* affection, emotion, sentiment, passion, feeling, tenderness, liking, regard, attraction, fervor, flame, rapture, adoration. *Ant.* hate, disaffection, estrangement, bitterness, antipathy, malice, loathing, abhorrence, aversion, abomination, contumely.

lovely—*Syn.* beautiful, attractive, inviting, nice, captivating, fascinating, enticing, delightful, gratifying, satisfying, lovable, graceful, exquisite. *Ant.* ugly, plain, homely, unseemly, unprepossessing, ill-favored, ungraceful, grim, forbidding, repulsive, shocking, repugnant.

low—*Syn.* below, beneath, under, depressed, sunken, inferior, soft, muffled, mean, debased, vulgar, disgraceful, dishonorable, degraded, cheap, inexpensive. *Ant.* high, elevated, upper, lofty, tall, prominent, loud, noisy, blatant, honorable, decent, estimable, respected, vigorous, strong, costly, inexpensive.

lucid—*Syn.* bright, shining, transparent, clear, plain, same, rational, sound. *Ant.* dark, murky, gloomy, obscure, dim, dusky, cloudy, unintelligible, incomprehensible.

lucky—*Syn.* fortunate, triumphant, thriving, flourishing, conquering, overcoming, winning, gaining. *Ant.* unlucky, unfortunate, unsuccessful, crushed, persecuted, ruined, overwhelmed.

ludicrous—*Syn.* comical, odd, farcical, ridiculous, droll, funny, whimsical, screaming, bizarre, quaint, eccentric, ridiculous. *Ant.* serious, solemn, sorrowful, grievous, depressing, pensive, grim, demure.

lunacy—*Syn.* insanity, mania, furor, aberration, delusion. *Ant.* sanity, rationality, normalcy, soundness, reason.

lure—*Syn.* attract, entice, draw, decoy, coax, cajole, snare, trap, entangle, induce, persuade, seduce. *Ant.* repel, dissuade.

luscious—*Syn.* sweet, palatable, pleasing, tasty, savory, delectable, delicious, exquisite. *Ant.* unsavory, acrid, tart, sharp, sour.

luster—*Syn.* brilliancy, gloss, glow, sheen, distinction, celebrity, reputation. *Ant.* darkness, gloom, obscurity, murk, shade, shadow, disrepute, dishonor, humiliation, shame, stigma.

luxuriant—*Syn.* exuberant, abundant, superabundant, profuse, dense, fertile. *Ant.* meagre, dwarfed, scanty, scarce, barren, infertile, fallow, unfruitful.

lying—*Syn.* untruthful, false, deceitful, fraudulent, dishonest, faithless, insincere, disingenuous, deceptive, low, contemptible. *Ant.* truthful, sincere, frank, honest, guileless, unreserved, ingenuous, honorable, trustworthy, reliable, straightforward, scrupulous.

M

mad—*Syn.* insane, crazy, deranged, distracted, wild, raging, furious, frantic, frenzied, violent, raving, fierce. *Ant.* normal, steady, settled, calm, cool, collected, sober, rational, lucid, sane, sagacious.

magic—*Syn.* occultism, legerdemain, witchery, superstition, sorcery, jugglery, soothsaying, fortune-telling, omen.

magnanimous—*Syn.* high-minded, generous, noble, exalted, honorable, lofty, dignified, heroic, sublime. *Ant.* selfish, mean, corrupt, depraved, mercenary, covetous, miserly, doubting, greedy.

magnificent—*Syn.* grand, splendid, noble, surpassing, glorious, superb, fine, artistic, majestic, spectacular. *Ant.* plain, common, ordinary, normal, informal, unpretentious, offensive, forbidding.

magnitude—*Syn.* size, volume, bulk, extent, greatness, measure, mass, quantity, enormity, multitude, might, power, intensity, expanse. *Ant.* small, thin, paucity, slenderness, insignificance, minimum.

maintain—*Syn.* support, sustain, hold, uphold, defend, contend, assert, bear, keep, continue, confirm. *Ant.* deny, reject, refuse, abandon, desert, leave, quit, depart, denounce.

majestic—*Syn.* stately, grand, impressive, august, dignified, splendid, imposing, mighty, eminent, renowned, prominent. *Ant.* low, small, diminutive, inferior, humble, shabby, petty, insignificant, obscure, unpretentious, unadorned.

make—*Syn.* do, form, construct, fabricate, forge, compose, produce, perform, execute, shape, create, establish, generate, complete. *Ant.* break, burst, destroy, wreck, scatter, abolish, ruin, overthrow, crash, batter, ravage, raze, level, mutilate, disfigure, deform, distort, twist, damage, eradicate, obliterate.

malediction—*Syn.* curse, execration, anathema, denunciation, wrath, disparagement. *Ant.* blessing, benediction, approval, approbation, praise, esteem.

malevolent—*Syn.* spiteful, malicious, evil, ill-intentioned, bitter, spiteful, treacherous. *Ant.* amiable, cordial, kind, tender, considerate, benevolent.

malice—*Syn.* spite, rancor, animosity, enmity, bitterness, antipathy, dislike. *Ant.* benevolence, unselfishness, kindliness, sympathy, goodwill, kindness, compassion.

maltreat—*Syn.* injure, abuse, punish, strike, damage, hurt, bruise, victimize. *Ant.* benefit, treat kindly, soothe, encourage, favor, help, aid, comfort, sustain, enliven, animate.

manage—*Syn.* regulate, govern, direct, show, control, conduct, administer, wield, guide, advise. *Ant.* mismanage, bungle, blunder, fumble, misdirect, misguide.

mangle—*Syn.* tear, mutilate, lacerate, injure, cripple, disfigure, cut, slay, bruise. *Ant.* heal, mend.

manifest, *a.*—*Syn.* clear, visible, evident, plain, apparent, open, obvious, definite, unmistakable, explicit. *Ant.* buried, concealed, hidden, cloaked.

manifest, *v.*—*Syn.* reveal, show, discover, exhibit, display, declare, unveil, divulge, expose, proclaim. *Ant.* bury, conceal, hide, cover, withhold, secrete, obscure.

manly—*Syn.* brave, courageous, fearless, firm, dignified, valiant, gallant. *Ant.* cowardly, timid, afraid.

manner—*Syn.* habit, behavior, appearance, aspect, look, way, style, mien, mode, expression, deportment, carriage, bearing.

mar—*Syn.* deform, distort, impair, injure, hurt, spoil, deface, harm, damage. *Ant.* beautify, adorn, repair, improve, refresh, vivify.

march, *n.*—*Syn.* journey, expedition, promenade, hike, saunter, tour, advancement, course.

march, *v.*—*Syn.* walk, move, advance, proceed, step, travel, journey. *Ant.* rest, pause, halt, stand, stay, stop.

margin—*Syn.* brink, edge, verge, lip, brow, skirt, rim, fringe, strand. *Ant.* interior, surface, area, width, breadth, depth.

maritime—*Syn.* nautical, naval, marine, oceanic, seagoing, seafaring, aquatic. *Ant.* earthly, terrestrial, inland, landlocked.

mark, *n.*—*Syn.* sign, symbol, token, design, brand, badge, line, trace, impression, stamp, engraving, device, type, character, figure, score, stripe, index.

mark, *v.*—*Syn.* stamp, impress, form, make, brand, label, sign, imprint, engrave, trace, insert, record, register, indicate, ticket, docket.

marriage—*Syn.* union, wedlock, nuptials, wedding, matrimony, match. *Ant.* celibacy, bachelorhood, spinsterhood, single.

martial—*Syn.* warlike, soldierly, courageous, belligerent, militant, combative, embattled. *Ant.* quiet, pacific, non-combatant, submissive, meek, mild, unresisting, pliant.

marvelous—*Syn.* wonderful, miraculous, phenomenal, amazing, astonishing, astounding, stupendous, prodigious. *Ant.* plain, common, normal, ordinary, simple, conventional, unimportant, inconsiderable, paltry.

masculine—*Syn.* manly, mannish, male, robust, daring. *Ant.* feminine, womanly, effeminate, female, delicate.

mask—*Syn.* conceal, cloak, cover, hide, screen, disguise, veil, camouflage, suppress. *Ant.* unmask, uncover, tell, explain, announce, relate, record, declare, proclaim.

mass—*Syn.* bulk, heap, lump, whole, sum, total, amount, aggregate, quantity, density, gravity, size, weight, solidity, thickness. *Ant.* buoyancy, lightness, fluff, froth, air.

massive—*Syn.* huge, heavy, dense, ponderous, weighty, large, bulky, solid. *Ant.* light, airy, volatile, flexble.

master—*Syn.* chief, leader, ruler, governor, director, lord, principal, overseer, superintendent, supervisor, preceptor, chieftain, commander. *Ant.* servant, follower, attendant, valet, subject, dependent, serf, disciple, beginner, laborer, hireling.

matchless—*Syn.* peerless, incomparable, inimitable, surpassing, unparralleled, supreme, perfect, complete, faultless, superior. *Ant.* common, ordinary, meagre, petty, paltry, inferior.

material—*Syn.* corporal, corporeal, physical, sensible, tangible, substantial. *Ant.* immaterial, airy, shadowy, misty, ethereal, discarnate, unearthly, spiritual, disembodied, ghostly.

matter—*Syn.* substance, element, object, article, thing. *Ant.* nothingness, immateriality, soul, ego, astral body, ghost, phantom, vision, imagination.

mature—*Syn.* adolescent, pubescent, ripe, nubile, adult, ready, fit, perfect, settled, maturated. *Ant.* immature, unripe, undeveloped, incomplete, fresh, rudimental, callow, raw, unfitted, unready, inexperienced.

mausoleum—*Syn.* tomb, crypt, vault, grave, sepulchre, catacomb, pit, tumulus, mound, barrow, cenotaph.

maxim—*Syn.* text, aphorism, precept, proverb, adage, saw, saying, byword, epigram, moral, wittism, repartee, axiom. *Ant.* absurdity, blunder, nonsense, quibble, joke, extravaganza, bull, jargon, gibberish, claptrap.

maze—*Syn.* tangle, twist, winding, convolution, intricacy, labyrinth, perplexity, difficulty, puzzle. *Ant.* simplicity, ease, facility, enlightment.

meager—*Syn.* thin, poor, small, slender, emaciated, scanty, barren, withered, dry, diminutive, deficient, insufficient. *Ant.* sufficient, ample, abundant, luxuriant, replete.

mean, *a.*—*Syn.* low, base, debased, ignoble, abject, paltry, shabby, stingy, miserly, mercenary, niggardly, selfish. *Ant.* generous, unselfish, liberal, honorable, helpful, compassionate, indulgent.

mean, *v.*—*Syn.* intend, purpose, signify, indicate, design, denote, decide, determine, propose, pursue, signify, allude to. *Ant.* jabber, confuse, mystify, puzzle, sidestep, pretend, deceive.

measure—*Syn.* quantity, magnitude, degree, amount, extent, scope, reach, outline, sketch, proposal, proposition.

meddle—*Syn.* interpose, interfere, tamper with. *Ant.* keep off, shun, refrain from, ignore, avoid.

meddlesome—*Syn.* obtrusive, intrusive, audacious, impertinent, obstructive, hindering, interfering. *Ant.* aiding, assisting, helping, encouraging, supporting.

meditate—*Syn.* study, contemplate, consider, ponder, revolve, project, reflect, deliberate. *Ant.* relax the mind, divert attention, be inattentive, turn from, neglect, ignore.

medium, *a.*—*Syn.* middle, mediocre, intermediate, commonplace, ordinary, normal. *Ant.* excellent, superior, fine, choice, rare, eminent, surpassing, inferior, useless.
medley—*Syn.* mixture, confusion, variance, miscellany, diversity, disorder. *Ant.* order, uniformity, proportion, system, orderliness, simplification, regularity, normalcy.
meek—*Syn.* humble, mild, gentle, unassuming, modest, yielding, compliant, demure, tranquil, quiet, reserved, placid. *Ant.* harsh, cruel, overbearing, haughty, vain, conceited, bold, presuming, obstinate, impertinent.
melancholy, *a.*—*Syn.* depressed, dispirited, gloomy, pensive, dejected, discontented, sad, sorrowful, despondent, heavy-hearted, dismal, dull, discouraged, forlorn. *Ant.* cheery, cheerful, gay, lively, merry, laughing, happy, smiling, bouyant, jolly, vivacious, agreeable, amiable.
mellow—*Syn.* ripe, mature, perfected, seasoned, full-flavored, aged, pleasing, hearty, gay. *Ant.* immature, hard, sour, acrid, tart, flat, stale, insipid, dull, sober, temperate, solemn.
melodious—*Syn.* musical, harmonious, pleasing, dulcet, clear, silvery. *Ant.* harsh, grating, unmusical, dissonant, discordant, raucous, shrill.
melody—*Syn.* music, harmony, symphony, unison, concord, syncopation. *Ant.* discord, dissonance, disagreement, harshness, discordance.
melt—*Syn.* dissolve, soften, mollify, thaw, render, decrease, diminish, waste. *Ant.* freeze, coagulate, thicken, densify, stick, adhere, solidify, congeal, condense.
memorable—*Syn.* extraordinary, uncommon, important, surpassing, unforgettable, crucial, remarkable, prominent, illustrous, famous, great, momentous. *Ant.* unimportant, trifling, trivial, petty, foolish, frivolous, inconsequential, irrelevant.
memorial—*Syn.* memento, souvenir, remembrance, monument, tablet, pillar, tombstome, headstone, column, shaft, obelisk, monolith, mausoleum, record, inscription.
memory—*Syn.* recollection, remembrance, retrospect, recollection. *Ant.* oblivion, forgetfulness, oversight, obliteration.
menace—*Syn.* threat, intimidation, warning, trepidation. *Ant.* peace, tranquillity, calmness.
mend—*Syn.* improve, repair, rectify, correct, amend, restore, ameliorate, refine, revive, refresh, renew. *Ant.* deteriorate, weaken, destroy, injure, hurt, impair, disfigure, deface.
mendacity—*Syn.* lying, falsehood, prevarication, calumny, perjury, deception, fabrication, distortion. *Ant.* veracity, candor, honesty, probity, sincerity.
mental—*Syn.* intellectual, psychological, rational, subjective, appercipient, subconscious. *Ant.* incogitant, fatuous, unreasoning, thoughtless, inane.
merciful—*Syn.* kind, lenient, gentle, tender, gracious, feeling, compassionate, sympathetic, humane. *Ant.* unkind, cruel, inhuman, ruthless, unmerciful.
mercurial—*Syn.* changeable, variable, fluctuating, inconstant, unstable, erratic, excitable. *Ant.* steady, stable, settled, constant, unvarying, immutable, steadfast, patient, calm.
mercy—*Syn.* pity, lenity, forbearance, charity, compassion, sympathy, humanity, clemency, leniency, tolerance, kindness. *Ant.* cruelty, severity, harshness, rigor, hardness, punishment, vengeance, justice.
merit—*Syn.* worth, worthiness, goodness, excellence, reward, regard, honor, appreciation, value, rectitude, stability, honor. *Ant.* vice, dishonor, demerit, shame, scandal, wrongdoing, betrayal, badness, corruption, injustice, wrong.
meritorious—*Syn.* worthy, praiseworthy, generous, noble, commendable, estimable, admirable, good, excellent, honorable, fine, unselfish. *Ant.* unworthy, dishonorable, shameless, immoral, corrupt, infamous.
merriment—*Syn.* gaiety, hilarity, frolic, joviality, mirth, cheer, glee, joy, laughter, fun, frolic. *Ant.* sorrow, sadness, dullness, gloom, melancholy, dejection.
merry—*Syn.* gay, cheerful, happy, jovial, jocular, joyous, mirthful, lively, rollicking, buoyant, jubliant, elated. *Ant.* sad, sorrowful, miserable, dull, wretched, gloomy, downcast, melancholy, moaning, groaning, weary, worried.
mess—*Syn.* mixture, combination, compound, glutinous, mass, waxy lump, medley, potpourri.
metaphorical—*Syn.* symbolical, allegorical, figurative, allusive, comparative, contrastive, antonomastic, euphuistic, ironic, colloquial.
method—*Syn.* order, system, arrangement, style, manner, custom, way, mode, course, routine, form, fashion. *Ant.* disorder, irregularity, discord, disunion, disarrangement, mixture, complication.
mettle—*Syn.* spirit, animation, character, stamina, courage, bravery, determination. *Ant.* fear, weakness, timidity.
mien—*Syn.* manner, aspect, appearance, condition, look, air, expression, carriage, deportment.
mighty—*Syn.* strong, powerful, great, foreceful, potent, muscular, vigorous. *Ant.* weak, puny, feeble, frail.
migratory—*Syn.* wandering, unsettled, transient, roving, roaming, vagrant. *Ant.* settled, permanent, fixed, established.
mild—*Syn.* soft, gentle, tender, kind, bland, easy, mellow, quiet, smooth, calm. *Ant.* rough, uncouth, harsh, unkind, bluff, boisterous.
mimic—*Syn.* imitate, repeat, echo, re-echo, mock, simulate, copy, emulate.
mind—*Syn.* intellect, understanding, inclination, desire, judgement, liking, thought, sense, reason, faculty, intelligence, reasoning. *Ant.* matter, substance, materiality.
mindful—*Syn.* attentive, thoughtful, observant, observing, alert. *Ant.* inattentive, heedless, careless, inadvertent, bemused, dreamy, preoccupied.
minister, *n.*—*Syn.* priest, parson, clergyman, preacher, divine, churchman, pastor, confessor, reverend, shepherd, servant, official, ambassador, plenipotentiary, consul, representative. *Ant.* layman, parishioner, diciple, follower, student.
minister, *v.*—*Syn.* serve, act, perform, help, succor, relieve, sustain, uphold, administer, attend. *Ant.* obstruct, impede, interdict, stop, encumber, embarrass, interfere, hamper, restrain.
minute—*Syn.* small, microscopic, diminutive, little, insignificant, miniature, infinitesimal, particular. *Ant.* large, heavy, bulky, unwieldly, huge, immense, great, colossal, vast, stupendous, spacious, infinite.
miraculous—*Syn.* wonderful, prodigious, marvelous, extraordinary, curious, monstrous, freakish, spectacular, wondrous, astonishing, amazing, astounding, unimaginable. *Ant.* common, ordinary, everyday, trivial, familiar, natural.
miscellaneous—*Syn.* mixed, mingled, promiscuous, various, combined, commixed, several, many, manifold. *Ant.* simple, uniform, unmixed, similar, homogenous.
mischief—*Syn.* damage, hurt, injury, detriment, evil, harm, grievance, accident. *Ant.* good, benefit, advantage, service, profit, improvement, kindness, favor, assistance, help, amity, vindication.
miscreant—*Syn.* wretch, villain, knave, rogue, ruffian, rascal, scamp, caitiff, sneak, scoundrel, culprit, deliquent, felon, criminal, roughneck, vagabond. *Ant.* model, exemplar, pattern, benefactor, saint, angel, demigod, good man, good woman, paragon.
miser—*Syn.* curmudgeon, shrew, skinflint, hoarder, niggard, churl. *Ant.* prodigal, spendthrift, squanderer, spender, wastrel.
miserable—*Syn.* unhappy, pained, afflicted, distressed, unfortunate, sickly, suffering, sad, meager, insufficient, mean, stingy, venal, mercenary. *Ant.* happy, smiling, prosperous, comfortable, cheerful, blithe, gay, contented, satisfied, buoyant.
misery—*Syn.* pain, grief, sorrow, depression, distress, unhappiness, despair, desolation, trouble, anguish, agony, annoyance, irritation, heaviness, despondency. *Ant.* pleasure, gratification, enjoyment, ease, comfort, gladness.
misfortune—*Syn.* calamity, adversity, harm, hurt, accident, misadventure, ill luck, sorrow, trouble, bereavement, mischance, mishap, disaster, hardship. *Ant.* prosperity, success, advantage, joy, good luck, good fortune, happiness, welfare, consolation.
mislead—*Syn.* delude, deceive, misrepresent, defraud, cheat, hoodwink, bilk, trick, hoax. *Ant.* advise, encourage, assist, aid, help, succor, relieve, counsel, inform, direct, protect, guard, defend, uphold.
mistake—*Syn.* blunder, error, omission, fallacy, failure, oversight, slip, flaw, oversight, misstatement, false. *Ant.* truth, reality, fact, accuracy, precision, answer.
mitigate—*Syn.* assuage, abate, alleviate, lighten, moderate, relieve, mollify, weaken, decrease, diminish. *Ant.* aggravate, increase, excite, augment, strengthen, intensify, stimulate, deepen.
mix—*Syn.* blend, mingle, confuse, unite, join, compound, combine, commix, intermix, alloy. *Ant.* purify, separate, shift, exclude, simplify, adjust, arrange, untangle, sort, segregate, assort, classify.
mob—*Syn.* crowd, gathering, populace, people, flock, drove, horde. *Ant.* nobility, gentry, quality, notables.
mode—*Syn.* fashion, style, manner, custom, rule, sort, state, habit, vogue, practice, plan, scheme. *Ant.* disuse, infringement, obsolescence, noncomformity.
model—*Syn.* prototype, original, standard, example, mold, form, facsimile, design, image, pattern, type, copy. *Ant.* misrepresentation, travesty, distortion, exaggeration.
moderate, *a.*—*Syn.* limited, medium, reasonable, fair, abstemious, temperate, modest, ordinary, sober, regulated, calm, tolerant. *Ant.* great, considerable, extensive, extended, excessive, extravagant, full, complete, abundant, liberal, ample, plenty, unlimited, fast, speedy, rapid.
moderate, *v.*—*Syn.* check, curb, restrain, lessen, allay, temper, reduce, qualify, control, limit, regulate. *Ant.* excite, rouse, incite, exasperate, inflame, exacerbate, stimulate, madden, irritate, agitate, enrage, strengthen.
modern—*Syn.* recent, fresh, new, novel, fresh. *Ant.* ancient, antique, old, primitive.
modest—*Syn.* bashful, retiring, reserved, diffident, shy, coy, humble, small, unpretentious, demure, pure, continent. *Ant.* extravagant, excessive, exorbitant, outrageous, mighty, immpressive, ostentatious, arrogant, haughty.
modesty—*Syn.* reserve, timidity, shyness, coyness, restraint, constraint, bashfulness, decency, decorum, innocence. *Ant.* boldness, confidence, audacity, pertness, defiance, effrontery, arrogance, presumption, swagger, conceit.
moist—*Syn.* damp, wet, humid, dank, watery, saturated, sodden, soppy. *Ant.* dry, arid, barren, sandy, dehydrated, parched, dried up.
molest—*Syn.* hurt, injure, annoy, disturb, worry, plague, bother, pester, harass, badger, irritate, vex, thwart, trouble, confuse, maltreat, misuse. *Ant.* comfort, console, soothe, aid, help, assist, hearten, encourage, cheer, benefit, praise, applaud, oblige, favor, commend, recommend.
mollify—*Syn.* assuage, mitigate, lessen, soften, ameliorate, moderate, appease, soothe, lull, smooth, temper, tranquillize, moderate, calm, pacify, restrain, repress, reconcile, console, please, allay. *Ant.* anger, enrage, infuriate, taunt, tempt, excite, incite, disturb, annoy, harass, agitate, worry, plague, torment, vex, irritate, provoke, exasperate, exacerbate, arouse, inflame, incense, chafe, nettle, madden.
momentous—*Syn.* important, consequential, weighty, memorable, notable, salient, eventful, stirring. *Ant.* unimportant, slight, trivial, trifling, insignificant, small, immaterial, irrelevant, uninteresting, common-

place, ordinary.
money—*Syn.* gold, silver, coin, cash, currency, bills, notes, funds, capital, bullion, wealth, stock, assets, wherewithal, means, opulence, treasure, resources, affluence, independence, riches.
monomania—*Syn.* madness, derangement, morbidity, mania, dementia, delirium, aberration, infatuation, obsession. *Ant.* sanity, lucidity, common sense, normalcy, soundness, steadiness, mental vigor, rationality, reasonableness.
monotonous—*Syn.* dull, tedious, wearisome, wearying, undiversified, irksome, uninteresting, humdrum. *Ant.* varied, versatile, interesting, droll, pleasant, amusing, entertaining, festive, pleasing, inviting, charming, appealing, captivating.
monstrous—*Syn.* horrible, terrible, atrocious, dreadful, awful, frightful, shocking, preposterous, marvelous, stupendous, vast, prodigious, terrifying, inconceivable, strange, incredible, huge, enormous, immense, anomalous. *Ant.* common, ordinary, normal, natural, conventional, formal, diminutive, graceful, shapely, plain, customary, expected, comformable, habitual, standard, average.
monument—*Syn.* tomb, shaft, column, pillar, vault, mausoleum, headstone, tombstone, grave-stone, memorial, shrine, statue, building, erection, pile, tower, obelisk, monolith, tablet, slab, stone. *Ant.* forgetfulness, oblivion, obliteration, extinction, annihilation.
mood—*Syn.* mode, manner, state, condition, temper, disposition, humor, vein, behavior, conduct, nature, principle, character, habit, temperament.
morbid—*Syn.* abnormal, pathological, unsound, unhealthy. *Ant.* sound, vigorous, robust, normal, lively, strong, well, hearty, hale.
moron—*Syn.* fool, simpleton. *Ant.* sage, philosopher, scholar, genius.
morose—*Syn.* gloomy, sour, sullen, morbid, depressed, acrimonious, gruff, dolorous, melancholy, perversive, sulky, crusty, grouchy, surly, moody, churlish, cantankerous. *Ant.* cheerful, bright, lively, animated, spirited, blithe, buoyant, sprightly, vivacious, keen, hilarious, amiable, pleasant, tender, mild, indulgent, gentle, friendly, genial.
mortal—*Syn.* deadly, fatal, lethal, deathly, serious, extreme, human, transient, temporal. *Ant.* refreshing, reinvigorating, reviving, vivifying, revivifying, curative, trivial, perpetual, eternal.
motion—*Syn.* movement, transition, change, transit, passage, act, movement, restlessness, stride, gait, pace, step. *Ant.* quiet, quiescence, rest, stop, pause, standstill, repose, lull, stagnation, stoppage, halt, cessation.
motionless—*Syn.* still, unmoving, torpid, dead, inert, quiescent, motionless, fixed, stationary, stagnant, immovable, becalmed, undisturbed, silent. *Ant.* moving, shifting, changing, movable, restless, flowing, floating.
mound—*Syn.* hill, pile, heap, grave, knoll, elevation, eminence, fortification, defense, earth bank, protection, shield, mole, rampart, ditch, fosse, scarp, parapet, embankment.
mount—*Syn.* rise, ascend, climb, tower, scale, arise, grow, increase, augment, swell, soar, surge. *Ant.* descend, decline, drop, fall, subside, lapse, collapse, sink, slump, alight, decrease, diminish, lessen, abate, curtail, abridge.
mourn—*Syn.* lament, deplore, grieve, fret, sorrow, bemoan, rue, regret, droop, languish, whimper, groan, wail. *Ant.* rejoice, exult, revel, cheer, shout, caper, frolic, gambol, play, express joy.
mournful—*Syn.* sorrowful, sad, heavy, doleful, lugubrious, downcast, unhappy, funeral, melancholy, joyless, cheerless, blue, heavy-hearted, pensive, disconsolate, forlorn, abandoned, heartsick, despairing. *Ant.* joyful, cheerful, merry, gay, light, buoyant, rejoicing, vivacious, lively, animated, enlivening, playful, jolly, exhilarated, gleeful, elated.
move—*Syn.* stir, advance, influence, actuate, instigate, impel, budge, shift, glide, walk, run, fly, travel, drift, go, propel, hustle, bustle, proceed, propose, induce, stimulate, rouse, persuade, agitate, excite, coax, bias, lure, whip, lash, spur, urge. *Ant.* stand, halt, pause, rest, cease, repose, stop, relax, sleep, doze, drowse, calm, suppress, restrain, mollify, pacify, dissuade, discourage, dishearten, quell, settle.
movement—*Syn.* motion, velocity, transition, change, flight, journey, travel, progress, advancement, progression, speed, activity, action, quickness, hustle, bustle, hurry, flurry, scurry, work, act, enterprise. *Ant.* inactivity, abandonment, resignation, cessation, stop, inaction, idleness, inertness, laziness, insensibility, slumber, sleep, indolence, remissness, inaction, stagnation, passiveness.
movies—*Syn.* moving pictures, motion pictures, cinema, cinematograph, silver screen, panorama, diorama, presentation, photoplay, entertainment.
muddle, *n.*—*Syn.* difficulty, confusion, dilemma, mixup, disorder, jumble, maze, turmoil, perplexity, mixture, complication, intricacy, entanglement, mess, botch, ferment, complexity. *Ant.* order, arrangement, method, plan, conformity, unity, system, orderliness, uniformity, ease, smoothness, classification, allocation, outline, regularity.
muddle, *v.*—*Syn.* foul, confuse, disarrange, disturb, mix, disorder, jumble, toss, turn, ruffle, disorganize, entangle, embroil, disconcert, confound. *Ant.* clarify, explain, elucidate, interpret, expound, arrange, regulate, adjust, unravel, untangle, sort, classify, allot, allocate.
multitude—*Syn.* crowd, throng, swarm, gathering, congregation, collection, assemblage, galaxy, army. *Ant.* scarcity, sparseness, part, portion, paucity, fraction, zero, nobody, minority, handful.
munificent—*Syn.* bountiful, generous, liberal, helpful, lavish, charitable, hospitable, unselfish, ample, unsparing, profuse. *Ant.* parsimonious, penurious, selfish, frugal, saving, niggardly, stingy, improvident, cautious, careful.
murder—*Syn.* kill, slay, butcher, slaughter, dispatch, assassinate, immolate, destroy, massacre. *Ant.* restore, vivify, animate, refresh, reinvigorate, vitalize, revive, propagate, produce.
murky—*Syn.* obscure, dark, filmy, dim, gloomy, dull, flat, overcast, clouded, somber, lowering, dreary, dismal, dusky, dingy. *Ant.* light, clear, bright, sunny, shining, glittering, sparkling, glowing, luminous, radiant, brilliant, dazzling, unobscured, cloudless.
murmur—*Syn.* whisper, mutter, grumble, trickle, drip, hum, meander. *Ant.* storm, thunder, peal, clang, swell, rend, split, roar, boom, explode, detonate.
muse—*Syn.* think, ponder, meditate, reflect, deliberate, study, consider, cogitate, contemplate, reason. *Ant.* relax, unbend.
music—*Syn.* harmony, melody, symphony, tune, air, concord, rhythm, syncopation, orchestration, instrumentation, harmonization. *Ant.* discord, dissonance, cacaphony, confusion, clash, disagreement, variance, discordance, incongruity, dissidence.
musical—*Syn.* melodious, harmonious, tuneful, pleasing, euphonic, agreeable, melodic, lyrical, symphonic, vocal, tonal, mellow. *Ant.* discordant, grating, jarring, jangling, disagreeable, dissonant, unmusical, incongruous, inharmonious.
musty—*Syn.* moldy, stale, sour, mildewed, rank, foul, smudged, grimy, dusty, soiled, rusty. *Ant.* clean, pure, unstained, sweet, green, cleansed, renewed.
mute—*Syn.* speechless, silent, still, noiseless, hushed, calm, inaudible. *Ant.* vocal, articulate, distinct, oral, talkative, clear, spoken, uttered.
mutilate—*Syn.* cripple, disable, disfigure, injure, impair, mangle, deface, lame, wound, hurt, distort, spoil, mar, deform, damage. *Ant.* form, restore, fix, shape, patch, replace, renovate, renew, revive, rectify, repair, rehabilitate, mend, reconstruct.
mutinous—*Syn.* rebellious, insubordinate, revolutionary, turbulent, insurgent, resistant, tumultuous, recalcitrant, insubordinate, insurgent, unruly, lawless, ungovernable, refractory. *Ant.* obedient, submissive, loyal, passive, subjective, resigned, compliant, faithful, devoted, peaceful, pacific, tranquil, observant, true, constant, dutiful, orderly.
mutual—*Syn.* joint, common, correlative, convertible, identical, coincident, equivalent, similar, like. *Ant.* separate, dissociated, disunited, distinct, detached, disconnected, dissimilar, unlike, different, disparate, divergent.
muzzle—*Syn.* bind, fasten, gag, restrain, trammel, restrict, repress, suppress, check, confine, prevent, stop, silence. *Ant.* free, liberate, unfasten, foster, encourage, approve, stimulate, impel, urge.
mysterious—*Syn.* occult, secret, obscure, enigmatic, covert, dark, hidden, incredible, inexplicable, puzzling, unrevealed, mystical, inscrutable. *Ant.* clear, plain, definite, apparent, distinct, obvious, evident, intelligible, lucid, explicit, graphic, vivid, comprehensible, known, overt, ostensible, discernible, indisputable, incontrovertible.
mystify—*Syn.* perplex, puzzle, confuse, dissemble, confound, embarrass, mislead, misguide, misrepresent, equivocate, obfuscate. *Ant.* clear, explain, illustrate, inform, declare, report, interpret, translate, define, render, elucidate, unravel, disentangle, enlighten, disclose, communicate. expound.

naked—*Syn.* bare, uncovered, open, exposed, unclothed, nude, undressed, unconcealed, manifest, plain, evident, undisguised, simple, definite, distinct, explicit, express, literal, divested, unclad. *Ant.* covered, clad, clothed, cloaked, dressed, arrayed, draped, robed, garbed, attired, wrapped, swathed, latent, concealed, secret, covert, unexposed, undisclosed, veiled.
name, *n.*—*Syn.* appellation, designation, title, denomination, epithet, surname, style, reputation, repute, character, distinction, sign, signature, autograph.
name, *v.*—*Syn.* style, call, denominate, term, title, head, specify, signify, denote, designate, mark, characterize, proclaim, label, define.
nameless—*Syn.* unnamed, anonymous, obscure, inglorious, shameful, degrading, humiliating, unmentionable, pseudo. *Ant.* named, acknowledged, signed, confirmed, designated, known, famous, celebrated, renowned, prominent, eminent, distinguished.
narrate—*Syn.* tell, relate, recite, detail, enumerate, describe, recount, portray, picture, proclaim, unfold, recapitulate, describe, paint, disclose, reveal. *Ant.* screen, cover, shade, withhold, veil, hide, conceal, disguise, suppress, repress, stifle, smother, restrain, stop.
narrow—*Syn.* restricted, close, cramped, contracted, shrunken, compressed, limited, scanty, constrained, tenuous, scrawny, attenuated, spare, prejudiced, bigoted. *Ant.* wide, expanded, ample, broad, extended, swollen, turgid, tumid, corpulent, bloated, fat, thick, dumpy, squat, thickset, stubby, plump, portly, stout, dilated, expanded, generous.
nasty—*Syn.* contaminated, offensive, unclean, tainted, defiled, impure, sloppy, slatternly, soiled, gross, grimy, rotten, beastly, corrupt, polluted. *Ant.* clean, pure, sweet, uncontaminated, pleasing, unsoiled, unsullied, spotless, pleasurable, gratifying, attractive, winsome, purified, stainless, disinfected, cleansed, bright, shiny, glittering, attractive, washed.
nation—*Syn.* state, realm, country, commonwealth, republic, empire, kingdom, principality, colony, population, populace, persons, folk, society, community, public.
native—*Syn.* indigenous, original, aboriginal, natural, inborn, vernacular, domestic, domesticated. *Ant.* foreign, alien, extraneous, outside, extrinsic, strange, distant, remote,

external, outward, assumed, unnatural, acquired.
natural—*Syn.* intrinsic, original, regular, normal, essential, true, consistent, probable, subjective, fundamental, inborn, innate, ingrained, inherited, genetic, incarnate, unintentional, simple, unaffected, plain. *Ant.* objective, extraneous, casual, contingent, incidental, subsidiary, outward, external, intentional, contemplated, intended, prepared, ready, ornamented, embellished, elaborated, decorated, beautified, unnatural.
nauseous—*Syn.* disgusting, abhorrent, loathsomme, unsavory, unpleasant, distasteful, abominable, disagreeable, offensive, revolting, repulsive, repellent, nasty, sickening. *Ant.* pleasing, pleasant, agreeable, sweet, savory, delectable, toothsome, delicious, luscious, satisfying, desirable, refreshing, appetizing.
nautical—*Syn.* marine, maritime, naval, oceanic, aquatic, sailing, seafaring, seagoing, navigable, floating, boating, yachting, rowing. *Ant.* peripatetic, wandering, ambulatory, vehicular, itinerant, sauntering, rambling, walking, running, jumping, flying, skating.
near—*Syn.* close, intimate, adjacent, bordering, neighboring, adjoining, proximal, approaching, next, prospective, expectant, imminent, impending, continguous, immediate, coming, brewing, looming, forthcoming, approximate. *Ant.* far, distant, remote, past, gone, expired, extinct, late, posthumous, adjourned, shelved, reserved, postponed, deferred, stopped, suspended, untimely, regressive, lavish, prodigal, extravagant, liberal, generous.
neat—*Syn.* tidy, shapely, trim, prim, clean, dapper, orderly, becoming, suitable, regular, correct, uniform, methodical, spotless. *Ant.* slovenly, ungainly, unkempt, ragged, untidy, careless, awkward, irregular, disorderly, straggling, negligent, sloppy, loose, slipshod, lax, clumsy, gawky, inept.
necessary—*Syn.* essential, requisite, expedient, needful, indispensable, required, unavoidable, undeniable, urgent, wanted, imperative, prerequisite, pressing, exigent, compulsory, inexorable. *Ant.* unnecessary, redundant, useless, prodigal, exorbitant, casual, extravagant, crammed, inoperative, inadequate, unsuitable, superfluous, undesirable, objectionable, unfit, inadmissible, unsatisfactory, contingent, optional.
necessity—*Syn.* need, want, emergency, privation, hunger, starvation, poverty, destitution, distress, urgency, compulsion, duress, enforcement, constraint, restraint, stress. *Ant.* determination, desire, wish, will, willingness, inclination, assent, compliance, zeal, enthusiasm, opulence, affluence, means, resources, income.
need, *n.*—*Syn.* want, privation, misery, destitution, penury, indigence, emergency, necessity, exigency. *Ant.* plenty, comfort, luxury, competence, riches, property, fortune, independence.
nefarious—*Syn.* wicked, detestable, abominable, atrocious, vile, sinister, vicious, depraved, foul, gross, disgraceful, scandalous, outrageous, dishonorable, brazen, immoral, improper, flagrant, infamous, inexcusable, disreputable. *Ant.* virtuous, good, innocent, righteous, praiseworthy, commendable, creditable, exemplary, worthy, inoffensive, inapproachable, meritorious, excellent, upright, honest, reputable, candid, frank, sincere, dependable, scrupulous, true, incorruptible, unselfish, magnanimous.
neglect, *n.*—*Syn.* slight, omission, default, indifference, disregard, thoughtlessness, oversight, inattention, evasion, indolence, dereliction. *Ant.* performance, execution, achievement, perpetration, work, labor, toil, vigilance, surveillance, alertness, concern, vigil, attention, obligation, action, zeal, ardor, enthusiasm, dash, application, perseverance, anxiety, caution, heed, precaution, management, solicitude.
neglect, *v.*—*Syn.* slight, overlook, disregard, ignore, defer, procrastinate, suspend, dismiss, discard, spurn, underestimate, scorn, disdain, forget. *Ant.* do, perform, watch, safeguard, protect, warn, advise, use, handle, manipulate, accomplish, achieve, consummate, complete, finish, conclude, effect, execute, satisfy, discharge, undertake, work, serve, obey, arouse, work, toil, labor.
negligent—*Syn.* careless, inattentive, thoughtless, remiss, inconsiderate, unmindful, neglectful, heedless, perfunctory, dreamy, unwary, indifferent, insouciant. *Ant.* careful, watchful, keen, sharp, quick, considerate, alert, vigilant, considerate.
neighborhood—*Syn.* environs, vicinity, locality, proximity, district, nearness. *Ant.* distance, remoteness, background, outpost, outskirt.
nervous—*Syn.* shaky, timorous, apprehensive, restless, quivering, shaking, trembling, perturbed, aghast, fidgety, frightened, alarmed, shocked. *Ant.* brave, fearless, strong, hardy, bold, seasoned, courageous, valiant, resolute, daring, dauntless, audacious, spirited, heroic, confident.
new—*Syn.* novel, fresh, recent, late, restored, green, raw, immature, young, untried, modern. *Ant.* old, ancient, worn, deteriorated, antique, venerable, prehistoric, antiquated, archaic, outworn, obsolete.
news—*Syn.* information, story, copy, message, bulletin, report.
newspaper—*Syn.* publication, press, journal, sheet, tabloid, magazine, gazette.
nice—*Syn.* pretty, comely, lovely, attractive, fascinating, captivating, exquisite, dainty, refined, delicate, charming, fair, graceful, elegant, pleasing, amiable, agreeable, winsome, precise, particular, punctilious, fastidious, correct. *Ant.* repellent, repulsive, revolting, abhorrent, unpleasant, rough, rude, boorish, grim, sour, unseemly, dowdy, squat, ungainly, odious, hideous.
niggardly—*Syn.* miserly, penurious, stingy, sparing, close, grudging, avaricioius, covetous, mean, sordid. *Ant.* generous, liberal, prodigal, lavish, unsparing, profuse, extravagant.
nimble—*Syn.* lively, quick, brisk, swift, spry, active, prompt, bustling, hustling, agile, fast, expeditious. *Ant.* slow, dull, tardy, slack, dilatory, languid, weary, apathetic, sluggish, gradual.
nobility—*Syn.* rank, gentility, aristocracy. *Ant.* commonalty, public, proletariat, rabble, the workingg class, riff-raff.
noble—*Syn.* grand, high, exalted, majestic, august, stately, imperial, princely, generous, magnificent, courtly, lofty, elevated, splendid, supreme, eminent, dignified, aristocratic, loyal, sincere, truthful, constant, faithful, upright. *Ant.* base, mean, corrupt, ignoble, treacherous, low, vile, contemptible, dishonest, perfidious, disreputable, turpid, immoral, debased, infamous, ignominious, scandalous, proletarian, common, subordinate, inferior.
noise—*Syn.* clatter, din, tumult, uproar, cry, sound, resonance, roar, racket, bomb, explosion, detonation, blare, blast, peal, boom, shouting, yelling, talk. *Ant.* silence, lull, calm, hush, stop, peace, oblivion.
noiseless—*Syn.* silent, still, hushed, calm, quiet, stifled, muffled, smothered, deadened, stifled, stopped. *Ant.* sonorous, noisy, resonant, audible, distinct, phonic, resounding, booming, shouting, bellowing, yelling, roaring.
noisome—*Syn.* noxious, putrid, mischievous, offensive, disgusting. *Ant.* good, fragrant, redolent, perfumed, aromatic, odorous, sweet, pleasing, delightful, pleasurable, refreshing, agreeable.
nominal—*Syn.* formal, mere, simple, mentioned, suggested, bare, ostensible, pretended, professed, trifling, low, insignificant, inexpensive. *Ant.* dear, costly, expensive, substantial, extravagant, exorbitant, high, above, ordinary, unusual, valuable, prized, uncommon, priceless.
nonchalant—*Syn.* indifferent, negligent, uncaring, neglectful, trifling, insouciant, supine, heedless, unheeding, frivolous, apathetic, impassive, imperturbable, easy-going, listless, lackadaisical. *Ant.* careful, considerate, thoughtful, patient, cautious, wary, solicitous, anxious, eager, spirited, enthusiastic, emotional, attentive, heedful, zealous, ardent, precautious, prudent, perturbed, excitable, agitated, vigilant, alert.
nonobservance—*Syn.* negligence, inadvertence, abstraction, preoccupation, absorption, disuse, neglect, disobedience, violation, repudiation, casualness, laxity, dereliction, failure, evasion, transgression. *Ant.* obligation, liability, responsibility, duty, observance, compliance, performance, obedience, habit, custom, usage, practice, consideration, alertness, circumspection, heed, conformity, performance.
nonsense—*Syn.* absurdity, folly, trash, jest, joke, bluster, pomposity, jabber, palaver, foolishness, shallowness, babble, rant, fudge, rubbish, inconsistency. *Ant.* wisdom, sense, truth, fact, reality, veracity, accuracy, reliability, significance, sincerity, intelligibility, clarity, lucidity, understanding, discernment, discrimination, adage, saw, epigram, precision, doctrine, principle, statute, law.
normal—*Syn.* ordinary, conventional, usual, natural, common, typical, average, rational, reasonable, orderly, methodical, habitual, medium, uniform, customary. *Ant.* irregular, unusual, extraordinary, unnatural, eccentric, odd, unconventional, diversified, uncustomary, strange, singular, peculiar, uncommon, rare.
notable—*Syn.* remarkable, famous, celebrated, renowned, distinguished, clever, skilled, eminent, illustrous, popular, significant, rare, striking, manifest, apparent, extraordinary, signal, conspicuous, prominent, worthy, honored, dignified, stately, imposing. *Ant.* unknown, obscure, humble, low, mean, debased, contemptible, unworthy, abject, common, unimportant, insignificant, petty, trivial, common, slight, ordinary, usual.
note—*Syn.* symbol, token, index, mark, figure, type, representation, device, trace, record, indication, register, explanation, commentary, interpretation, rendering, translation, letter, dispatch, paper, order, repute, renown, fame, celebrity, distinction, reputation, tone.
nothing—*Syn.* not anything, nonbeing, nothingness, annihilation, extinction, oblivion, unreality, spectre, vision, illusion, ghost, phantom, naught. *Ant.* thing, something, anything, object, article, matter, reality, actuality, existence, fact, substance, body, creature, person, stuff, element, entity, being, life.
notice, *n.*—*Syn.* intimation, notification, remark, note, heed, attention, respect, consideration, information, intelligence, instruction, direction, observation, cognizance, regard, hint, enlightenment, publicity, mention, advice. *Ant.* neglect, omission, evasion, laxity, exemption, disrespect, contempt, slight, disdain.
notice, *v.*—*Syn.* observe, heed, regard, mark, respect, mention, see, distinguish, warn, salute, remember, compliment, greet, hail, welcome. *Ant.* ignore, shun, avoid, despise, reject, repel, disdain, spurn, elude, eschew.
notify—*Syn.* announce, publish, inform, tell, acquaint, express, intimate, impart, communicate, signify, specify, convey, disclose, indicate, proclaim, advertise, circulate, spread, diffuse, disseminate, divulge, reveal, report. *Ant.* screen, cover, mask, secrete, camouflage, withhold, reserve, cloak, suppress, evade, smother, dissemble, disguise, shuffle, shift, deny, equivocate, avoid, maneuver, dodge.
notion—*Syn.* idea, conception, sentiment, opinion, understanding, inclination, imagination, belief, knowledge, impression, perception, reflection, theory, claim, viewpoint, presumption, conviction, tenet, dogma, doctrine, principle, surmise, insight, consciousness, consideration.
notorious—*Syn.* infamous, disreputable, shameful, disgraceful, despicable, outrageous, vile, base, dishonorable, disgraced, immoral, depraved, profligate, flagrant, unprincipled. *Ant.* virtuous, noble, honorable, honest, decent, true, moral, elevated, respected, reputable, righteous, kind, commmendable, admirable, exemplary, famous, celebrated, distinguished, honored, renowned, notable.
notwithstanding, *adv.*—*Syn.* how-

ever, nevertheless, yet.
notwithstanding, *prep.*—*Syn.* despite, in spite of, for all that.
notwithstanding, *conj.*—*Syn.* however, nevertheless, though, although, but, still, yet.
nourish—*Syn.* supply, sustain, support, nurture, cherish, minister, serve, attend, tend. *Ant.* starve, deprive, exhaust, weaken, debilitate, enervate, reduce, impair, sap, neglect, abandon.
nourishment—*Syn.* food, supply, sustenance, nutrition, diet, upkeep, meal, repast, maintenance, support, provisions. *Ant.* starvation, hunger, deprivation, destitution, detriment, damage, deficiency, lack scarcity.
novel—*Syn.* new, unusual, strange, rare, modern, recent, late, fresh, untried, unique, odd, strange, unparalleled. *Ant.* old, ancient, primitive, antiquated, outworn, hoary, familiar, usual, customary, frequent, common, ordinary, similar.
novice—*Syn.* beginner, learner, neophyte, pupil, follower, disciple, recruit, apprentice. *Ant.* master, instructor, trainer, tutor, teacher, professor, preacher, guide, director, mentor, adviser, expositor, mentor, preceptor, scholar.
noxious—*Syn.* baneful, pernicious, poisonous, injurious, deleterious, dangerous, unwholesome, deadly, virulent, toxic, offensive, putrid, rotten, malodorous, stinking, tainted, contaminated, foul, bad, rank, nocuous, unhealthy, destructive. *Ant.* healthy, wholesome, salubrious, bracing, strengthening, invigorating, harmless, innocuous, beneficial, healing, remedial, useful, profitable, antiseptic, inoffensive, harmless.
nude—*Syn.* naked, unclothed, undraped, uncovered, stripped, divested, undressed, exposed. *Ant.* dressed, robed, covered, cloaked, screened, draped, attired..
nullify—*Syn.* cancel, invalidate, quash, vacate, annul, destroy, abrogate, counteract, upset, suppress, obliterate, erase, countermand, delete, dispel, revoke, rescind, ignore, infringe, discard, disobey. *Ant.* uphold, support, affirm, conform, consent, concur, agree, harmonize, cooperate, record, note, list, indorse, commemorate, observe, obey, respect. execute, perform.
number—*Syn.* enumerate, estimate, reckon, compute, calculate, check, tell, score, call, muster, recapitulate.
numerous—*Syn.* various, sundry, manifold, profuse, crowded, teeming, populous. *Ant.* scarce, sparse, scant, lacking, reduced, diminished, small, fractional, decimated, thin, deficient.

O

oath—*Syn.* affirmation, declaration, assertion, curse, affidavit, denunciation, swearing, profanity, cursing, reprobation, anathema, sworn statement, profane swearing, ban, vow. *Ant.* benediction, blessing, approval, approbation, sanction, admiration, commendation, acclamation, praise, acclaim.
obdurate—*Syn.* stubborn, callous, hard, unyielding, headstrong, obstinate, immovable, dogged, resolute, perverse, dogmatic, tenacious, inflexible, inexorable, pigheaded. *Ant.* amendable, gentle, tractable, yielding, changing, erratic, whimsical, flighty, careless, capricious, inconsistent, fanciful.
obedient—*Syn.* compliant, submissive, respectful, loyal, faithful, devoted, resigned, subjective, pliant, yielding, submitting. *Ant.* obstinate, disobedient, contemptuous, rude, obdurate, contumacious, insubordinate, insurgent, unruly, riotous, obstreperous, defiant, unyielding, stubborn, unwilling.
obese—*Syn.* fat, corpulent, fleshy, rotund, stout, burly, bulky, ponderous, puffy, swollen. *Ant.* lean, thin, slender, lanky, delicate, withered, shrunken, shriveled, scrawny, skinny, gaunt.
obey—*Syn.* comply, submit, respond, assent, accede, concur, yield, act, perform, serve.
object, *n.*—*Syn.* thing, anything, something, substance, matter, article, person, body, element, part, person. *Ant.* nothingness, vision, shadow, appearance, dream, imagination, illusion, emptiness, space.
object, *v.*—*Syn.* oppose, discard, reject, dislike, shun, avoid, disapprove, hesitate, scruple. *Ant.* like, desire, wish, want, need, covet, request, solicit, demand, implore, ask, crave, petition, beseech, invite, assent, accept, comply, concur, consent, applaud, approve, admire.
objective, *n.*—*Syn.* goal, aim, aspiration, purpose, intention, design, scheme, outlook. *Ant.* premise, beginning, introduction, preface, foreword, cause, origin, inception, initiation.
oblige—*Syn.* accommodate, gratify, please, constrain, compel, drive, enforce, require, insist, necessitate, restrain, command. *Ant.* free, release, exempt, discharge, acquit, excuse, renounce, accede, grant.
obloquy—*Syn.* contumely, reproach, defamation, shame, disrepute, abasement, dishonor, stigma, brand, reproach. *Ant.* repute, fame, character, dignity, reputation, renown, distinction, prestige.
obnoxious—*Syn.* offensive, disagreeable, displeasing, reprehensible, detestable, distressing, abhorrent, abominable, repellent, revolting, irritating. *Ant.* pleasing, beneficial, attractive, inviting, charming, seductive, winsome, satisfying, gratifying, welcome, refreshing.
obscene—*Syn.* impure, lewd, indelicate, coarse, indecent, immoral, nasty, unclean, smutty, soiled, grimy, foul, abominable, offensive, defiled, polluted. *Ant.* upright, clean, spotless, unstained, unspotted, virtuous, unsullied, innocent, decent, modest, particular, respectable.
obscure—*Syn.* dim, dark, doubtful, mysterious, cloudy, complex, intricate, indistinct, hidden, concealed, profound, ambiguous, incomprehensible, dense, complicated, casual, uncertain, dubious, vague, indeterminate, indefinite. *Ant.* plain, clear, evident, axiomatic, undisputed, unquestionable, apparent, unimpeachable, conclusive, irrefutable, incontrovertible, indubitable, definite, intelligible, unequivocal, explicit, lucid, distinct, positive, absolute, unambiguous, manifest, visible, unmistakable, known.
obsequious—*Syn.* cringing, slavish, sycophantic, deferential, servile, subject, subordinate, groveling, spineless, crouching, abject. *Ant.* insolent, impudent, bold, defiant, swaggering, presumptuous, contemptuous, hardened, intimidating, arrogant, imperious, haughty, assertive, arbitrary, overbearing, assuming, brazen.
observant—*Syn.* attentive, watchful, careful. *Ant.* heedless, careless, unmindful, indifferent, abstracted, preoccupied, thoughtless, nonobservant.
obsolete—*Syn.* disused, archaic, antique, ancient, antiquated, rare, old, traditional, obscure, neglected, outworn. *Ant.* new, novel, recent, modern, fresh.
obstinate—*Syn.* stubborn, headstrong, opinionated, contumacious, inflexible, resolute, immovable, perverse, unaffected, determined, resolved, intractable, firm, dogged, obdurate, persistent, unyielding, decided, firm, fixed. *Ant.* complaisant, courteous, obliging, yielding, tractable, submissive, obedient, pliable, gentle, compliant, agreeable, amenable, irresolute, acquiescent, humble, passive, manageable.
obstruct—*Syn.* impede, oppose, retard, embarrass, stay, check, clog, arrest, stop, block, hinder, prevent, close, plug, shut, bar, bolt, lock, interrupt, circumvent, thwart, frustrate, counteract, contravene, cramp, hamper, handicap. *Ant.* aid, assist, help, encourage, favor, succor, support, sustain, expedite, patronize, advance, further, champion, advocate, promote, forward, uphold, reenforce, accelerate.
obtain—*Syn.* acquire, procure, get, attain, gain, win, secure, collect, gather, pick, inherit, salvage, effect, realize, save, hoard. *Ant.* disburse, scatter, spend, waste, squander, lose, forfeit, give, expend, dispense, present, consign, contribute, award, subscribe, grant, bequeath, yield, distribute, allocate, assign.
obvious—*Syn.* plain, clear, evident, self-evident, manifest, apparent, distinct, lucid, intelligible, precise, definite. *Ant.* complex, complicated, mixed, confused, intricate, puzzling, unintelligible, obscure, indefinite, ambiguous, latent.
occasion—*Syn.* opportunity, cause, reason, need, time, necessity, circumstance, situation, origin, contingency, emergency, occurrence, crisis, turn, plight, source, spring. *Ant.* consequence, resultant, conclusion, effect, outcome, outgrowth, development.
occasional—*Syn.* incidental, irregular, contingent, uncertain, doubtful, dubious, vague, indefinite, equivocal, indeterminate. *Ant.* certain, sure, dogmatic, authoritative, conclusive, indubitable, authentic.
occult—*Syn.* latent, hidden, mysterious, esoteric, secret, unknown, unrevealed, dark, ambiguous, unintelligible, unknowable, obscure, enigmatic, unfathomable, impenetrable, elusive, undiscernible, mystical, inscrutable, inexplicable, incomprehensible, recondite. *Ant.* see SYNONYMS for **obvious** above.
occupation—*Syn.* vocation, trade, profession, pursuit, business, craft, office, employment, undertaking, concern, mission, duty, work, job, enterprise, function, work.
occurrence—*Syn.* happening, incident, accident, event, occasion, circumstance, juncture, provision, exigency, crisis, proceeding, transaction, adventure, experience.
odd—*Syn.* uneven, single, strange, peculiar, quaint, sole, remaining, residual, irregular, extraordinary, unusual, uncommon, abnormal. *Ant.* uniform, even, regular, ordinary, symmetrical, normal, methodical, common, conventional, standard, constant, steady, reliable, reasonable, cultivated, dainty, usual.
odious—*Syn.* hateful, abhorrent, repellent, disgusting, abominable, offensive, detestable, disagreeable, repugnant, hideous, shocking, horrid, obnoxious, repulsive, distasteful, coarse, vulgar, impure, rotten. *Ant.* pleasing, attractive, inviting, engaging, fascinating, winning, charming, enticing, cheerful, refreshing, clean, pure, wholesome, honorable, amiable, refined, fine, splendid.
offense—*Syn.* misdeed, misdemeanor, transgression, trespass, fault, affront, resentment, attack, assault, insult, aggression, onset, battery, hurt, injury, misconduct, corruption, guilt. *Ant.* innocence, harmlessness, good, conduct, morality, righteousness, excellence, credit, good behavior, rectitude, nobility, generosity, character.
offensive—*Syn.* insolent, impudent, impertinent, abusive, disagreeable, rude, scurrilous, abhorrent, reprehensible, infamous, forward, brazen, arrogant. *Ant.* humble, gentle, mild, docile, pliable, agreeable, ready, compliant, courteous, amiable, refined, modest, retiring, tidy, neat, affable, bland.
office—*Syn.* charge, function, business, calling, employment, duty, performance, transaction, engagement, undertaking, mission, trade, craft, profession, vocation, avocation, service, appointment, post, station, agency, cue, action.
official—*Syn.* authoritative, authentic, genuine, true, proper, real, certain, sure, reliable, assured, positive, clear, decided, decisive, conclusive, governmental, definite. *Ant.* doubtful, indecisive, vague, indeterminate, disputable, questionable, obscure, uncertain, contingent, ambiguous, unofficial.
offspring—*Syn.* progeny, issue, descendants, children, siblings, generation, posterity, blood, seed, family, heirs, heredity, succession. *Ant.* ancestry, ancestors, progenitors, forefathers, fathers, stem, line, stock, family, tribe, clan, pedigree, lineage, genealogy.
oily—*Syn.* lustrous, brilliant, shining, greasy, smeary, slippery, servile, flattering, coaxing, plausible, sanctimonious. *Ant.* dull, dim, lustreless, rough, dry, coarse, impudent, saucy, presumptuous, impertinent, flippant, insolent.

old—*Syn.* ancient, primitive, antique, antiquated, obsolete, early, prehistoric, immemorial, hoary, venerable, timeworn, olden, remote, decrepit, aged. *Ant.* new, modern, recent, late, fresh, budding, young, juvenile, puerile, renovated, freshened.

omen—*Syn.* portent, sign, indication, warning, precursor, presage.

ominous—*Syn.* threatening, foreboding, suggestive, portentous, premonitory, unpropitious, inauspicious, presaging, indicating, precursive, significant, prescient, prophetic. *Ant.* cheering, comforting, consoling, appealing, encouraging, pleasing, exhilarating, auspicious.

omit—*Syn.* exclude, overlook, disregard, bar, except, preclude, repudiate, prohibit, eliminate, neglect, discard, nullify, retract, cancel, void. *Ant.* insert, enter, include, record, introduce, inject, register, enroll, chronicle, accept, docket, inscribe, mark, indicate.

onerous—*Syn.* troublesome, difficult, oppressive, responsible, heavy, serious, laborious, irksome, arduous, formidable, cumbersome. *Ant.* easy, light, trivial, agreeable, pleasant, facile, immaterial, insignificant, little, unessential, common, unnecessary, normal, ordinary.

opaque—*Syn.* obscure, non-transparent, dim, dull, shady, smoky, murky, misty, cloudy, filmy. *Ant.* clear, transparent, lucid, bright, shining, diaphonous, glassy, translucent, luminous.

open, *a.*—*Syn.* accessible, unsealed, unobstructed, unrestricted, ajar, agape, expanded, fullblown, clear manifest, apparent, definite, plain, evident, ostensible, explicit, candid, frank, simple, sincere, undisguised, unaffected, ingenuous, guileless, innocent. *Ant.* closed, shut, barred, stopped, blocked, obstructed, tight, contracted, compressed, hidden, concealed, buried, latent, secret, underhand, covert, involved, cryptic, subtle, deep, intriguing, designing, tricky, shifty, astute, sharp, shrewd.

open, *v.*—*Syn.* unlock, uncover, begin, start, inauguarate, admit, clear, render, split, divide, rend, separate, discover, explain, speak, initiate. *Ant.* bar, close, refuse, admittance, turn away, deny, stop, block, plug, screen, cover, hide, secrete, conceal, close, finish, terminate, conclude, exclude, reject, repudiate, prevent, hinder, restrain, prohibit, inhibit.

operate—*Syn.* work, perform, sustain, execute, manipulate, transact, practice, buy, sell, manage, direct, guide, superintend, produce, manufacture, construct, contrive, constitute, accomplish, achieve. *Ant.* dissolve, overthrow, smash, destroy, quash, dismantle, disorganize, disuse, relinquish, neglect, discard.

operation—*Syn.* action, execution, performance, act, effect, process, production, work, procedure, employment, labor, deed, proceeding, transaction, achievement, result. *Ant.* inaction, inefficiency, ineffectiveness, idleness, indolence, relaxation, rest, inertia.

opinion—*Syn.* notion, view, judgement, sentiment, conception, idea, estimation, conviction, impression, surmise, conclusion, inference, tenet, creed, principle. *Ant.* doubt, misgiving, incredibility, scepticism, dissent, demur, incredulity, uncertainty, vagueness.

opponent—*Syn.* rival, antagonist, competitor, challenger, assailant, contestant, litigant, enemy, adversary. *Ant.* friend, confidant, associate, companion, comrade, ally, colleague, helper, crony, consort.

oppose—*Syn.* resist, check, combat, contravene, withstand, restrain, deny, thwart, confront, retaliate, rebuff, contradict, protest, taunt, defy, antagonize, impede, hinder, overcome, invert. *Ant.* cooperate, concur, combine, federate, ratify, confirm, indorse, sanction, commend, certify, attest, support, sustain, approve, praise, acclaim, coalesce.

opprobrious—*Syn.* infamous, disgraceful, shameful, scurrilous, offensive, derogatory, abusive, contemptuous, degrading, ignominious, dishonorable, humiliating, defamatory, slanderous, outrageous, flagrant, nefarious, wanton, abhorrent, abominable, shocking, disreputable. *Ant.* worthy, commendable, deserving, creditable, estimable, meritorious, reputable, respectable, decent, virtuous, distinguished, eminent, proper, respected, righteous, trustworthy, good, just, upright, dignified, incorruptible, dependable.

oppugnant—*Syn.* opposing, resisting, unfavorable, unpropitious, unfriendly, adverse, recalcitrant. *Ant.* favorable, propitious, helpful, sympathetic, conciliatory.

optimistic—*Syn.* hopeful, cheering, cheerful, sanguine, elated, enthusiastic, promising, encouraging. *Ant.* pessimistic, gloomy, despairing, doubtful, dejected, inconsolable.

oracular—*Syn.* ambiguous, obscure, mystical, cryptic, vague, hazy, dubious, doubtful. *Ant.* plain, easy, lucid, intelligible, clear, distinct, definite.

oration—*Syn.* speech, discourse, address, talk, declaration, rhetoric, bombast, lecture, sermon. *Ant.* silence, reticence, suppression.

ordain—*Syn.* install, institute, appoint, enact, decree, dictate, order, prescribe, impose, commission, delegate, warrant, call, induct, consecrate. *Ant.* abrogate, cancel, revoke, rescind, repeal, dismiss, invalidate, prohibit, disqualify, annul, abolish, nullify, disestablish, retract.

order, *n.*—*Syn.* command, mandate, injunction, direction, regulation, requirement, prohibition, rule, system, plan, method, precept, custom, condition, state, rank, class, management, arrangement. *Ant.* disorder, confusion, chaos, irregularity, mixture, medley, tangle, complexity, maze, labyrinth, huddle, muddle, infringement, unconventionality, allowance, consent, leave, liberty, license, permission, permit.

order, *v.*—*Syn.* command, appoint, direct, rule, dictate, enjoin, bid, demand, instruct, request, decree, charge, proclaim, exact. *Ant.* beg, petition, solicit, crave, entreat, beseech, implore, supplicate, seek, pray, appeal.

orderly—*Syn.* methodical, regular, systematic, peaceable, quiet, correct, neat, tidy, regulated, symmetrical, classified, formal. *Ant.* disorderly, confused, irregular, tangled, disorganized, promiscuous, gnarled, snarled, intricate, complex, untidy.

ordinary—*Syn.* common, regular, usual, conventional, formal, customary, conformable, typical, consistent, habitual, accustomed, familiar, trite, prevalent, stereotyped, current, simple, unaffected, natural, plain. *Ant.* uncommon, extraordinary, informal, unconventional, eccentric, arbitrary, irregular, exceptional, strange, unnatural, unique, curious, unusual, egregious.

origin—*Syn.* rise, beginning, *alpha. [Gr.]*, commencement, source, cause, outset, start, birth, dawn, foundation, spring, origination. *Ant.* end, termination, effect, result, consequence, harvest, conclusion, finish, finality, close, goal, fulfillment, destiny, destination.

original—*Syn.* first, primary, primeval, primordial, rudimentary, casual, formative, aboriginal, constitutive, elementary. *Ant.* individual, special, peculiar, formal, conventional, accruing, deriving, following, emanating, evolved, derivative.

ornamental—*Syn.* decorative, embellishing, garnishing, decorated, ornate, gilt, adorned, emblazoned, embossed, bespangled, arrayed, illuminated, painted. *Ant.* dull, tarnished, soiled, discolored, disfigured, botched, stained, unadorned, unseemly, smeared.

ostensible—*Syn.* apparent, avowed, specious, professed, notable, pronounced, striking, probable, likely, expected, anticipated, seeming, obvious, evident, plain. *Ant.* improbable, unlikely, unexpected, obscure, shadowy, vague, latent, concealed, unknown, covert, veiled, hidden, indirect, unrevealed.

ostentation—*Syn.* show, display, bravado, brag, vaunt, boast, pomposity, pompousness, flourish pageant, pretension, spectacle, exhibition. *Ant.* modesty, humility, diffidence, timidity, unobtrusiveness, shrinking, retirement, reserve, unostentation, constraint, humiliation, submissiveness.

oust—*Syn.* eeject, dispossess, evict, dislodge, remove, dismiss, deprive, expel, depose, disinherit, banish, discharge. *Ant.* restore, reinstate, commission, delegate, depute, install, induct, authorize, admit, welcome, empower, appoint, ordain, constitute.

outbreak—*Syn.* eruption, violence, outburst, explosion, quarrel, brawl, row, disturbance, fight, scrimmage, revolt, irruption, rebellion, insurrection. *Ant.* peace, tranquillity, quiet, brotherhood, friendship, compliance, subjection, allegiance, loyalty, passivity, fidelity, servility, concord, harmony, agreement, union, understanding, tolerance, patience, endurance.

outcast—*Syn.* vagrant, vagabond, reprobate, castaway, rogue, scamp, rowdy, criminal. *Ant.* model, paragon, exemplar, hero, pattern, leader, chief, gentleman, guardian, worthy, heroine.

outlandish—*Syn.* strange, odd, queer, peculiar, bizarre, grotesque, unfamiliar, barbarous, uncouth, ridiculous, extraneous, unseemly, comic, eccentric, quaint, unusual, abnormal, unconventional. *Ant.* normal, regular, common, usual, familiar, seemly, becoming, conventional, decorous, plain, consistent, typical, formal, strict, natural, universal, customary, current, simple, homely, uniform, symmetrical, prevalent, suitable, adapted, fit, apt, proper, meet, congruous.

outline—*Syn.* delineation, sketch, drawing, draft, plan, contour, boundary, skeleton, profile, silhouette, perimeter, periphery, circumference, circuit, shape, figure, appearance, representation, design. *Ant.* distortion, misrepresentation, amorphism, irregularity.

outrage—*Syn.* insult, abuse, affront, offense, injury, indignity, assaut, fury, wrong, grievance, persecution, maltreatment, malice, damage. *Ant.* innocence, benefit, favor, kindness, gentleness, feeling, respect, regard, estimation, amiability, consideration, praise, advantage, calm, tranquillity, peace.

outrageous—*Syn.* wanton, flagrant, nefarious, atrocious, heinous, excessive, scandalous, disgraceful, abusive, shameful, despicable, notorious, shocking, disreputable, ignominious, disorderly, insulting, unbearable, vehement, frenzied, furious, frantic, infuriate, desperate, fierce. *Ant.* calm, peaceful, quiet, patient, tolerant, tranquil, dispassionate, passive, cool, imperturbable, submissive, composed, collected, resigned, unruffled, untroubled.

outward—*Syn.* external, outside, superficial, exterior, outer, extraneous, foreign, ecdemic. *Ant.* inner, interior, internal, inward, inmost, endemic.

overbearing—*Syn.* oppressive, haughty, domineering, imperious, proud, arrogant, insolent, brazen, dictorial, swaggering, blustering, intimidating, pedantic, egotistic, egomaniacal, audacious, chauvinistic, saucy. *Ant.* meek, mild, humble, submissive, servile, cringing, sycophantic, retiring, bashful, modest, parasitical, abject, cowering, sneaking.

overflow—*Syn.* exuberance, abundance, superabundance, congestion, oversupply, superfluity, plethora, glut, inundation, deluge, avalanche. *Ant.* scarcity, sparseness, insufficiency, deficiency, depression, reduction, curtailment, shortening, shortage, want, dearth, inadequacy, depletion.

oversight—*Syn.* supervision, management, inspection, direction, guidance, control, watch, surveillance, regulation, failure, omission, mistake, error, slip, inattention, abstraction, preoccupation, misconception, fault, flaw. *Ant.* care, consideration, circumspection, inspection, scrutiny, observance, heed, heedfulness, accuracy, precision, exactness, realism, truth, verity, fact.

overthrow—*Syn.* subvert, upset, overturn, demolish, defeat, rout, invert, subvert, abolish, disrupt, disorganize, wreck, raze, level, obliterate, smash, crush, shatter. *Ant.* construct, rehabilitate, produce, form, make, fashion, manufacture, establish, organize, develop, contrive, erect, constitute, fabricate, raise, build, prove, verify.

overwhelm—*Syn.* overcome, crush, inundate, defeat, vanquish, rout, ruin, destroy, ravage, dismantle, disrupt, demolish, upset, conquer, overpower, master, suppress, triumph, worst, subdue, subjugate. *Ant.* fail, lose, miss, flounder, weaken, falter, give up, avoid, shun, flee, desert, recede, restore, reproduce, assist, succor, help, befriend, save, rescue.

overwrought—*Syn.* emotional, affected, excited, tired, spent, exhausted, perturbed, impassioned, agitated, ruffled, flustered, shaken, disturbed, hysterical. *Ant.* calm, collected, cool, unruffled, silent, quiet, composed, peaceful, content, tranquil, quiescent, undisturbed, restrained, satisfied, complacent, contented, resigned, stoical.

P

pacific—*Syn.* peaceful, tranquil, calm, placid, untroubled, halcyon, smooth, gentle, quiet, still, appeasing, conciliating, composed, restful, unruffled. *Ant.* rough, turbulent, warlike, quarrelsome, hostile, contentious, belligerent, militant, bellicose, combative, sanguinary, armed, soldierly.

pack, *n.*—*Syn.* bundle, blanket, kit, package, burden, parcel, load, baggage, grip, bag, valise, trunk, luggage, lot, amount, assemblage, gathering, number, group, collection, flock.

pack, *v.*—*Syn.* stuff, squeeze, tie, bind, brace, girdle, gather, collect, go, depart, hasten, condense, compress, contract, press, stow, arrange. *Ant.* unpack, untie, unbind, loosen, scatter, disperse, dispose, sort, distribute, allocate, apportion.

padre—*Syn.* clergyman, priest, minister, monk, parson, divine, shepherd, pastor, confessor, reverend, missionary, preacher, revivalist, Bible-reader, gospel, dean, deacon, archdeacon, prebendary, chaplain.

pagan—*Syn.* gentile, pantheist, heathen, heretic, unbeliever, infidel, freethinker, atheist, agnostic. *Ant.* Christian, Jew, Mohammedan, believer, Catholic, Protestant, apostle, missionary, churchman, ritualist, theosophist, Christian Scientist, spiritualist, Puritan, Mormon, Unitarian, Lutheran, Baptist, Congregationalist.

pageantry—*Syn.* pomp, show, spectacle, exhibition, display, ostentation, parade, flourish, array, fuss, magnificence, glitter, splendor, revel, carnival, festivity. *Ant.* modesty, unobtrusiveness, diffidence, privacy, reserve, humility, lowliness, weariness, boredom, tedium, tediousness, humdrum.

pain—*Syn.* torment, agony, woe, anguish, distress, ache, twinge, pang, rack, discomfort, misery, laceration, cramp, disorder, malady, sickness, grief, worry, anxiety, etc. *Ant.* good health, physical and mental well-being, pleasure, enjoyment, delectation, joy, bliss, felicity, transport, cheerfulness, ecstasy, happiness, delight, comfort, ease, rapture, contentment, peace, relief, solace.

pale—*Syn.* pallid, wan, ghastly, faded, bleached, blanched, ashen, luster, dim, lurid. *Ant.* florid, red, flushed, blooming, bright, glowing, luminous, shiny, radiant, gleaming, pink, reddish, ruddy, inflamed.

palliate—*Syn.* extenuate, screen, hide, conceal, cover, veil, mitigate, varnish, veneer, whitewash, soften, excuse, moderate, defend, justify, alleviate. *Ant.* blame, accuse, censure, check, denounce, implicate, reproach, tax, inculpate, brand, incriminate, indict, arraign, impeach, disapprove, condemn, reprehend.

palpable—*Syn.* plain, unmistakable, obvious, discernible, perceivable, distinct, definite, striking, prominent. *Ant* latent, obscure, hidden, concealed, involved, complex, intricate, complicated, covert, secret.

pamper—*Syn.* indulge, spoil, pet, coddle, fondle, gratify, humor, please, satisfy, satiate, flatter. *Ant.* deny, refuse, punish, chasten, correct, disappoint.

panic—*Syn.* alarm, fright, apprehension, awe, dread, dismay, fear, tremor, quivering, nervousness. *Ant.* peace, tranquility, calm, placidity, calmness, security, hope, confidence, bravery, courage, daring.

paradox—*Syn.* contradiction, ambiguity, absurdity, enigma, inconsistency, puzzle, perplexity, uncertainty. *Ant.* proverb, maxim, axiom, truism, postulate, adage, clearness, precision, vividness, clarity, explicitness, distinctness.

parallel—*Syn.* correspondent, congruous, concurrent, correlative, analogous, concentric, similar, like, uniform, regular. *Ant.* irregular, distorted, askew, crooked, skewed, zigzag, disimilar, divergent, unlike.

paramount—*Syn.* supreme, eminent, preeminent, superior, excellent, utmost, unequaled, unsurpassed, inimitable, peerless, foremost. *Ant.* inferior, subordinate, minor, less, unimportant, secondary, least, trivial, common, ordinary, normal, slight, inconsiderable, inconsequential, meager.

parasite—*Syn.* flatterer, slave, flunky, sycophant, craven, groveler, puppet, dupe, loafer, dependent. *Ant.* master, director, leader, ringleader, driver, superior, tyrant, rowdy.

pardon, *n.*—*Syn.* forgiveness, mercy, acquittal, forbearance, amnesty, remission, exoneration, discharge, release, respite, reprieve, immunity, impunity, freedom. *Ant.* condemnation, conviction, punishment, penalty, restraint, detention.

pardon, *v.*—*Syn.* forgive, absolve, remit, quash, reprieve, forget, exonerate, exculpate, excuse, condone, acquit, pass over, liberate. *Ant.* avenge, retaliate, castigate, banish, expel, ostracize, boycott, convict, condemn, proscribe, exile, transport.

paroxysm—*Syn.* violence, agitation, emotion, anger. fit, furor, fury, outbreak, frenzy, passion, explosion, quiver, seizure, rage, perturbation. *Ant.* equanimity, steadiness, restraint, composure, repression, suppression, calm, rest, mildness.

part—*Syn.* portion, share, piece, fragment, section, component, constituent, member, particle, segment, partition, element, fraction, detachment, bit, slice, scrap. *Ant.* whole, all, total, aggregate, sum, entirety, bulk, mass, amount, gross, combination, unity, integration.

particle—*Syn.* atom, iota, jot, scrap, shred, mite, bit, molecule, morsel, piece, whit, element. *Ant.* mass, quantity, lot, whole, entirety, aggregate.

particular—*Syn.* exact, distinct, exclusive, specific, definite, precise, actual, appropriate, careful, observant, attentive, singular. *Ant.* general, indefinite, inaccurate, erroneous, fallacious, inconsiderate, imprudent, negligent, slovenly, untidy.

partition—*Syn.* distribution, apportionment, separation, division, barrier, compartment, detachment, segregation. *Ant.* juncture, connection, conjunction, attachment, union.

patience—*Syn.* resignation, forbearance, fortitudee, composure, submission, endurance, moderation. *Ant.* impatience, uneasiness, petulance, excitement, flurry, fluster, hurry, anger, rage.

patient—*Syn.* passive, submissive, meek, composed, cool, calm, enduring, quiet, serene, resigned, imperturbable, placid, dispassionate, tolerant, gentle. *Ant.* impatient, excitable, boisterous, vehement, irritable, feverish, hysterical, fiery, turbulent, fussy, furious, raging, hasty.

patron, —*Syn.* benefactor, helper, protector, supporter, advocate, customer, client. *Ant.* opponent, adversary, vendor, auctioneer, salesman.

pause—*Syn.* rest, stop, intermission, cessation, halt, suspension, truce, stay, respite, stillness, break, recess. *Ant.* continuance, perseverance, endurance, repetition, extension, continuity, progression.

pay, *n.*—*Syn.* compensation salary, reward, remuneration, fee, wages, stipend, honorarium, earnings, atonement, retribution, settlement, satisfaction, clearance. *Ant.* penalty, fine, forfeit, damages, confiscation, seizure, nonpayment, default, disbursement, distribution.

pay, *v.*—*Syn.* compensate, reward, recompense, expend, defray, remunerate, discharge, settle, satisfy, liquidate, refund, reimburse, indemnify. *Ant.* defraud, victimize, bilk, circumvent, embezzle, steal.

peace—*Syn.* calm, repose, tranquility, order, pacification, conciliation, concord, harmony, quiet, amity, hush, lull, rest, armistice. *Ant.* discord, variance, difference, dissension, division, split, rupture, disruption, disunion, fracas, dispute, disturbance, enmity, anger, skirmish, clamor, explosion, war, warfare.

peaceable—*Syn.* pacific, peaceful, quiet, tranquil, composed, calm, gentle, mild, serene, amiable, friendly, undisturbed, moderate, conciliatory, harmless, sympathetic. *Ant.* turbulent, rough, roisterous, violent, tumultuous, disorderly, furious, angry, impetuous, irritating, exasperating, raging, roaring, blustering, uproarious, fierce.

peerless—*Syn.* unequaled, supreme, best, perfect, glorious, unique, unrivaled, inimatable, superior, maximum, culminating, paramount, matchless, superlative, surpassing. *Ant.* inferior, subordinate, imperfect, secondary, minor, commonplace, ordinary, inconsiderable, defective, faulty, mediocre, average.

peevish—*Syn.* fretful, fretting, captious, perverse, obstinate, cantankerous (*colloq.*), cross, growling, grumbling. *Ant.* suave, courteous, pleasant, agreeable, amiable, polite, civil, gentle, kind.

penetrate—*Syn.* bore, pierce, perforate, enter, insert, infiltrate, permeate, comprehend, understand, grasp, absorb. *Ant.* emerge, exude, leak, drain, seep, discharge, recede.

penetrating—*Syn.* sharp, keen, subtle, astute, acute, shrewd, sagacious, pointed, piercing, incisive, keen. *Ant.* dull, shallow, blunt, thick, heavy, obtuse, muddled, confused, stolid.

penetration—*Syn.* entrance, ingress, infiltration, insertion, invasion, perception, acuteness, understanding, acumen. *Ant.* egress, emergence, exit, evacuation, discharge, incapacity.

people—*Syn.* persons, humanity, mankind, race, populace, population, community, individuals, inhabitants, tribe, nation, state, commonwealth, multitude, crowd, mass, mob, folks, residents, mortals, society, world, proletariat.

perceive—*Syn.* note, observe, discern, distinguish, sense, comprehend, conceive, understand, see, realize, apprehend, infer, behold, discover, recognize. *Ant.* mistake, misunderstand, misjudge, overlook, grope, search, feel, ignore, miss, lose.

peremptory—*Syn.* arbitrary, absolute, dictatorial, harsh, overbearing, decisive, authoritative, firm, compulsory, rigorous, dominant, imperious, strict, stern, rigid, uncompromising, positive, emphatic, insistent, determined, binding, obligatory, express, distinct, explicit, precise. *Ant.* mild, indulgent, tolerant, compassionate, loose, wavering, shallow, indeterminate, irresolute, indecisive, capricious, optional, discretionary, erratic, inconsistent.

perfect—*Syn.* consummate, conclusive, crowning, thorough, mature, faultless, unblemished, spotless, impeccable, intact, entire, whole, absolute, august, grand, dignified, sublime, supreme. *Ant.* imperfect, deficient, incomplete, unfinished, lacking, short, damaged, spoiled, faulty, tainted, inferior.

perfume—*Syn.* scent, fragrance, aroma, smell, odor, bouquet. *Ant.* decay, stench, malodor.

perhaps—*Syn.* possibly, maybe, perchance, probably. *Ant.* incredibly, unlikely, immprobably.

peril—*Syn.* danger, risk, jeopardy, hazard, exposure. *Ant.* safety, caution.

period—*Syn.* epoch, age, era, cycle, circuit, term, duration, end, limit, conclusion, lifetime, generation, term, year, decade.

periodical—*Syn.* regular, recurring, intermittent, alternate, serial, hourly, daily, weekly, monthly, yearly, annual, centennial, occasional. *Ant.* irregular, uncertain, erratic, desultory, variable, changeable, constant, perpetual, lasting, permanent.

permanent—*Syn.* durable, lasting, abiding, constant, unchanging, persistent, enduring, indestructible, perpetual, imperishable, chronic, continual, settled, unalterable, confirmed, habitual, invariable, stable. *Ant.* fleeting, passing, short, brief, changing, uncertain, temporary, transitory, momentary, transient, impermanent, temporal, inconstant, variable, mutable, erratic, alternating, fluctuating, spasmodic, capricious.

permission—*Syn.* leave, liberty, consent, license, permit, allowance, authority, tolerance, authorization, dispensation. *Ant.* prohibition, injunction, embargo, restraint, inhibition, opposition, exclusion, restriction, hindrance.

permit—*Syn.* allow, tolerate, warrant, authorize, empower, charter, license, sanction, legalize, let, grant, indulge, favor. *Ant.* deny, refuse, disallow, veto, proscribe, hinder, prevent, forbid, inhibit, ban, bar, withhold, exclude, restrict, prohibit, enjoin, stop, restrain, circumscribe.

pernicious—*Syn.* destructive, deadly, evil, mischievous, virulent, harmful, injurious, detrimental, perverting, perversive, malignant, prejudicial. *Ant.* good, healthy, invigorating, wholesome, pure, innocuous, advantageous, inoffensive, excellent, fine, favorable, curative, healing, useful, serviceable, efficacious, reviving.

perpetual—*Syn.* continual, unceasing, constant, incessant, permanent, lasting, uninterrupted, everlasting, enduring, perennial, continued, endless, immortal. *Ant.* momentary, temporary, short, brief, transient, fleeting, passing, ephemeral, transitory, temporary, impermanent.

perplex—*Syn.* puzzle, mystify, bewilder, baffle, confound, disconcert, amaze, annoy, irk, trouble, agitate, mock, entangle, daze, astonish, confuse, mislead, abash, dismay, fluster, flurry, muddle. *Ant.* assure, convince, guarantee, prove, determine, arrange, place, regulate, satisfy, gratify, delight, instruct, inform, enlighten, acquaint, disclose, impart, teach, tell, explain, interpret, expound, elucidate.

perplexity—*Syn.* doubt, embarrassment, distraction, disturbance, bewilderment, astonishment, confusion, amazement, complexity, complication, intricacy, ferment, agitation, uncertainty. *Ant.* certainty, facilility, easiness, smoothness, disentanglement, feasibility, capability, perception, knowledge, cognition, recognition, familiarity, apprehension, grasp, understanding, lucidity, precision, sense, understanding, conception.

persecute—*Syn.* oppress, torment, worry, afflict, annoy, harass, aggrieve, inflict, victimize, abuse, outrage, molest, maltreat, badger, provoke, roil, rile. *Ant.* reward, recompense, redress, remunerate, benefit, serve, favor, recommend, please, gratify, satisfy, indulge, comfort, refresh, help, support, sustain, oblige, accommodate, console, assuage.

perseverance—*Syn.* steadfastness, tenacity, persistence, constancy, perpetuation, endurance, resolution, determination, stamina. *Ant.* sloth, laziness, languor, inactivity, idleness, indolence, ennui, stupor, lethargy, cessation, halt.

perspicuity—*Syn.* clearness, lucidity, clarity, comprehensibility, transparency, discernment. *Ant.* obscurity, vagueness, incomprehensibility, uncertainty, perplexity, paradox, puzzle, confusion, embarrassment, intricacy, complexity.

persuade—*Syn.* coax, entice, urge, allure, convince, impel, lead, influence, dispose, move, incline, exhort, prompt, instigate, lure, decoy, bribe, induce, stimulate, cajole. *Ant.* dissuade, discourage, curb, restrain, remonstrate, expostulate, dampen, check, prevent, repress, hinder, coerce, stop, suppress, withhold, constrain, restrict, prohibit.

pertness—*Syn.* impertinence, flippancy, forwardness, self-assertion, pride, pretension, assumption, egotism, self-confidence, conceit, arrogance, impudence, boldness. *Ant.* shyness, modesty, humility, diffidence, timidity, coyness, constraint, restraint.

perturbation—*Syn.* discomposure, trepidation, worry, derangement, disorganization, agitation, quiver, shock, turmoil, tumult, disturbance, commotion, flurry, fluster, rage, fury, anger, excitement, paroxysm, voilence, alarm, consternation, dread, horror. *Ant.* peace, quietness, tranquillity, composure, quietude, silence, resignation, endurance, moderation, repression, apathy, inertia.

perverse—*Syn.* obstinate, contrary, stiff, unyielding, petulant, factious, contrary, obdurate, resolute, intractable, irascible, sullen, grouchy, querulous, contentious, cranky, headstrong. *Ant.* docile, mild, amendable, gentle, yielding, complacent, soft, willing, capricious, changeable, agreeable, condescending, conceding, pliant, consenting, manageable.

petition—*Syn.* appeal, request, entreaty, requisition, application, invocation, proposal, solicitation. *Ant.* expostulation, protest, remonstrance, opposition, disapproval, condemnation, denunciation, censure.

petty—*Syn.* small, trivial, trifling, insignificant, weak, frivolous, meager, paltry, little, shallow, unimportant. *Ant.* large, great, important, significant, prominent, leading, salient, beneficial, advantageous, useful, helpful, principal, essential, necessary, valuable, vital, worthy, remarkable, capacious.

philanthropic—*Syn.* kind, benevolent, humanitarian, considerate, feeling, generous, liberal, charitable, beneficient, munificent, bountiful, compassionate. *Ant.* misanthropic, selfish, pitiless, harsh, cruel, oppressive, miserly, sordid, stingy, parsimonious, gripping, grasping, greedy.

philosophical—*Syn.* thoughtful, collected, cool, unmoved, impassive, patient, reflective, cogitative, studious, imperturbable, composed, serious, solemn, tolerant, placid, wise, prudent, considerate, sagacious, rational, judicious, sensible, profound, erudite. *Ant.* imprudent, rash, precipitate, thoughtless, inexperienced, dull, shallow, unphilosophical, frivolous, unreasonable, simple, eccentric.

phlegmatic—*Syn.* dull, indifferent, cold, sluggish, heavy, inexcitable, stolid, moody, morose. *Ant.* lively, quick, keen, acute, sharp, fussy.

physical—*Syn.* material, tangible, natural, substantial, sensible, vigorous, vital, muscular. *Ant.* immaterial, mental, sublimated, ethereal, intellectual, subjective.

picture—*Syn.* image, likeness, portrait, painting, effigy, representation, appearance, description, illustration, scene.

picturesque—*Syn.* artistic, pictorial, graphic, scenic, grateful, attractive, pleasing, vivid, striking. *Ant.* forbidding, repellent, ungraceful, grim, squalid, dingy, awkward, distorted, homely, haggard.

piercing—*Syn.* shrill, acute, deafening, sharp, penetrating, entering, perforating, sounding, harsh, blaring, raucous. *Ant.* soft, low, murmuring, modulated, faint, stifled, muffled, inaudible, whispered, soothing, inaudible.

pillage—*Syn.* plunder, loot, spoil, injury, damage, hurt, theft, desecration, robbery, impairment, ravage, wreck, ruin. *Ant.* restoration, repair, restitution, compensation, recompense, satisfaction.

pious—*Syn.* religious, reverent, devout, devotional, righteous, saintly, pure, spiritual, sacred, solemn. *Ant.* impious, wicked, sinful, blasphemous, sacrilegious, profane, unholy.

piquant—*Syn.* spirited, clever, smart, lively, charming, racy, bright, sparkling. *Ant.* unsavory, unpalatable, flat, insipid, sweet, saccharine, honied, cloying, nauseating.

pique, *n.*—*Syn.* umbrage, resentment, offense, displeasure, grudge, irritation, indignation, anger, ire, wrath. *Ant.* pleasure, gratification, enjoyment, satisfaction, contentment, delight, approval.

pique, *v.*—*Syn.* irritate, fret, goad, offend, displease, anger, provoke, rouse, taunt, inflame, agitate, perturb, chafe, gall, roil, rile, affront, incense, excite. *Ant.* please, delight, charm, interest, allure, attract, fascinate, captivate, bewitch, refresh, gratify.

pitiful—*Syn.* wretched, miserable, mournful, pitiable, compassionate, distressing. *Ant.* happy, cheerful, contented.

pitiless—*Syn.* merciless, obdurate, unfeeling, malevolent, ruthless, unmerciful, spiteful, harsh, cruel, unfeeling, truculent. *Ant.* merciful, kind, gentle, compassionate, benevolent, cordial, sympathetic, indulgent, charitable, friendly, humane, comforting, kindly.

pity—*Syn.* compassion, sympathy, kindness, charity, philanthropy, tenderness, goodness, forbearance, humanity, clemency, mercy, devotion. *Ant.* severity, malevolence, mercilessness, truculence, tyranny, ferocity, brutality, persecution, rigor, rancor, sternness, revenge, vengeance, inhumanity.

place, *n.*—*Syn.* locality, situation, position, point, site, post, station, area, region, section, habitation.

place, *v.*—*Syn.* appoint, establish, settle, fix, put, set, induct, arrange, locate, dispose, allot, group, allocate, assign, distribute, deposit, install, store. *Ant.* displace, remove, dislodge, empty, unload, discompose, disarrange, disorder, disturb, eject, unsettle.

plain—*Syn.* open, evident, manifest, obvious, clear, visible, distinct, perceptible, exposed, indubitable, express, comprehensible, lucid, positive, unadorned, undistinguished, ordinary, level, flat, even, smooth. *Ant.* obscure, complex, complicated, intricate, difficult, puzzling, hard, unknowable, illegible, inscrutable, cryptic, cloudy, occult, incomprehensible, indistinct, hidden, concealed.

plan, *n.*—*Syn.* arrangement, scheme, design, drawing, sketch, cut, draft, delineation, device, map, project, scope, view, outline, model, proposal, proposition, policy, method, device, contrivance, program.

plan, *v.*—*Syn.* devise, shape, outline, delineate, depict, picture, sketch, represent, illustrate, project, prepare, plot, draft. *Ant.* distort, misrepresent, twist, confuse, muddle, shuffle, falsify, render, mix, obscure, delete, erase, cancel, tangle.

play, *n.*—*Syn.* amusement, sport, game, contest, action, exhibition, show, drama, tragedy, comedy, melodrama, scene, act, representation, theatricals, vaudeville. *Ant.* work, toil, labor, oppression, drudgery, boredom, monotony.

play, *v.*—*Syn.* act, perform, participate, represent, imitate, entertain, divert, revel. *Ant.* mope, whine, grieve, mourn.

plead—*Syn.* implore, beg, ask, solicit, argue, advocate, urge, press, beseech, entreat, request, petition, appeal, testify, respond. *Ant.* deprecate, protest, reject, deny, expostulate, refuse, decline, forswear, discourage, dishearten, deter, warn, check, admonish, decry.

pleasant—*Syn.* agreeable, gratifying, pleasing, enjoyable, cheerful, pleasurable, kind, cordial, engaging, winning, jocund, jolly, funny, entertaining, diverting. *Ant.* unpleasant, disagreeable, dissatisfying, dull, painful, annoying, disturbing, dolorous, unsatisfactory.

please—*Syn.* gratify, satisfy, humor, delight, gladden, captivate, indulge, flatter, amuse, attract, allure. *Ant.* displease, offend, injure, hurt, pain, afflict, persecute, mortify, taunt, mock, shame, irritate, worry, annoy.

pleasure—*Syn.* gratification, enjoyment, satisfaction, indulgence, joy. *Ant.* displeasure, sorrow, woe, grief, suffering, dissatisfaction, uneasiness, adversity, infelicity, trouble, unhappiness.

plentiful—*Syn.* abundant, ample, plenty, fruitful, profuse, lavish, full, sufficient, liberal, replete, luxuriant, unstinted. *Ant.* scarce, few, short, small, deficient, exhausted, impoverished, sparing, inadequate, niggardly, poor, skimpy, barren, depleted, minute, lacking, sparse.

pliant—*Syn.* limber, supple, bending, lithe, flexible, ductile, docile, tractable, vacillating, submissive. *Ant.* hard, unbending, unyielding, rigid, determined, resolute, self-possessed, experienced, tough, stable, obstinate, obdurate.

plight—*Syn.* difficulty, dilemma, predicament, state, condition, situation, position, lot, quandary, form, shape, circumstance, doubt, hesitation, perplexity. *Ant.* assurance, surety, certainty, regularity, security, confidence, capability, facility, easy circumstances.

plot, *n.*—*Syn.* intrigue, conspiracy, combination, plan, scheme, design, project, proposal, outline, sketch, draft, program, platform, plank, slate, idea, forcast, prospectus, land, area, patch, lot, section.
plot, *v.*—*Syn.* plan, scheme, contrive, sketch, devise, invent, frame, project, intrigue, concoct, draft, organize, conspire, propose, suggest.
pluck—*Syn.* courage, boldness, bravery, determination, grit *(colloq.)*, spirit, resolution, decision, firmness, energy. *Ant.* fluctuation, wavering, indecision, hesitation, irresolution, uncertainty.
plump—*Syn.* fleshy, portly, full, round, fat, bouncing, corpulent, lusty, hulking, puffy, swollen, florid. *Ant.* lean, thin, puny, shrunken, spare, withered, shriveled.
poetry—*Syn.* poem, verse, song, numbers, rime, rhyme, rhythm, meter, metrical composition, poesy, stanza, epic, idyll, pastoral, rondeau, elegy, ballad, lyric, ode, song, sonnet. *Ant.* prose, prosaic, speech, essay, story, history, sermon, speech, address, oration.
poise—*Syn.* balance, gravity, equilibrium, ballast, equality, calm, composure, imperturbability, patience. *Ant.* disparity, levity, vehemence, turbulence, anger, fury, agitation, passion, excitement, paroxysm, frenzy, ferocity, outburst.
poisonous—*Syn.* bad, noxious, harmful, dangerous, virulent, vicious, corrupt, deleterious, morbid, fatal, toxic, deadly, destructive. *Ant.* good, healthy, invigorating, stimulating, salubrious, wholesome, nourishing, tonic, bracing, sanitary, preserving, remedial, strengthening.
polite—*Syn.* civil, courteous, genteel, polished, refined, urbane, suave, amiable, cultured, cultivated, affable, agreeable, behaved. *Ant.* rude, rough, unmannerly, uncivil, churlish, boorish, ungracious, impolite, vulgar, insulting, abusive, offensive.
politic—*Syn.* cunning, wary, adroit, foxy, discreet, judicious, sagacious, diplomatic, wise, provident, prudent, wily, watchful, calculating, sage, crafty, subtle, intriguing, timesaving, deceptive, shrewd, sharp, astute, acute. *Ant.* dull, stolid, simple, unsophisticated, blunt, slow, artless, ingenuous, incautious, rash, foolhardy, careless.
pollute—*Syn.* soil, stain, taint, corrupt, debase, tarnish, smear, smudge, smirch, befoul, contaminate, impair, voilate, disgrace, dishonor, degrade. *Ant.* cleanse, purify, wash, clean.
pompous—*Syn.* arrogant, haughty, proud, domineering, boastful, ostentatious, vain, egotistical, blustering, inflated, flambuoyant, affected, supercilious. *Ant.* unobtrusive, retiring, unpretentious, mild, coy, shy, unassuming, humble, meek, submissive.
ponderous—*Syn.* dull, heavy, lifeless, inanimate, inert, massive, unwieldly. *Ant.* light, volatile, fluffy, imponderable, ethereal, buoyant.
poor—*Syn.* indigent, penniless, destitute, poverty-stricken, distressed, paltry, miserable, pitiable, weak. *Ant.* rich, wealthy, affluent, opulent, strong, robust, vigorous, husky, powerful, important, prominent, assertive, compelling, commanding, happy, joyous, strong, large, great.
popular—*Syn.* favorite, liked, approved, recommended, pleasing, suitable, general, familiar, prevailing, common, current, demanded, sought, fashionable, customary, stylish, conventional, beloved, polished, esteemed, estimable, notable. *Ant.* abhorrent, abominable, detestable, repellent, revolting, offensive, disagreeable, troublesome, unwelcome, unpopular, undesirable, depressing, annoying, repugnant, wicked, heinous, disgraceful, abandoned, exiled.
portion—*Syn.* division, share, part, fraction, parcel, quantity, allotment, fragment, section. *Ant.* whole, all, entirety, embodiment, aggregation, amount, sum, total, unity, completeness.
position—*Syn.* place, station, state, condition, circumstance, posture, attitude, rank, office, employment, situation, status, standing, post, environment, ground, location, site, seat, spot.
positive—*Syn.* certain, absolute, decided, assertive, precise, real. *Ant.* uncertain, doubtful, questionable, erroneous.
possessor—*Syn.* holder, owner, proprietor, occupant.
possible—*Syn.* likely, contingent, achievable, attainable. *Ant.* impossible, unlikely, improbable, unreasonable.
postpone—*Syn.* defer, delay, procrastinate, adjourn, suspend, waive, protract, shelve. *Ant.* proceed, continue, expedite, hasten, sustain, maintain.
potent—*Syn.* strong, influential, able, effective, dynamic, sturdy, stalwart. *Ant.* weak, delicate, fragile, powerless.
poverty—*Syn.* distress, want, indigence, deficiency, dearth, insufficiency, inadequacy. *Ant.* wealth, riches, affluence, plenty, substance.
power—*Syn.* efficacy, strength, vigor, force, energy, might, command, sway, authority, energy, domination, leadership, prestige. *Ant.* weakness, impotence, disability, ineptitude, inability, fatigue, exhaustion, timidity.
praise, *n.*—*Syn.* adulation, plaudit, commendation, approval, cheer, tribute, acclaim. *Ant.* censure, disapproval, denunciation.
praise, *v.*—*Syn.* laud, commend, recommend, extol, cheer, acclaim, indorse, sanction, exalt. *Ant.* censure, condemn, decry, disapprove, dislike.
precarious—*Syn.* doubtful, uncertain, dubious, unsettled, unsteady, equivocal, risky, uncertain, insecure. *Ant.* certain, assured, undoubted, unquestionable, undeniable, sure, firm.
percept—*Syn.* doctrine, law, rule, principle.
precious—*Syn.* valuable, costly, estimable, beloved, superior, excellent, select, important, worthy, fine. *Ant.* worthless, insignificant, inconsiderate, valueless, trifling.
precise—*Syn.* accurate, definite, scrupulous, exact. *Ant.* inexact, careless, negligent, faulty.
predicament—*Syn.* strait, quandary, plight, dilemma, diffulty, fix, imbroglio. *Ant.* firmness, resolution, certainty, confidence.
prediction—*Syn.* prognostication, announcement, prophecy.
predominant—*Syn.* prevailing, ruling, controlling, paramount. *Ant.* light, slight, trivial, powerless.
prejudice—*Syn.* partiality, bias, prejudgement. *Ant.* appreciation, admiration, esteem, approval, approbation.
premature—*Syn.* untimely, precipitate, early, impending, unprepared, raw. *Ant.* late, delayed, ripe, ready.
presumptuous—*Syn.* arrogant, insolent, bold, rash, overconfident, presuming, haughty, brazen. *Ant.* modest, bashful, humble, timid, diffident, coy, unpretentious, unassuming, unobtrusive, reserved, shy.
pretense—*Syn.* pretext, excuse, trick, mask, cloak, seeming. *Ant.* candor, honesty, truth, openness, sincerity, veracity.
pretty—*Syn.* handsome, beautiful, fine, nice, becoming, attractive. *Ant.* homely, ordinary, common.
prevailing—*Syn.* prevalent, general, universal, common, comprehensive. *Ant.* isolated, sporadic, particular, individual, definite, uncertain.
prevent—*Syn.* prelude, obviate, block, stop, thwart, impede, check, inhibit. *Ant.* allow, permit, aid, help, sustain, uphold, further, abet.
previous—*Syn.* antecedent, prior, preceding, anterior, preparatory, foregoing, earlier, aforementioned. *Ant.* succeeding, following, after, subsequent.
price—*Syn.* expenditure, expense, cost, value, figure, impost, valuation, appraisement. *Ant.* allowance, concession.
pride—*Syn.* vanity, conceit, self-esteem, egotism. *Ant.* humility, self-effacement, humiliation, abasement, modesty, timidity.
primeval—*Syn.* ancient, primitive, primal, primary, pristine, olden. *Ant.* modern, recent, present, prospective, future, expectant, new, fresh, young.
princely—*Syn.* royal, regal, august, grand, fine, magnificent, superb. *Ant.* mean, miserly, ignoble, low, coarse.
principal—*Syn.* leading, chief, first, head, prime, main, foremost, essential, capital, important, highest, prominent, paramount. *Ant.* inferior, minor, negligible, secondary, supplemental, subsidiary, contributory, additional, trivial.
principally—*Syn.* chiefly, mainly, essentially. *Ant.* slightly, somewhat, tolerably.
principle—*Syn.* law, doctrine, precept, tenet, purpose, decree, rule, policy, maxim, integrity.
privilege—*Syn.* favor, advantage, prerogative, right, permission, sanction. *Ant.* assumption, unsurpation, prohibition, restriction, injunction.
probity—*Syn.* honesty, honor, integrity, rectitude, fairness, righteousness. *Ant.* dishonor, dishonesty, deception, perfidy, injustice.
problematic—*Syn.* problematical, uncertain, doubtful, questionable, disputable. *Ant.* certain, sure, undoubted, indubitable, evident, authoritative, dogmatic, doubtless.
proceeding—*Syn.* action, process, transaction, experiment, incident, movement, procedure, manoeuver. *Ant.* inactivity, quiescence, passiveness, cessation.
prodigious—*Syn.* immense, extraordinary, enormous, vast, wonderful, great, amazing, marvelous, astonishing, overwhelming, impressive. *Ant.* common, ordinary, small, insignificant, inconsiderable, unimpressive, slight, diminutive.
prodigy—*Syn.* marvel, portent, wonder, miracle, scholar, extraordinary. *Ant.* normalcy, regularity, universality.
produce, *n.*—*Syn.* product, fruit, harvest, result, return, effect, amount, profit, outcome, outgrowth. *Ant.* cause, origin, beginning, source, agent, detriment, privation.
produce, *v.*—*Syn.* bear, yield, impart, afford, effect, cause, make, breed, swell, extend, create. *Ant.* waste, consume, destroy, overthrow, deny, diminish, abolish, hide, close, discard.
profession—*Syn.* calling, trade, business, vocation, employment, occupation, craft, sphere, line, field, declaration.
profit—*Syn.* gain, benefit, advantage, improvement, return, proceeds, receipts, value. *Ant.* loss, damage, failure, ruin, hurt, injury, indebtedness, obligation, waste, ruin.
profligate—*Syn.* abandoned, corrupt, degenerate, wicked, vile, flagitious, satanic. *Ant.* virtuous, ujpright, noble, refined, modest, innocent, uncorrupted, undefiled.
profound—*Syn.* deep, solemn, learned, scholarly, accomplished, knowing, knowledgeable, intellectual, wise, consummate, enlighted, sage, comprehensive, serious. *Ant.* shallow, slight, light, superficial, unsettled, erratic, eccentric, simple, unenlightened, ignorant, absurd.
profuse—*Syn.* lavish, prodigal, extravagant, abundant, liberal, excessive, plentiful, overflowing. *Ant.* scarce, meager, insufficient, inadequate, scanty, limited, curtailed.
progress—*Syn.* advancement, progression, development, growth, improvement, increase, movement. *Ant.* rest, stagnation, immobility, pause, stay, delay, relapse, decrease, decline.
prohibit—*Syn.* bar, hinder, prevent, block, forbid, disallow, inhibit, exclude, ban, refuse, deny. *Ant.* allow, permit, tolerate, license, concede, grant, warrant.
prolix—*Syn.* diffuse, wordy, tiresome, prolonged, long, lengthy, prosy. *Ant.* short, concise, explicit, clear, terse, condensed, pointed, succinct, summary.
prominent—*Syn.* extended, jutting, conspicuous, embossed, extended, remarkable, notable, protruding, eminent, popular, famous, renowned, distinguished. *Ant.* depressed, sunken, flat, level, obscure, unknown, humble, common, rude.
promiscuous—*Syn.* confused, indiscrimate, undistinguished, mingled, irregular, composite, miscellaneous. *Ant.* select, unadulterated, simple, regular, orderly, discrimate.
promote—*Syn.* advance, encourage, organize, equip, prefer, push, foster, help, excite. *Ant.* lower, reduce, sink, humiliate, degrade, damage, harm.
promulgate—*Syn.* publish, declare, proclaim, announce, advertise,

herald, circulate, disseminate. *Ant.* hide, conceal, suppress, smother, withhold, cover, silence.
propagate—*Syn.* breed, engender, create, generate, spread, disseminate, multiply, produce, impregnate, implant. *Ant.* destroy, suppress, crush, exterminate.
proper—*Syn.* just, right, fair, decent, suitable, appropriate. *Ant.* improper, incongruous, wrong, unfit, inappropriate, incorrect, unsuitable.
propitiate—*Syn.* conciliate, appease, atone, calm, soothe, mollify, satisfy, placate, reconcile. *Ant.* excite, annoy, anger, aggravate, scorn, nettle, displease.
propitiation—*Syn.* conciliation, reconciliation, reparation, indemnification, satisfaction. *Ant.* impenitence, guilt, delinquincy.
propitious—*Syn.* favorable, pleasing, satisfactory. *Ant.* unfavorable, harmful, unkind, hopeless, unfortunate.
proposal—*Syn.* scheme, design, suggestion, plan, proposition, program, outline, bid, appeal. *Ant.* protest, expostulation, refusal, renunciation, dissent, denial, disapproval.
propose—*Syn.* plan, project, design, suggest, offer, move, contend, enunciate, assert, state. *Ant.* discount, belittle, denounce, renounce, dispute.
propriety—*Syn.* decency, good manners, correctness, justice. *Ant.* impropriety, misconduct, misbehavior.
proscribe—*Syn.* banish, exile, prohibit, forbid, interdict, ostracize, boycott, reject, repudiate, exclude, disallow, inhibit. *Ant.* invite, solicit, entreat, welcome, greet.
prosperity—*Syn.* success, welfare, affluence, attainment, achievement, riches. *Ant.* adversity, failure, misfortune, ruin, poverty.
protract—*Syn.* postpone, defer, procrastinate, prolong, lengthen, elongate, continue, delay. *Ant.* shorten, abbreviate, abridge, curtail, contract, limit, lessen, condense, shrink.
proverb—*Syn.* maxim, adage, aphorism, precept, saw, saying, motto, dictum, axiom. *Ant.* absurdity, nonsense, silliness.
proverbial—*Syn.* general, unquestioned, undoubted, ackowledged, familiar, noted, recognized, established. *Ant.* unknown, strange, deceptive, erroneous.
provoke—*Syn.* rouse, excite, stir, move, incite, inflame, enrage, anger, taunt, irritate, infuriate, aggravate, madden, agitate, perturb. *Ant.* mollify, placate, please, pacify, flatter, soothe, calm, comfort, restrain, please, soften.
prudence—*Syn.* discretion, caution, judgement, forecast, deliberation, wisdom, care, discernment, discrimination. *Ant.* negligence, carelessness, imprudence, rashness, deferment.
prudent—*Syn.* wise, careful, discreet, cautious, throughtful, frugal, judicious, heedful, particular, alert. *Ant.* rash, impetuous, foolish, silly, heedless, careless, imprudent, precipitate, shallow, simple, indiscreet, injudicious, unwise.
prurient—*Syn.* longing, craving, desiring, desirous, wishful, solicitous, ardent, fervent, impure, lewd, wanton, salacious, pornographic, indecent, unclean, immoral, smutty, foul, coarse. *Ant.* indifferent, neutral, easygoing, phlegmatic, supine, listless, desire, impotent.
puerile—*Syn.* inexperienced, immature, foolish, puny, childish, fatuous, shallow. *Ant.* experienced, wise, sensible, sharp, sage, clearheaded, farsighted, philosophical, shrewd.
punctilious—*Syn.* formal, particular, exact, precise, scrupulous, definite, cautious, observant, constant, dutiful. *Ant.* careless, negligent, neglectful, heedless, uncaring, inattentive, regardless.
punctual—*Syn.* prompt, precise, particular, exact, expeditious, steady. *Ant.* unreliable, desultory, rambling, uncertain, irregular, wavering, inconstant, variable, fluctuating.
pungent—*Syn.* sharp, acid, tart, biting, penetrating, acute. *Ant.* sweet, mild, pleasant, soothing, agreeable.
punish—*Syn.* chastise, correct, lash, discipline, castigate, inflict, afflict, strike. *Ant.* clear, free, acquit, exculpate, exonerate, defend, praise, cheer, laud.
purchase—*Syn.* obtain, acquire, get, procure, secure, buy. *Ant.* lose, miss, sell, spend, dispose of.
pure—*Syn.* spotless, stainless, unblemished, unsullied, clean, incorrupt, upright, perfect, clear, genuine. *Ant.* impure, gross, coarse.
purify—*Syn.* cleanse, chasten, clear, refine, wash, filter, correct. *Ant.* tarnish, stain, corrupt, pollute, taint.
purpose—*Syn.* design, intention, goal, consummation, meaning, object, aim, scope, desire, mind, realization. *Ant.* chance, indefiniteness, speculation, gamble, risk, uncertainty.
push—*Syn.* impel, propel, shove, press, urge, force, advance, proceed. *Ant.* idle, lag, dawdle, recede, withdraw, halt.
put—*Syn.* place, lay, set, deposit, seat, station, lodge, quarter, install, establish, fix, lay down, plant, insert. *Ant.* move, remove, displace, misplace, shift, dislodge, transfer, abstract, oust, transport.
putrefy—*Syn.* rot, decay, decompose, corrupt, putresce, taint, defile, pollute, contaminate. *Ant.* cleanse, purify, renew, restore, freshen, invigorate, refresh.
putrid—*Syn.* corrupt, rotten, decayed, polluted, putrescent, contaminated, rancid. *Ant.* clear, pure, whole, wholesome, sound, uncontaminated, fresh, health-giving.
puzzle, *n.*—*Syn.* perplexity, difficulty, mystery, embarrassment, doubt, uncertainty, bewilderment, conundrum, enigma, vagueness, ambiguity, obscurity, labyrinth, complexity, muddle, quandary. *Ant.* certainty, plainness, clearness, lucidity, explicitness, fact, truth.
puzzle, *v.*—*Syn.* perplex, confuse, confound, mystify, bewilder, complicate, involve, muddle, jumble, disconcert, discompose, mix, mingle. *Ant.* clarify, illustrate, explain, assure, certify, demonstrate, evince, manifest, prove, confirm, elucidate, show, exhibit, display, expound, unravel, solve.
puzzling—*Syn* obscure, ambiguous, uncertain, perplexing, extraordinary, mystifying, confused, mixed, complicated, complex. *Ant.* clear, lucid, plain, evident, factual, explicit, precise, intelligible, comprehensible, undoubted, indubitable.

Q

quack—*Syn.* imposter, charlatan, mountebank, sophist, pretender, empiric, boaster, deceiver, dissembler, fourflusher, swindler, knave, rogue, simpleton.
quaint—*Syn.* odd, queer, curious, old, fanciful. *Ant.* ordinary, common, regular, usual.
qualified—*Syn.* capable, able, adequate, competent, proficient, experienced, fitted, equipped. *Ant.* inept, incapable, incompetent, unfit, deficient, unable, disqualified.
quality—*Syn.* nature, character, peculiarity, characteristic, attribute, state, condition, qualification, faculty, capability, tendency, inclination, susceptibility.
quarrel—*Syn.* wrangle, dispute, contention, feud, strife, bickering, argument, row, tiff, embroilment. *Ant.* peace, quiet, tranquillity, agreement, concord, harmony, accord, unanimity.
quarrelsome—*Syn.* factious, fractious, turbulent, unruly, pugnacious, contentious, irritable, fiery, excitable, brawling, bickering. *Ant.* peaceful, quiet, inoffensive, modest, retiring, agreeable, fraternal, placid, calm, composed.
queer—*Syn.* odd, strange, peculiar, unique, eccentric, quaint, whimsical, unusual. *Ant.* common, normal, regular, usual, ordinary, natural, conventional.
quell—*Syn.* subdue, stop, reduce, allay, quiet, check, overcome, stem, moderate, pacify, curb. *Ant.* torment, excite, inflame, encourage, incite, urge, stimulate, promote, exacerbate, infuriate, agitate, disturb, irritate, anger, incense.
querulous—*Syn.* fretful, fretting, peevish, touchy, tetchy, censorious, disagreeable, irritable. *Ant.* cheerful, happy, joyous, merry, gay, carefree, unconcerned, satisfied, buoyant, animated, spirited.
question, *v.*—*Syn.* inquire, interrogate, examine, search, put, propose, propound, query, probe, investigate, scrutinize, analyze. *Ant.* answer, reply, depose, state, inform, assent, ackowledge, declare, attest, confirm, allege.
questionable—*Syn.* uncertain, dubious, equivocal, disputable, suspicious, vague, unsettled, unconfirmed. *Ant.* certain, sure, unequivocal, obvious, assured, reliable, positive, definite, unmistakable, unquestionable, dogmatic, evident, satisfactory, axiomatic, believable, clear, convincing, logical, exact, authentic, genuine.
quibble—*Syn.* evade, prevaricate, equivocate, straddle, shift, cavil, dissemble. *Ant.* play the game (*colloq.*), stand patt (*colloq.*), be firm, act conscientiously, act squarely, speak plainly, be guileless.
quick—*Syn.* swift, nimble, agile, active, brisk, alert, lively, sharp, ready, prompt, expeditious, fleet, rapid, speedy, mercurial, instantaneous, peppery, fast. *Ant.* slow, creeping, crawling, tardy, dilatory, languid, sluggish, apathetic, phlegmatic, indolent, slothful, weary, drowsy, irksome, dull, flat, leaden.
quicken—*Syn.* accelerate, expedite, stimulate, refresh, revive, speed, urge, hasten, advance, drive, facilitate, further, force, excite, incite, animate, inspire, enthuse, sharpen, whet, impel, goad, spur, urge, propel. *Ant.* hinder, impede, obstruct, retard, drag, delay, clog, check, counteract, cumber, encumber, handicap, cramp, hamper, thwart, frustrate, baffle, circumvent, cripple, dishearten, repress, suppress, inhibit, override, overcome, oppose, curb, intercept, preclude, block.
quiet—*Syn.* peaceful, calm, tranquil, still, unruffled, smooth, pacific, placid, pleased, contented, meek, satisfied, gentle, moderate, cool, silent, quiescent, motionless, stationary, hushed, muffled. *Ant.* noisy, sonorous, loud, tinkling, blatant, thunderous, shrieking, screaming, deafening, shrill, piercing, uproarious, explosive, detonating, ringing, reverberating.
quit—*Syn.* abandon, leave, forsake, relinquish, cease, stop, depart, vacate, evacuate, withdraw, remove, abscond, desert, yield, surrender, resign. *Ant.* remain, retain, hold, keep, occupy, appropriate, corner, possess, engross, forestall, safeguard, defend, protect, guard, watch, preserve, secure.
quote—*Syn.* cite, adduce, repeat, note, exemplify, illustrate, recite, excerpt, extract, elucidate, explain, instance, evidence, allege, verify, attest, ratify, confirm, corroborate, endorse, establish, authenticate, substantiate.

R

rabid—*Syn.* mad, frantic, furious, infuriated, berserk, raging, fanatical, deranged, crazy, maniacal, frenzied, daft, distraught, frenetic. *Ant.* sane, normal, lucid, reasonable, normal.
race—*Syn.* breed, family, nation, stock, tribe, people, order, class, division, genus, species, variety, caste, kind, type, coterie, assortment, set, house, ancestry, lineage, pedigree, paternity, parentage, tribe.
rack—*Syn.* torture, torment, harass, annoy, distress, irritate, afflict, oppress, strain, stretch, lacerate, agonize. *Ant.* cheer, encourage, sustain, support, enliven, animate, soothe, assuage, comfort, alleviate.
racket—*Syn.* noise, clamor, commotion, confusion, uproar, clatter, din, brawl, squabble, scuffle, wrangle, agitation, stir, turmoil, turbulence. *Ant.* peace, quietude, concord, harmony, unison, love, agreement.
racy—*Syn.* pungent, piquant, spicy, sharp, smart, clever, keen, bright, lively, interesting, entertaining *Ant.*

dull, insipid, tasteless, watery, vapid, unsavory.

radiance—*Syn.* brightness, brilliance, splendor, glow, sheen, shine. *Ant.* darkness, shade, shadow, murkiness.

rage, *n.*—*Syn.* anger, fury, ferocity, violence, wrath, bluster, agitation, ferment, frenzy, raving, uproar, explosion. *Ant.* calm, composure, patience, resignation, submission, restraint, rest, quiescence, unconcern.

rage, *v.*—*Syn.* rave, storm, fume, shout, swear, foam, flash, flare, seethe, excite, boil, rant, roar, explode, rampage, fulminate. *Ant.* soothe, calm, placate, soften, allay, alleviate, assuage, appease, tranquilize, lull, pacify, hush, curb, mollify.

raise—*Syn.* lift, elevate, hoist, heighten, erect, grow, increase, produce, aggravate, excite, cause, collect, construct, establish, acquire, gather, borrow. *Ant.* lower, reduce, decrease, curtail, abridge, abate, lessen, diminish.

ramble—*Syn.* roam, wander, range, stroll, stray, prowl, saunter, patrol, traverse. *Ant.* lead, steer, direct, guide, condense, illuminate.

rampant—*Syn.* violent, vehement, abrupt, impetuous, turbulent, furious, infuriate, unruly, prevalent, dominant, impulsive, intolerant. *Ant.* mild, meek, modest, gentle, unobtrusive.

rancid—*Syn.* rank, tainted, fetid, impure, offensive, disagreeable, decaying, rotten. *Ant.* sweet, pure, wholesome, enjoyable, innocuous, good, pleasing.

rancor—*Syn.* spite, hatred, malice, enmity, malevolence, animosity, hostility, bitterness, unfriendliness. *Ant.* friendship, love, regard, respect, sympathy, confidence.

rank, *n.*—*Syn.* line, range, series, row, file, division, reputation, class, order, position, standing. *Ant.* disrepute, debasement.

rank, *adj.*—*Syn.* musty, rancid, foul, offensive. *Ant.* fresh, green, new, pleasing, wholesome, fragrant.

ransack—*Syn.* pillage, plunder, ravish, sack, raid. *Ant.* restore, return, recoup, repay, compensate.

rapacious—*Syn.* grasping, greedy, avaricious, ransacking, cruel, predatory, merciless, voracious. *Ant.* liberal, bountiful, prodigal, profuse.

rapid—*Syn.* quick, swift, speedy, accelerated, flying, expeditious, fast. *Ant.* slow, creeping, crawling, slack, dilatory, sluggish, idle, listless, lethargic.

rapture—*Syn.* ecstasy, delight, joy, bliss, happiness, glee, enjoyment, pleasure. *Ant.* sorrow, distress, melancholy, annoyance, irritation.

rare—*Syn.* uncommon, scarce, singular, unparalleled, unprecedented, unusual, curious, extraordinary, strange, superlative, matchless, incomparable, exclusive, select. *Ant.* common, ordinary, general, universal, typical, normal, profuse, worthless, trivial, inexpensive.

rash—*Syn.* hasty, precipitate, foolhardy, reckless, careless, thoughtless, impetuous, unthinking, inconsiderate. *Ant.* careful, cautious, prudent, thoughtful, deliberate.

rate—*Syn.* ratio, proportion, degree, price, valuation, measure, amount. *Ant.* discount, rebate, concession, reduction.

ratify—*Syn.* confirm, indorse, approve, sanction, establish, warrant, vouch for, attest, support, corroborate, consent, acquiesce. *Ant.* refuse, oppose, renounce, denounce, contradict, deny, disclaim, abrogate, repudiate.

rational—*Syn.* wise, sensible, judicious, sane, reasonable, sagacious, conscious, mental, subjective, ratiocinative, logical. *Ant.* foolish, absurd, ridiculous, weak, erratic, eccentric, shallow.

ravage—*Syn.* pillage, overrun, devastate, destroy, desolate, damage, wreck, waste, disrupt, overwhelm, extinguish. *Ant.* upraise, restore, erect, build, institute, organize, achieve, reinstate, replace, renovate.

ravish—*Syn.* charm, enchant, cheer, gladden, rejoice, captivate, attract, seize. *Ant.* displease, disgust, annoy, harass, worry, grieve, disturb.

raze—*Syn.* destroy, demolish, dismantle, ruin, scatter, overturn. *Ant.* build, raise, erect, rear, construct, restore, repair.

reach—*Syn.* arrive, attain, land, meet. *Ant.* start, go, depart, embark, begin.

ready—*Syn.* prompt, prepared, suitable, proper, fit, enthusiastic. *Ant.* unprepared, unsuitable, improper, remiss.

real—*Syn.* actual, genuine, true, certain, firm, essential. *Ant.* nonexistent, unreal, imaginary.

realize—*Syn.* achieve, effect, acquire, comprehend, gain, get, accomplish, perfect, execute, believe, imagine. *Ant.* fail, slip, neglect, undo, flounder, falter, topple, tumble.

reap—*Syn.* gain, get, acquire, obtain, win, procure, gather, collect, glean, produce, profit. *Ant.* scatter, disperse, forfeit, lose, miss, fail, decline.

reason, *v.*—*Syn.* conclude, deduce, infer, question, contend, dispute, prove, establish, debate, demonstrate, explain, think, reflect, cogitate, consider, meditate, ponder. *Ant.* equivocate, hedge, dodge, evade, elude, prevaricate, shift, mislead, confuse.

reasonable—*Syn.* fair, just, right, honest, rational, wise, agreeable, sound, sensible, lenient. *Ant.* outlandish, excessive, immoderate, unreasonable, ridiculous, outrageous, excessive, expensive, costly, exorbitant.

rebellion—*Syn.* insurrection, revolt, revolution, debacle, overthrow, uprising, mutiny, riot, outbreak, tumult, disturbance. *Ant.* peace, quiet, quietness, tranquillity, submission, endurance, armistice.

rebellious—*Syn.* mutinous, unmanageable, recalcitrant, uncontrollable, pugnacious, quarrelsome, refractory, insubordinate, disobedient. *Ant.* docile, dutiful, obedient, subservient, tractable, yielding, manageable, willing, agreeable, loyal.

recant—*Syn.* recall, retract, abjure, deny, revoke, cancel, renounce, disavow, disclaim, withdraw, abrogate, repudiate, nullify. *Ant.* ackowledge, admit, proclaim, commission, accredit, indorse, sanction, confirm, strengthen, uphold, affirm, insist.

recede—*Syn.* regrade, retrograde, retreat, retire, withdraw, recoil, return. *Ant.* proceed, advance, approach, progress.

receive—*Syn.* accept, admit, take, entertain, acquire, gather, collect, inherit, include, incorporate. *Ant.* reject, refuse, renounce, exclude, expel, dislodge.

recess—*Syn.* receptacle, corner, niche, cell, hole, nook, drawer, ambush, seclusion, vacation, intermission, interlude, interregnum, cessation, pause, rest, interval. *Ant.* space, extension, range, expansion, room, void, level, plain, continuance, prolongation, persistence.

recover—*Syn.* regain, obtain, improve, increase, revive, procure, salvage, realize, retrieve, collect, resume, regain. *Ant.* lose, miss, mislay, forfeit, squander, waste.

recreation—*Syn.* pastime, amusement, sport, game, play, fun, diversion, relaxation, pastime. *Ant.* drudgery, toil, plodding, struggle, weariness.

redeem—*Syn.* purchase, repurpurchase, rescue, liberate, recover, deliver, free, recoup, redress, regain. *Ant.* sell, lose, barter.

redress—*Syn.* restoration, repair, remedy, relief, remission, diminution, replacement, rehabilitation, renewal, renovation, amends, compensation, payment, remuneration. *Ant.* penalty, retribution, forfeiture, assessment.

reduce—*Syn.* lower, lessen, decrease, diminish, abate, modify, curtail, subdue, shorten, decimate. *Ant.* increase, augment, enlarge, expand, swell, extend, amplify.

refinement—*Syn.* culture, civilization, scholarship, learning, erudition, elegance, cultivation, purification, cultivation, enlightenment, polish. *Ant.* rudeness, roughness, coarseness, boorishness, brutality, vulgarity, ignorance.

reflect—*Syn.* contemplate, consider, ponder, think, meditate. *Ant.* relax, disregard, neglect, dream, idle.

reform—*Syn.* amend, correct, improve, better, restore, convert, resolve, remodel, reorganize, revise. *Ant.* deteriorate, relapse, degenerate, wither, totter, tumble, corrupt, taint, pollute.

refuge—*Syn.* shelter, retreat, asylum, protectory, haven, harbor, protection, home, anchorage, covert, sanctuary, seclusion, solitude. *Ant.* abyss, chasm, pitfall, snare, trap, exposure, danger, jeopardy, casualty.

refuse, *v.*—*Syn.* decline, reject, repel, rebuff, disavow, disown, deny, repudiate, decline. *Ant.* accept, acquiesce, accede, acknowledge, assent, consent, sanction.

refute—*Syn.* disprove, repel, confound, rebut. *Ant.* support, sustain, indorse, encourage, sanction.

regard—*Syn.* observe, consider, estimate, heed, esteem, approve, admire, respect, honor, revere, appreciate, notice, mark. *Ant.* disregard, overlook, shun, ignore, neglect.

regret—*Syn.* grief, sorrow, lamentation, remorse, repentance, dissatisfaction. *Ant.* contentment, satisfaction, serenity, comfort.

regular—*Syn.* ordinary, orderly, stated, uniform, consistent, systematic, conventional. *Ant.* irregular, inconstant, inconsistent, noncomformable, variable, uncommon.

regulate—*Syn.* arrange, adjust, organize, govern, rule, order. *Ant.* disorder, disarrange, confuse, mix, muddle, entangle, involve.

relevant—*Syn.* appropriate, fit, proper, pertinent, becoming, pertaining to, apt, congruous. *Ant.* disparate, separate, antagonistic, irrelevant, inconsistent, isolated.

reliable—*Syn.* dependable, true, faithful, trusty, devoted, attached, positive, absolute, unequivocal, unimpeachable, authentic. *Ant.* unreliable, flimsy, false, fallacious, doubtful, uncertain.

reliance—*Syn.* confidence, trust, hope, faith, optimism, conviction, expectation, belief, assurance. *Ant.* despair, dependency, gloom, doubt.

relief—*Syn.* succor, help, assistance, alleviation, support, maintenance, remedy. *Ant.* hinderance, impediment, obstruction, obstacle, burden, disapproval.

religion—*Syn.* piety, devotion, morality, righteousness, theology, theism, divinity, persuasion, faith, worship, pietism. —*Syn.* atheism, ungodliness, sacriliege, blasphemy, agnosticism.

relinquish—*Syn.* renounce, forego, leave, abandon, quit, resign, forsake, surrender, abjure, secede, discard, claim. *Ant.* hold, keep, grip, persevere, continue, persist, maintain.

reluctant—*Syn.* unwilling, averse, opposed, tardy, adverse, remiss. *Ant.* willing, eager, favorable, desirous, inclined, predisposed.

remain—*Syn.* continue, endure, stay, exist, prevail, survive. *Ant.* depart, vanish, fade.

remedy—*Syn.* cure, restorative, reparation, redress, relief, antidote, drug. *Ant.* pain, agony, torment, weakness, disease, affliction.

remit—*Syn.* release, relax, absolve, pardon, acquit, exonerate, forgive, send, forward, transmit. *Ant.* hold, withhold, persist.

remnant—*Syn.* remainder, residue, rest, surplus. *Ant.* whole, entire, principal part, entirety.

remonstrate—*Syn.* expostulate, check, criticize, censure, reprimand, discourage, recriminate. *Ant.* commend, praise, indorse, sanction, laud.

remorse—*Syn.* regret, contrition, penitence, self-reproach, sorrow. *Ant.* obduracy, induration, pretension.

remote—*Syn.* distant, far away, unconnected, unrelated, alien, separate, secluded, inaccessible. *Ant.* near, close, contiguous, adjoining, adjacent, touching, bordering, affiliated.

remove—*Syn.* displace, transfer, transport, separate, abstract, unseat. *Ant.* place, settle, remain, stay, establish, root.

remunerate—*Syn.* compensate, recompense, reward, pay, satisfy, acknowledge.. *Ant.* deprive, forfeit, confiscate, appropriate.

render—*Syn.* give, present, return, restore, apportion, assign, distribute, deliver. *Ant.* withhold, withdraw, keep, retain, hold, secure, take, deduct, ignore.

renounce—*Syn.* repudiate, recant, refuse, reject, abandon, deny, disavow, revoke, recall, disclaim, disown, abrogate, forsake. *Ant.* persist, maintain, remain, stay, keep, continue, uphold.

reparation—*Syn.* satisfaction, re-

turn, repair, remuneration, compensation, recompense, restoration, restitution. *Ant.* confiscation, tax, impost, penalty, appropriation.
repentance—*Syn.* sorrow, remorse, regret, penitence, contrition. *Ant.* hardness, obduracy, comfort, approval, content, obstinacy.
replace—*Syn.* restore, substitute, reinstate, rehabilitate, refund, restore, reconstruct, repair, mend, supersede. *Ant.* change, exchange, barter, shuffle, alternate, transform, shift, deviate.
report, *n.*—*Syn.* statement, account, description, narrative, record, recital, narration, announcement, rumor, news. *Ant.* concealment, secret, reserve, suppression, evasion, deletion, distortion.
report, *v.*—*Syn.* announce, relate, tell, recite, describe, detail, communicate, record, publish, disclose, impart. *Ant.* conceal, hide, secrete, veil, reserve, suppress.
reprobate, *n.*—*Syn.* sinner, transgressor, rascal, villain, scoundrel. *Ant.* exemplar, guide, paragon.
reproof—*Syn.* censure, rebuke, blame, disapproval, reproach, admonition. *Ant.* credit, commendation, recommendation, approval, indorsement, praise, adulation.
reprove—*Syn.* disapprove, berate, scold, disparage, condemn, blame, censure. *Ant.* approve, applaud, acclaim, sanction, indorse, instigate.
repudiate—*Syn.* disavow, disown, discard, renounce, reject, disclaim, exclude, banish. *Ant.* acknowledge, avow, affirm, assert, profess, admit, incorporate, approve, assent.
repugnant—*Syn.* antipathetic, disagreeable, distasteful, inimical, hostile, unwilling, opposed, offensive, contrary, adverse, antagonistic, conflicting. *Ant.* agreeable, pleasant, harmonious, suitable, congruent, identical, equivalent, sympathetic.
repulsive—*Syn.* forbidding, horrid, hideous, repellent, disagreeable, detestable, abominable, terrible. *Ant.* pleasing, agreeable, enticing, inviting, attractive, delicate.
reputable—*Syn.* honorable, worthy, creditable, respectable, celebrated, distinguished, popular, dignified. *Ant.* dishonorable, untrue, unscrupulous, undignified.
requite—*Syn.* repay, exchange, reciprocate, compensate, reward, retaliate, return. *Ant.* slight, pardon, overlook, extenuate, justify, release.
rescind—*Syn.* abrogate, revoke, cancel, reverse, void, vacate, discard, abolish, repeal, reverse, dissolve, countermand. *Ant.* commission, delegate, command, appoint, advance, permit, allow, propose.
rescue—*Syn.* save, deliver, preserve, recover, liberate, free, redeem, extricate, release, emancipate, ransom. *Ant.* prevent, incarcerate, impede, check, hinder, retain, block.
resemblance—*Syn.* likeness, similarity, match, companion, effigy, simile, image, duplicate, replica. *Ant.* difference, divergence, dissimilarity, distinction, variety, disagreement, discrepancy.
resentment—*Syn.* anger, wrath, ire, indignation, displeasure, animosity, acerbity, bitterness. *Ant.* cheer, friendship, affection, concord, cordiality, enthusiasm.
reside—*Syn.* dwell, abide, live, inhabit, stay. *Ant.* absent, shun, vacate, retire, leave, abandon.
resist—*Syn.* oppose, hinder, check, withstand, obstruct, baffle, disappoint, refuse, impede. *Ant.* comply, concur, cooperate, collaborate, help, assist, contribute.
resolute—*Syn.* steady, firm, determined, decided, bold, persevering, resolved. *Ant.* irresolute, wavering, vacillating, unsteady, timorous, afraid, cautious.
respite—*Syn.* reprieve, suspension, commutation, delay, postponement, pause, interval, stop, intermission. *Ant.* condemnation, conviction.
responsible—*Syn.* accountable, amendable, liable, binding, imperative, obligatory. *Ant.* irresponsible, exempt, immune, unbound, uncontrolled, unrestrained.
rest—*Syn.* quiet, tranquillity, intermission, cessation, stop, stay, pause, death. *Ant.* unrest, movement, commotion, stir, tumult.
restless—*Syn.* agitated, disturbed, uneasy, nervous, unsettled, anxious, excited, worried, annoyed, agitated. *Ant.* steady, tranquil, calm, composed, cool, quiet.
restrain—*Syn.* check, curb, bridle, restrict, suppress, keep, constrain. *Ant.* loosen, unbind, free, liberate, release, arouse, encourage.
retain—*Syn.* hold, keep, secure, maintain, hire, engage, preserve, detain, bind, reserve. *Ant.* relinquish, dismiss, surrender, discard, render.
retract—*Syn.* revoke, deny, disown, recall, withdraw, annul, repudiate, renounce, disclaim, contradict. *Ant.* affirm, confirm, assert, reassert, depose, declare, announce.
reveal—*Syn.* divulge, disclose, impart, discover, expose, uncover. *Ant.* veil, hide, conceal, cover.
revenge, *n.*—*Syn.* retaliation, retribution, avenging, implacability. *Ant.* forgiveness, pardon, amnesty, reprieve, exoneration, reconciliation, compassion, acquital.
revenue—*Syn.* income, result, receipts, proceeds, interest, means, earnings. *Ant.* expenditure, expenses, disbursements, costs.
reverence—*Syn.* honor, respect, admiration, regard, esteem, veneration. *Ant.* disrespect, irreverence, affront, dishonor, insult.
revise—*Syn.* review, reconsider, edit, correct, alter, amend, overhaul. *Ant.* neglect, dismiss, discard, ignore, distort, confuse, complicate.
revive—*Syn.* refresh, renew, renovate, animate, resuscitate, reproduce, recall, reinforce. *Ant.* weaken, lessen, deteriorate.
revolution—*Syn.* revolt, rebellion, insurrection, insubordination, destruction, mutiny, sedition, tumult, riot, anarchy, confusion, uprising. *Ant.* government, domination, dominion, obedience, authority, command, law, order, rule, supremacy, control, peace, submission, fealty.
reward—*Syn.* remuneration, recompense, gain, compensation, reparation, retribution, payment. *Ant.* penalty, damages, divestment, seizure, forfeiture, fine, tax, loss.
ribald—*Syn.* low, base, vulgar, rude, outlandish, coarse. *Ant.* graceful, refined, polished, courteous, polite, decent.
rich—*Syn.* wealthy, opulent, affluent, ample, copious, sumptuous, abundant, plentiful. *Ant.* poor, impoverished, mean, lowly, humble, indigent.
riddle—*Syn.* conundrum, paradox, puzzle, obscurity, enigma, charade, rebus, secret, dilemma. *Ant.* answer, solution, explanation, interpretation, meaning.
right, *adj.*—*Syn.* true, correct, suitable, lawful, proper, straight, just, undeviating, regular, sincere, accurate, precise, actual, real, genuine, legitamite. *Ant.* wrong, false, erring, partial, unjustifiable, illegitimate, unbecoming, erroneous, misleading, inaccurate, incorrect, unreliable, uncertain.
right, *n.*—*Syn.* privilege, prerogative, immunity, claim, exemption, license, liberty, ownership, possession, domain, territory, equity, justice. *Ant.* dishonor, disgrace, turpitude, corruption, evasion, transgression, violation, subjection.
righteous—*Syn.* just, upright, virtuous, good, honest, deserving, worthy, moral, pure. *Ant.* wrong, unjust, unprincipled, immoral, disreputable.
rigid—*Syn.* stiff, unyielding, hard, firm, unbending, stony, stern, austere, severe, exact, precise. *Ant.* soft, pliant, plastic, flexible, mobile, yielding, tolerant, compassionate.
ripe—*Syn.* mature, mellow, complete, finished, ready, prepared, maturated, seasoned, consummate. *Ant.* immature, young, raw, unprepared, unripe, unready, inexperienced, recent, undeveloped.
rise—*Syn.* arise, ascend, mount, climb, scale, issue, spring, begin, grow, progress, commence, originate. *Ant.* decline, descend, sink, settle, fall, drop, recede, retrograde.
rival, *n.*—*Syn.* opponent, competitor, antagonist, enemy, contestant, adversary. *Ant.* patron, helper, assistant, supporter.
rival, *v.*—*Syn.* oppose, complete, contest, dispute, collide, conflict, resist, confront, encounter, struggle, combat. *Ant.* aid, assist, help, uphold, support, strengthen.
road—*Syn.* route, path, way, highway, street, avenue, roadway, viaduct, track, thoroughfare, pathway, boulevard, tramway.
roam—*Syn.* ramble, range, rove, wander, walk, traverse, perambulate. *Ant.* rest, stop, stay, remain, stand, halt, pause, anchor, settle.
robust—*Syn.* strong, lusty, vigorous, stout, sturdy, stalwart, athletic, brawny, powerful, hardy. *Ant.* weak, feeble, debilitated, frail, shaky, infirm, fragile, languid.
rout—*Syn.* overcome, overthrow, scatter, beat, defeat, conquer, surmount, overpower, vanquish, subjugate. *Ant.* fail, lose, succumb, falter, flounder, recede, withdraw, retire.
royal—*Syn.* kingly, princely, majestic, magnificent, splendid, regal, noble, dignified, dominant, paramount, sovereign, imperial. *Ant.* low, poor, humble, plebeian, ignoble.
rude—*Syn.* rough, uneven, rugged, uncouth, coarse, rustic, ignorant, illiterate, uncivilized, savage, brutal. *Ant.* polite, polished, refined, genteel, well-bred, cultured, cultivated, courteous, urbane.
rule—*Syn.* government, sway, control, regulation, direction, order, method, precept, guide, maxim, standard, authority, power, command, jurisdiction. *Ant.* revolt, insubordination, confusion, insurrection, strife, disorder.
rumor—*Syn.* report, story, news, gossip, tattle, hearsay. *Ant.* silence, lull, rest, hush, secret, concealment.
rustic—*Syn.* countrified, bucolic, pastoral, rural, country, rough, simple. *Ant.* accomplished, cultured, refined, elegant, urban, polished.
ruthless—*Syn.* savage, brutal, cruel, tyrannical, merciless, unrelenting, inhuman, harsh, unkind, unfriendly, ferocious, truculent, inexorable, unrelenting. *Ant.* kind, forgiving, amiable, tender, placable, conciliatory, compassionate, lenient.

S

sagacious—*Syn.* keen, quick, discerning, perspicacious, intelligent, shrewd, sensible, sage, penetrating, farsighted, brainy, tactful, circumspect. *Ant.* shortsighted, vacuous, thoughtless, careless, simple, inept, incapable, undiscerning, unimaginative ignorant, unintelligent.
sale—*Syn.* change, exchange, barter, trade, bargain, deal, auction, traffic, commerce, enterprise, speculation, auction, transaction, business, negotiation. *Ant.* purchase, buying, marketing, dealing, trading, investment, acquisition, expenditure.
salutary—*Syn.* wholesome, healthful, salubrious, beneficial, advantageous, useful, good, profitable, healthy, nutritious. *Ant.* deleterious, harmful, noxious, poisonous, unhealthy.
sanction, *n.*—*Syn.* confirmation, approval, commendation, authority, ratification, permission, warrant, authorization, liberty, privilege, license. *Ant.* disapproval, denunciation, stricture, objection, blame, censure, prohibition, injunction, restraint.
sanction, *v.*—*Syn.* confirm, encourage, support, sustain, ratify, authorize, countenance, indorse, approve, favor, commend, praise, compliment, acclaim. *Ant.* denounce, disparage, disapprove, censure, blame, disallow, interdict.
sane—*Syn.* rational, normal, lucid, sensible, steady, reasonable, sound. *Ant.* insane, irrational, delirious, mad, deranged, unsound, odd, eccentric, frenetic, distraught.
sanguine—*Syn.* hopeful, expectant, buoyant, optimistic, enthusiastic, trustful, confident, elated, reassured. *Ant.* despairing, despondent, pessimistic, dejected, depressed.
sarcasm—*Syn.* satire, irony, banter, derision, jeer, contempt, scoffing, flouting, ridicule, jibe, criticism, invective, censure. *Ant.* flattery, approval, appreciation.
sarcastic—*Syn.* scornful, mocking, ironical, satirical, taunting, derisive, sardonic, hostile, acrimonious, biting. *Ant.* pleasant, pleasing, polite, courteous, civil, agreeable, complaisant, amiable, flattering, affable,

gracious.

satisfy—*Syn.* pay, repay, settle, disburse, bestow, lend, give, confer, bequeath, defray, liquidate, accommodate, redeem, reimburse, cure, delight, amuse, please, content, gratify, indulge. *Ant.* deny, deprive, discourage, displease, repel, revolt, restrict, refuse.

saucy—*Syn.* impudent, impertinent, insolent, presumptuous, brazen. *Ant.* modest, retiring, bashful, meek, humble.

savage—*Syn.* wild, barbarous, cruel, inhuman, fierce, ferocious, brutal, terrible, rude, untamed, uncultivated, violent, frenzied, infuriate, frantic, incontrollable. *Ant.* meek, mild, gentle, genteel, soft, tranquil, peaceful, modest, calm, cool, temperate, yielding, placid, serene.

savory—*Syn.* palatable, pleasing, appetizing, tasty, tempting, ambrosial. *Ant.* unsavory, tasteless, insipid, flat, vapid, bitter, acrid, offensive.

scandal—*Syn.* shame, disgrace, infamy, turpitude, crime, discredit, slander, disrepute, defamation. *Ant.* praise, adulation, flattery, admiration, laudation.

scanty—*Syn.* scarce, few, little, small, bare, ragged, insufficient, thin, emaciated. *Ant.* big, large, grand, great, many, much, rich, luxuriant.

scatter—*Syn.* spread, strew, disseminate, disperse, dispel, dissipate, diffuse, disband, intersperse, separate. *Ant.* collect, gather, assemble, unite, concur, pack.

science—*Syn.* art, knowledge, skill, craftsmanship, comprehension, cognition, enlightenment, scholarship. *Ant.* ignorance, illiteracy, shallowness.

secret—*Syn.* concealed, hidden, secluded, private, latent, clandestine, covert, unknown, ambiguous, veiled. *Ant.* open, unconcealed, apparent, evident, obvious, plain, conspicuous, unmistakable, undisguised, explicit, transparent, clear, defined.

security—*Syn.* pledge, surety, bail, safety, protection, watch, shelter, guarantee, pledge, certainty, promise, warranty, contract, compact, understanding, stipulation. *Ant.* uncertainty, doubt, perplexity, difficulty, hesitation, possibility, timidity, contingency, unreliability, improbability, precariousness, incredibility.

seduce—*Syn.* decoy, allure, entice, abduct, attract, tempt, bait, induce, excite, stimulate, persuade, coax, attract, charm, defile. *Ant.* protect, guide, preserve, warn, advise, discourage, admonish, restrain, deter.

seize—*Syn.* grasp, take, catch, apprehend, comprehend, appropriate, grip, clasp, clutch, abstract, commandeer, grab, snatch, abduct, steal, loot, pillage, plunder, sack. *Ant.* restore, return, compensate, recompense, reward, repair, disgorge, remit, indemnify, remunerate, spare, leave, relinquish.

send—*Syn.* transmit, despatch, forward, delegate, emit, discharge, impel, consign, carry, convey, deliver. *Ant.* give, get, receive, hold, keep, retain, grip, withhold, secure, maintain, hide.

sensation—*Syn.* sense, feeling, emotion, perception, impression, sensibility, susceptibility, consciousness, wonder, awe, amazement, surprise, astonishment, admiration, impression. *Ant.* apathy, insensibility, inertia, coma, lethargy, sleep, inactivity, unconsciousness, impassiveness, trance.

sense—*Syn.* understanding, reason, mind, instinct, intellect, intelligence, spirit, soul, thought, brains, consciousness, perception, discernment. *Ant.* incapacity, simplicity, foolishness, nonsense.

sensible—*Syn.* wise, intelligent, sagacious, thoughtful, sharp, acute, penetrating, rational, subtle, sage. *Ant.* foolish, shallow, simple, stupid, stolid, fatuous, irrational.

sensible—*Syn.* material, physical, tangible, ponderable, substantial. *Ant.* immaterial, airy, ethereal, bodied, imponderable, intangible.

sensual—*Syn.* voluptuous, luxurious. *Ant.* ascetic, chaste, temperate, rigorous, moderate, abstemious.

separate, *a.*—*Syn.* apart, disunited, disjointed, divergent, unconnected, individual, alone, parted, distant. *Ant.* joined, united, tied, connected, bound, welded, fused, entwined, mixed, entangled, associated.

separate, *v.*—*Syn.* divide, disunite, sever, sunder, dissolve, disengage, part, detach, disconnect, unravel, disintegrate, dislocate, disperse, dissect, scatter, isolate. *Ant.* combine, collect, gather, assemble, lump, unite, connect, link, blend, compound, fuse, interfuse, twine, weld.

serene—*Syn.* clear, limpid, unruffled, undisturbed, tranquil, composed, calm, cool, sedate, content, satisfied, placid. *Ant.* confused, disturbed, ruffled, violent, furious, excited.

settle—*Syn.* regulate, adjust, straighten, arrange, decide, determine, conclude, dispose, allocate, distribute, rule, adjudicate. *Ant.* derange, discompose, disturb, perturb, disorganize, displace, confuse, ravel, shift.

several—*Syn.* diverse, sundry, various, plural, different, distinct, some, restricted, few. *Ant.* many, numerous, multiple, manifold, crowded, profuse.

severe—*Syn.* harsh, cruel, tyrannical, rigid, strict, stern, stringent, rigorous, stiff, unrelenting, austere, uncompromising, exacting, obdurate. *Ant.* lenient, easy, complacent, gentle, tractable, mild, courteous, tolerant.

shabby—*Syn.* mean, low, abject, meager, faded, reduced, impoverished, paltry, poor, miserable. *Ant.* flourishing, prosperous, thriving, comfortable, affluent.

shake—*Syn.* tremble, vibrate, quiver, shiver, flutter, oscillate, shudder, quake, wave, agitate, brandish, flutter, tremble. *Ant.* fix, place, fasten, tie, settle, solidify, set, stabilize, establish, confirm, strengthen, steady, resist, restrain, condense, coagulate.

shallow—*Syn.* superficial, slight, flimsy, trifling, simple, empty, trivial. *Ant.* deep, profound, unfathomable, depressed, wise, sage, learned, scholarly, educated, erudite.

shame—*Syn.* disgrace, dishonor, infamy, reproach, derision, contempt, disrepute, obloquy, scandal, humiliation. *Ant.* respect, nobility, dignity, fame, celebrity, exaltation, praise, applause, appreciation, approval, commendation, tribute.

shameful—*Syn.* disgraceful, dishonorable, contemptible, degrading, scandalous, unworthy. *Ant.* creditable, worthy, virtuous, commendable, reputable, respectable, honorable, illustrious, deserving.

shameless—*Syn.* disgraceful, immodest, impudent, bold. *Ant.* decent, upright, righteous, respectable, respected, honorable, fair, commendable, proper, candid.

shape, *n.*—*Syn.* form, fashion, model, mold, stamp, appearance, conformation, structure, trim. *Ant.* shapelessness, deformity, disfigurement, malformation, distortion, irregularity, unconformity.

shape, *v.*—*Syn.* form, mould, cast, regulate, fashion, make, create, design, construct, carve, chisel, cut, sketch, block out, hammer out, model, build, erect. *Ant.* deface, disfigure, cut, twist, distort, contort, warp, mangle.

shapeless—*Syn.* amorphic, unshaply, formless, unsymmetrical, irregular. *Ant.* shapely, symmetrical, regular, uniform, regulated, uniform, proportioned, proper.

share, *n.*—*Syn.* part, portion, lot, allotment, quantity, quota, contingent, consignment, residue, division, participation. *Ant.* total, entire, whole, all, combine, combination, aggregate, aggregation.

share, *v.*—*Syn.* give, allot, divide, apportion, part, participate, appropriate, deal, partition, assign. *Ant.* amass, aggregate, combine, unite, secure, keep, retain, hold, maintain.

sharp—*Syn.* acute, keen, penetrating, biting. *Ant.* dull, blunt, rough, uneven, jagged, ragged, gnarled, notched.

shelter—*Syn.* screen, cover, hide conceal, guard, ward, harbor, defend, protect, shield, secure, preserve, safeguard, surround, enclose, house. *Ant.* expose, evict, endanger, banish, ignore, imperil, uncover, strip, exclude, prohibit, disallow, inhibit, refuse.

shine—*Syn.* glare, glitter, radiate, sparkle, scintillate, gleam, shimmer, glisten. *Ant.* shade, cloud, veil, darken, cover, curtain, obscure, dim, shadow, lower.

shock, *n.*—*Syn.* concussion, percussion, impact, collision, crash, blow, stroke. *Ant.* peace, calm, quietness, rest, silence.

shock, *v.*—*Syn.* agitate, frighten, scare, alarm, dismay, terrify, startle, intimidate, threaten. *Ant.* soothe, calm, lull, pacify, soften.

short—*Syn.* brief, concise, succinct, summary, imcomplete, insufficient, abridged, abbreviated, curtailed, condensed, reduced, squat, compact, compressed. *Ant.* long, attenuated, lengthened, prolonged, protracted, extended, elongated, lengthy, interminable, unending, profuse.

shortsighted—*Syn.* myopic, nearsighted, partial, superficial, undiscerning, opinionated. *Ant.* farsighted, thoughtful, prudent, reasoning, circumspect, careful, wise, acute, sagacious.

shrewd—*Syn.* knowing, cunning, clever, discerning, calculating, cool, careful, observant, watchful, guarded. *Ant.* rash, unreasoning, silly, immpetuous, thoughtless, obtuse.

sick—*Syn.* ill, ailing, impaired, unhealthy, morbid, invalid, infirm, unhealthy. *Ant.* healthy, hearty, fine, strong, vigorous, robust, blooming, hale, hardy, unimpaired, sound, powerful.

sign, *n.*—*Syn.* omen, symbol, portent, token, emblem, symptom, signal, indication, mark, manifestation, indentification, index, note, cipher, device, motto, figure, representation, track, trail, footprint, clew.

sign, *v.*—*Syn.* affix, append, write, print, signal, convey, attract, contract, pledge, agree, guarantee, indicate, mark, note, imprint, score, impress, engrave, stamp, trace, gesture, gesticulate.

significant—*Syn.* important, material, critical, prominent, outstanding, weighty, suggestive, meaningful, expressive, notable, remarkable, serious. *Ant.* unimportant, trivial, petty, shallow, weak.

simple—*Syn.* plain, easy, common, ordinary, unmixed, uncompounded, pure, unadorned, isolated, absolute. *Ant.* sage, wise, knowing, alert, experienced, sensible, discerning, discriminating, deep, profound, learned.

simulate—*Syn.* pretend, imitate, cheat, deceive, misrepresent, prevaricate, distort.

sin—*Syn.* evil, vice, transgression, guilt, fault, wrong, falsification, lying, cheating, chicanery, immorality, perjury, depravity, vice, deliquency, crime, offense, wrongdoing, corruption. *Ant.* virtue, purity, morality, decency, right, rectitude, excellence, merit, worth, honesty, truth, kindness.

sincere—*Syn.* honest, truthful, honorable, frank, aboveboard, unreserved, true, candid, hearty, pure, genuine, real, fair, just, faithful. *Ant.* false, lying, perjured, insincere, dishonest.

sing—*Syn.* chant, carol, hum. *Ant.* cry, shout, howl, roar, shriek, growl.

single—*Syn.* one, only, sole, solitary, individual, separate, unmarried, celibate, secluded, elemental, isolated. *Ant.* many, numerous, accompanied, attended, associated, coupled, mixed, blended, combined.

sinister—*Syn.* bad, corrupt, dishonest, foreboding, disastrous, dire, woeful, deleterious. *Ant.* auspicious, lucky, fortunate, opportune, hopeful, timely, propitious.

sketch—*Syn.* portrayal, picture, draft, drawing, design, outline, form, shape, plan, painting, skeleton, figure, figuration, configuration, depiction, illustration, tracing, copy, likeness, description, report, summary, brief, monograph, memoir. *Ant.* erasure, deletion, cancellation, obliteration, blot, distortion, travesty, caricature, daub, derangement, travesty.

skilful—*Syn.* handy, proficient, efficient, apt, ingenious, adroit, adept, capable, smart. *Ant.* unskilled, bungling, blundering, inept, unqualified, untrained, incompetent.

slander—*Syn.* asperse, defame, malign, calumniate, detract, depreciate, defame, belittle, criticize,, malign. *Ant.* praise, applaud, eulogize, vindicate, defend, laud, flatter, magnify, admire, commend, boost, approve.

slavery—*Syn.* servitude, drudgery, bondage, captivity, subjection, serfdom, restraint, involuntary, servitude. *Ant.* freedom, liberty, immunity, exemption, right, privilege, liberation, emancipation, independence.

sleep—*Syn.* slumber, doze, drowse, nap, hibernate. *Ant.* exercise, walk, run.

slow—*Syn.* sluggish, slack, lingering, inert, inactive, delaying, deliberate, dilatory, gradual, moderate, delaying, belated, late, passive, languid, torpid, remiss. *Ant.* fast, quick, active, agile, swift, spry, speedy, sprightly, lively, alert, brisk, bustling.

smell—*Syn.* fragrance, odor, scent, perfume, exhalation, emanation. *Ant.* deodorization, cleanliness, purity, purification, disinfection.

smooth, *a.*—*Syn.* even, level, mild, uniform, regular, undeviating, unvarying, unwrinkled, tranquil, calm. *Ant.* rough, rugged, uneven, scraggy, jagged, corrugated, furrowed, rumpled.

sneer—*Syn.* mock, scoff, jeer, taunt, disparage, blame, slight, scorn. *Ant.* flatter, laud, applaud, praise, exalt, cheer, encourage.

soak—*Syn.* drench, wet, immerse, merge, drench, water, sponge, infiltrate, saturate. *Ant.* dry, remove, press, squeeze, drain, dehydrate, evaporate.

social—*Syn.* sociable, friendly, communicative, companionable, convivial. *Ant.* unsociable, disagreeable, discourteous, inhospitable, secluded, morose, sullen, solitary.

soft—*Syn.* gentle, meek, mild, pliant, yielding, pliable, bland, tender, supple, flexible. *Ant.* hard, rocky, rigid, stubborn, stiff, unbending.

solemn—*Syn.* grave, serious, formal, sober, important, notable, outstanding, momentous, salient, prominent. *Ant.* unimportant, common, ordinary, mean, paltry, undignified, trivial.

solicit—*Syn.* ask, request, beg, importune, implore, entreat, desire, petition, conjure, invoke. *Ant.* protest, deprecate, disapprove, oppose.

solitary—*Syn.* sole, only, alone, single, lonely, separate, desolate, individual, secluded. *Ant.* sundry, various, many, numerous, manifold, crowded.

sorry—*Syn.* grieved, paltry, insignificant, dismal, unimportant, base. *Ant.* glad, joyous, rejoicing, happy, contented.

sound, *a.*—*Syn.* healthy, wholesome, unimpaired, whole, entire, vigorous, hale, strong, hardy, stanch, robust, sturdy, stalwart, perfect, unblemished, intact, stable, durable, unyielding, sterling, substantial, good, prime, excellent, genuine, reliable. *Ant.* decayed, impaired, injured, defective, deficient, broken, cracked, weak, delicate, affected, unsound, sick, sickly, wasted, deteriorated.

sound, *n.*—*Syn.* noise, tone, note, resonance, intonation, din, clamor, outcry, shout, roar, racket, hullabaloo, fanfare, peal, jangle, boom, explosion, detonation, bellow, thunder. *Ant.* silence, hush, lull, stillness, oblivion, quiet, stagnation.

sour—*Syn.* acid, tart, bitter, astringent, morose, crusty. *Ant.* sweet, pleasant, agreeable, cheerful, serene, civil, urbane, kind.

source—*Syn.* origin, cause, beginning, ancestor, foundation. *Ant.* effect, result, consequence, derivation, aftermath, issue, outcome, end, termination, conclusion.

speak—*Syn.* talk, utter, deliver, tell, say, express, pronounce, enunciate, declare, articulate, converse, communicate, proclaim, report. *Ant.* refrain, stop.

special—*Syn.* specific, particular, distinctive, exceptional, appropriate, extraordinary, uncommon, individual, determinate, definite, marked, typical. *Ant.* general, embracing, comprehensive, prevailing, wide, broad, all, every, universal.

specious—*Syn.* plausible, ostensible, probable, presumable, presumptive, credible, likely, apparent. *Ant.* improbable, unlikely, incredible, unexpected, inconceivable, unreasonable, doubtful, obscure.

speech—*Syn.* speaking, utterance, language, discourse, talk, oration, address, dissertation, delivery, lecture, communication, conversation. *Ant.* silence, stillness.

spend—*Syn.* expend, exhaust, sonsume, waste, dissipate, squander, empty, deplete, disperse, dispense, contribute, give. *Ant.* save, hoard, collect, gather, take in, acquire, get, receive, recover, gain, profit, win, earn, inherit.

spontaneous—*Syn.* involuntary, instinctive, unintentional, impulsive, automatic, unforced, irresistible, unintentional, unconscious. *Ant.* willing, intended, designed, devised, determined, premeditated, calculated, considered, driven.

sporadic—*Syn.* infrequent, rare, uncommon, isolated, separate, scattered. *Ant.* grouped, clustered, conglomerate, concentrated, frequent, constant, habitual, prevalent, general.

sport—*Syn.* play, game, diversion, amusement, fun, frolic, mockery, mirth, jest, entertainment. *Ant.* boredom, weariness, lassitude, tedium, monotony.

spread—*Syn.* disperse, diffuse, scatter, expand, extend, propagate, disseminate, prepare, dispense, distribute, strew. *Ant.* assemble, collect, muster, unite, herd, crowd.

spring—*Syn.* fountain, source, beginning, origin, cause, principle, rise, commencement, inception, start, outset, opening, initiation. *Ant.* end, finish, effect, result, termination, completion, consummation, finale.

spry—*Syn.* nimble, active, vigorous, quick, agile, lively, frisky, swift, fast, keen, alert, brisk. *Ant.* dull, dejected, weary, depressed, gloomy, heavy, sullen, weak, tottering, infirm.

spurious—*Syn.* counterfeit, fictitious, false, fraudulent, dishonest, erroneous, deceptive, faked, fabricated, misrepresented. *Ant.* genuine, real, true, proven, tested, authorized, positive, undeniable, immutable, indisputable.

squalid—*Syn.* dirty, filthy, unclean, poor, grimy, soiled, foul, reeking, nasty, abominable, odious, repellent, musty, offensive. *Ant.* clean, spotless, sweet, attractive, spruce, neat, tidy, trim, washed, disinfected, comfortable.

stable—*Syn.* unchanging, lasting, abiding, fixed, durable, enduring, steady, constant, firm, established, steadfast, immutable, settled. *Ant.* movable, unsteady, shaking, unsettled, mobile, wavering, variable, restless, erratic.

stain—*Syn.* blot, speck, spot, tarnish, blur, blotch, mark, tinge, color, discolor, soil, tint, dye, sully, disgrace, dishonor, blemish, impair. *Ant.* clean, wash, purify, clarify, decorate, embellish.

state, *n.*—*Syn.* commonwealth, realm, government, empire, monarchy, republic, sovereignty, dominion, territory, principality, command, sway, rule, property, estate, assets, means, chattels, resources, condition, character, predicament, dilemma.

state, *v.*—*Syn.* declare, testify, tell, inform, avow, certify, assert, specify, depose, allege, pronounce, claim, say, protest, swear, propound, aver, affirm, express, maintain, assure, predicate, report, mention, communicate, signify, disclose, announce. *Ant.* contradict, repudiate, disprove, dispute, deny, refute, waive, retract, controvert, oppose, conceal, hide, suppress, withhold, disclaim, disown, renounce, forswear, retract, impugn, ignore, recant, dissent.

stately—*Syn.* dignified, imposing, elevated, proud, majestic, grand, magnificent, imperious, haughty, stiff. *Ant.* humble, poor, obscure, modest, retiring, abashed, timid, timorous, unostentatious, reserved.

sterile—*Syn.* barren, unproductive, unfruitful, destitute, bare, impotent, incomplete, unfinished, unprofitable, infertile. *Ant.* fertile, productive, fruitful, prolific, copious, plentiful, proliferous, luxuriant, profuse.

stern—*Syn.* severe, austere, rigorous, harsh, cruel, unrelenting, unfeeling, determined, resolute, unyielding, unbending, grim, resolved, firm, strict. *Ant.* gentle, kind, considerate, lenient, compassionate, indulgent, easy.

storm—*Syn.* agitation, tempest, hurricane, disturbance, commotion, perturbation, turmoil, turbulence, fury. *Ant.* tranquillity, calm, quiet, rest, silence, stillness, solemnity, serenity.

stormy—*Syn.* rough, boisterous, tempestuous, raging, violent, excitable, angry, excited, fierce, furious, agitated, turbulent. *Ant.* cool, calm, collected, composed, patient, demure, steady, gentle.

story—*Syn.* novel, tale, anecdote, fable, fiction, myth, legend, narrative, sketch, account, incident. *Ant.* annals, history, biography, memoirs, chronicle, autobiography, essay, commentary.

straight—*Syn.* direct, right, rectilinear, undeviating, unswerving, upright, erect, regular, honest, reliable, honorable, good. *Ant.* crooked, distorted, twisted, bent, curved, deviating, swerving, wavering, unreliable, deceptive.

strange—*Syn.* unrelated, irrelevant, remote, detached, apart, inapplicable, dissociated, irregular, wandering, unaccustomed, queer, quaint, extraordinary. *Ant.* common, commonplace, ordinary, trite, expected, unimportant, trivial, trifling, usual, well-known, plain, regular, formal, familiar, normal, average, prevailing.

strong—*Syn.* robust, sturdy, powerful, forceful, mighty, muscular, vigorous, energetic, tough, virile. *Ant.* weak, feeble, delicate, ailing, infirm, ill, emaciated, fragile.

stupid—*Syn.* dull, foolish, obtuse, senseless, stolid, heavy, sluggish, unintelligent, shallow. *Ant.* quick, sharp, keen, alert, comprehensive, comprehending.

stupidity—*Syn.* slowness, apathy, inertia, insensibility, shallowness, asininity, incompetence, ineptitude. —*Syn.* quickness, sense, sensibility, sagacity, cleverness, alertness, acuteness, intelligence, brilliancy.

stupor—*Syn.* insensibility, lethargy, apathy, coma, fainting, swooning, unconsciousness, torpor, trance. *Ant.* feeling, susceptibility, consciousness, sensibility.

subject—*Syn.* liable, submissive, obedient, susceptible, responsible, accountable, subjugate, servile, inferior. *Ant.* unconstrained, uncontrolled, unrestricted, unlimited, absolute, free, superior, above, exempt.

subsequent—*Syn.* succeeding, following, after, afterward, consequent, secondary, next, ensuing, later. *Ant.* preceding, prior, antecedent, earlier, previous, former, aforesaid, aforegoing.

subsidy—*Syn.* grant, gift, bonus, tribute, gratuity, allowance, aid, bounty, support. *Ant.* check, barrier, prevention, restraint, hindrance, restriction, opposition, objection, impediment.

substantial—*Syn.* solid, durable, lasting, strong, firm, material, ponderable. *Ant.* immaterial, incorporal, tenuous, intangible.

subvert—*Syn.* overturn, overthrow, suppress, supplant, supersede, invert, depress, upset, reverse. *Ant.* erect, raise, heighten, uplift, construct, build, organize, accomplish, establish, preserve, sustain.

succeed—*Syn.* prevail, accomplish, get, obtain, achieve, attain, flourish, win, thrive, acquire, procure, profit, realize, recover, retrieve, gain, overcome, surmount, conquer, triumph. *Ant.* fail, lose, forfeit, give up, abandon, miss, blunder.

suffer—*Syn.* feel, bear, experience, sustain, permit, allow, tolerate, submit, endure, support, allow, admit, collapse. *Ant.* conquer, vanquish, banish, exclude, discard, overcome.

suggestion—*Syn.* hint, intimation, insinuation, innuendo, implication, plan, scheme, opinion, project, design, proposition, outline, sketch, draft, copy, prospectus, recommendation, charge, exhortation. *Ant.* reserve, silence, suppression, concealment, taciturnity, secrecy, reticence, reservation.

superficial—*Syn.* flimsy, cursory, hasty, desultory, shallow, summary, partial, outward, external. *Ant.* deep, bottomless, submerged, profound, learned, accomplished, informed, shrewd, astute, discerning, intelligent, experienced.

superfluous—*Syn.* unnecessary, excessive, inordinate, exorbitant, extravagant, profuse, saturated. *Ant.* scarce, scanty, few, little, small, wanting, lacking, innsufficient, inadequate, devoid.

supernatural—*Syn.* superhuman, spectral, occult, mysterious, secret, unknown, unrevealed, dark, mystic, mythical, legendary, inscrutable, undiscernible, obscure, invisible. *Ant.* natural, plain, common, ordinary, known, usual, explainable, intelligible, manifest, evident.

support—*Syn.* prop, maintain, uphold, hold up, sustain, bear, carry, cherish, preserve, guard, aid, assist, help, contribute, subscribe, forward, advance, expedite, advocate, defend. *Ant.* abandon, desert, destroy, hinder, impede, obstruct, encumber, frustrate, discourage, undermine.

suppose—*Syn.* conjecture, guess, surmise, imagine, presume, infer, deduce, suspect, assume, fancy, speculate, presuppose. *Ant.* ascertain, know, prove, discover, conclude, determine, trace, detect, decide, define, resolve, settle.

surrender—*Syn.* sacrifice, yield, capitulate, cede, give, relinquish, abandon, submit, comply. *Ant.* conquer, overcome, triumph, surmount, defeat, outdo, override, repulse, rebuff.

surround—*Syn.* encompass, circle, enclose, beset, besiege, blockade. *Ant.* intervene, interfere, insert, introduce.

suspend—*Syn.* discontinue, cease, desist, check, halt, interrupt, delay, postpone, defer, delay, adjourn, reserve. *Ant.* continue, persist, maintain, expedite, accelerate, support, sustain, brace.

sustain—*Syn.* maintain, support, bear, uphold, assist, relieve, endure, contribute, relieve. *Ant.* hinder, impede, prevent, thwart, frustrate, weaken, stop, block, oppose, contradict, forsake.

sway, *n.*—*Syn.* rule, influence, power, dominion, control, domination, force, weight, prerogative, jurisdiction, strength. *Ant.* impotence, inability, disability, incapacity, ineptitude, futility.

sweet—*Syn.* pleasant, agreeable, fragrant, gentle, melodious, attractive. *Ant.* sour, acid, astringent, vinegary, repellent, repulsive, revolting.

sycophant—*Syn.* parasite, sponger, hangeron, puppet, groveler, sniveler. *Ant.* master, dictator, commander, chief, overlord, leader, director.

symmetry—*Syn.* proportion, arrangement, order, equality, regularity, conformity, agreement, finish, evenness, balance, equilibrium. *Ant.* disproportion, inequality, irregularity, disparity, difference, disagreement, deformity, contortion, distortion.

sympathy—*Syn.* compassion, condolence, cordiality, harmony, alliance, concord, tenderness, pity, kindness. *Ant.* hatred, enmity, animosity, bitterness, aversion, dislike, hostility.

synonymous—*Syn.* same, like, similar, equivalent, identical, correspondent, corresponding, alike, interchangable, covertible, apposite, compatible, coincident. *Ant.* unlike, dissimilar, diverse, different, opposed, opposite, contrary, conflicting, divergent, unidentical, disparate, contradictory, converse, reverse, incongruous.

system—*Syn.* method, plan, order, regularity, rule, manner, mode, scheme, way, policy, artifice, operation, arrangement, program. *Ant.* chaos, confusion, disorder, derangement, disarrangement, irregularity, complication.

systematic—*Syn.* regular, orderly, methodical, precise, punctual, formal, uniform, steady, constant, habitual, customary, recognized. *Ant.* confused, irregular, informal, rare, unconventional, desultory, disorderly, uncertain.

systematize—*Syn.* plan, arrange, organize, order, contrive, project, devise, design. *Ant.* confuse, disorder, disarrange, mess, unsettle, complicate, entangle.

T

taboo—*Syn.* prohibit, inhibit, interdict, forbid, prevent, ban, disallow. *Ant.* permit, allow, sanction, license, grant, privilege, admit.

taciturn—*Syn.* reserved, reticent, uncommunicative, silent, mute, laconic. *Ant.* garrulous, talkative, loquacious.

tact—*Syn.* perception, discrimination, judgement, acuteness, penetration, intelligence, ability, aptness. *Ant.* vulgarity, coarseness, misconduct, misbehavior, blunder.

tainted—*Syn.* infected, diseased, decayed, corrupt, vitiated, contaminated, rank, rancid, polluted, impaired, damaged. *Ant.* pure, fresh, clean, sound, wholesome, good, excellent, unblemished, strong, vigorous.

take—*Syn.* accept, receive, acquire, pocket, appropriate, seize, abstract, snatch, capture, collar, clutch, recover, remove, obtain. *Ant.* give, donate, contribute, bestow, present, deliver, allow, leave, grant, relinquish, restore, return, redeem, render.

tasteful—*Syn.* delicious, delectable, pleasing, gratifying, esthetic. *Ant.* coarse, vulgar, rough, rude, harsh, low, ribald, gaudy, gross, clumsy, distasteful, offensive, fulsome.

tax—*Syn.* custom, duty, impost, excise, toll, levy, assessment, rate, tribute, contribution, tariff, dues. *Ant.* discount, rebate, allowance, reduction, deduction, favor.

teach—*Syn.* educate, instruct, tutor, train, school, enlighten, indoctrinate, initiate, inform, drill, imbue, disseminate, expound, prepare, qualify, coach, illustrate, explain. *Ant.* learn, acquire, gain, receive, study, read, cultivate, follow, imbibe, master, copy, imitate, peruse, glean.

tease—*Syn.* taunt, tantalize, disturb, annoy, irritate, harass, spite, aggravate, bother, pester, badger, anger, thwart, discomfort, provoke. *Ant.* comfort, console, solace, please, satiate, satisfy, indulge, flatter, refresh, stimulate, encourage.

tedious—*Syn.* slow, wearisome, tiresome, irksome, tardy, lingering, uninteresting, monotonous, drowsy. *Ant.* light, cheerful, lively, exhilerating, animating, diverting, interesting, compelling.

temerity—*Syn.* audacity, boldness, rashness, presumption, precipitation, indiscretion, imprudence, impetuosity. *Ant.* caution, foresight, deliberation, care, prudence, discretion, coolness, vigilance, circumspection, calculation, wisdom, waiting.

temperate—*Syn.* cool, calm, impassionate, mild, moderate, genial, quiet, still, smooth, unruffled, dispassionate, unperturbed, unexcited, patient, sparing, abstemious. *Ant.* forceful, boisterous, vehement, shocking, outrageous, furious, mad, angry, raging, tempestuous, stormy, enraged, exasperated, boiling, rampaging, ranting, raving, roaring, uncontrolled, frantic, frenetic.

temporary—*Syn.* transitory, transient, fleeting, short, brief, momentary, impermanent. *Ant.* lasting, permanent, unchangeable, fixed, durable, persistent, chronic, protracted, persistent, prolonged, extended, endless, perpetual.

tenacious—*Syn.* tough, perverse, stubborn, obstinate, persistent, unyielding, retentive, sticky, cohesive, inseparable, resisting, persevering, resolute, determined, uncompromising. *Ant.* loose, lax, detached, fragile, frail, vacillating, unstable, timid.

tendency—*Syn.* aim, drift, scope, leaning, bias, tone, bent, turn, trend, disposition, inclination, aptitude, aim, direction, object, goal. *Ant.* aimlessness, thoughtlessness, oversight, negligence, neglect, omission, default, inattention, apathy.

tenet—*Syn.* view, conviction, belief, position, faith, trust, opinion, impression, doctrine, system, principle, presumption, assumption. *Ant.* disbelief misbelief, misgiving, mistrust, scruple, qualm, doubt, distrust, suspicion, uncertainty, vagueness, incredulity.

term—*Syn.* expression, phrase, word, name, denomination, member, article, condition, time, period, limit, boundary, end, finish, season, course, cycle, interval, interim, confine. bourne, border, verge, terminal, landmark, margin, line of demarcation, appellation, designation, title, head, caption, cognomen, patronymic, nickname, nomenclature, station, rank, degree, status, standing.

terse—*Syn.* short, succinct, laconic, compact, neat, concise, brief, exact, pointed. *Ant.* tedious, wearisome, vapid, tiresome, profuse, wordy, long, lengthy, diffuse, redundant, rambling.

testimony—*Syn.* proof, evidence, affirmation, confirmation, affidavit, witness, deposition, certification, attestation, declaration, warrant, credentials, voucher. *Ant.* protestation, refutuation, subversion, contraventionn, opposition, rebuttal, denial, dissent.

thankful—*Syn.* grateful, obliged, gratified, contented, satisfied, pleased, kindly, disposed, molified, assuaged. *Ant.* ungrateful, unmindful, careless, insensible, ingrate, forgetful, unsatisfied, grumbling, critical, censorious, dissatisfied, discontented.

thaw—*Syn.* melt, dissolve, flow, run, calm, cool. *Ant.* freeze, solidify, congeal, refrigerate, chill, petrify, incite, become, excited, rage, rampage, storm, act.

theatrical—*Syn.* dramatic, showy ceremonious, affected, spectacular, ostentatious, melodramatic, pretentious, formal, prim, prudish, simpering, sentimental, gradiose, demonstrative, pompous, overbearing. *Ant.* humble, modest, reserved, retiring, bashful, diffident, coy, sheepish, timid, unassuming, unpretentious, unaffected, unobtrusive, unostentatious, demure, shy, unpretending, nervous.

theft—*Syn.* robbery, depredation, pillage, plunder, appropriation, burglary. *Ant.* restoration, amends, restitution, return, indemnification, indemnity.

theme—*Syn.* subject, topic, test, essay, writing, dissertation, proposition, matter, thesis, discourse, composition, conversation, tale, story, legend, talk, feature, statement, report, narrative, description.

theory—*Syn.* hypothesis, conjecture, speculation, scheme, plea, supposition, surmise, attribution, perception, assumption. *Ant.* ignorance, darkness, blindness, chance, probability, possibility, guess, indetermination, contingence.

therefore—*Syn.* accordingly, consequently, hence, because, wherefore, for, since, by reason, for this reason, on account of.

thick—*Syn.* dense, close, crowded, solid, compact, coagulated, solidified, consolidated, heavy. *Ant.* rare, rarefied, airy, tenuous, subtle, unsubstantial, light, spongy, compressible, clear, transparent.

thin—*Syn.* slight, slender, slim, flimsy, lean, skeletal, gaunt, attenuated, tenuous, rare, spare, scarce, scanty. *Ant.* thick, fat, ample, solid, abundant, profuse, full, heavy, massive, ponderous, obese, swollen, inflated, puffed.

think—*Syn.* cogitate, muse, ponder, imagine, suppose, expect, fancy, guess, conjecture, consider, meditate, reckon, deem, believe, contemplate, reflect, conceive, regard, hold, esteem, deliberate, study, spec ulate, reason, ruminate. *Ant.* put away thought, relax the mind.

thorough—*Syn.* complete, perfect, reliable, trustworthy, accurate, correct, full, absolute, exhaustive, sweeping, radical. *Ant.* shallow, superficial, incomplete, inadequate, inefficient, unsatisfactory, unreliable, sketchy, crude, perfunctory, deficient, imperfect, garbled.

thought—*Syn.* sentiment, conception, consideration, reflection, imagination, supposition, opinion, view, idea, reflection, notion, provision, deliberation, mediation, speculation, image, perception, sentiment, apprehension, contemplation. *Ant.* thoughtlessness, vacancy, inanity, fatuity, incogitance, inattention, unreasoning, emptiness.

thoughtful—*Syn.* thinking, meditative, cogitative, absorbed, pensive, philosophic, studious, speculative, deliberative, reflective, sedate, acute, sharp, quick, cautious, rational, intelligent, discerning, wise, sagacious. *Ant.* thoughtless, heedless, careless, indifferent, shallow, stupid, heavy, obtuse.

throng—*Syn.* multitude, mass, assembly, crowd, jam, press, muster, gathering, meeting, congregation, group, company, body, clan, colloc tion, cluster, pack, mass, conglomeration. *Ant.* scarcity, sparsity, paucity, fraction, handful, scattering, dispersion, distribution, spread.

tie, *n.*—*Syn.* band, ligament, ligature, yoke, fastening, security, link, connection, bond, coupling, strap, tackle, bandage, brace. *Ant.* separation, division, break, severance, detachment.

tie, *v.*—*Syn.* bind, restrain, restrict, secure, unite, join, shackle, tether, hitch, fetter, fasten, fix, engage, moor, attach. *Ant.* loose, free, unloose, unbind, unfasten, detach, displace, unfix, loosen, change, disturb, separate.

time—*Syn.* duration, age, period, season, era, eon, epoch, term, sequence, while, course, succession, date, span, spell, stage, interval, interim, cycle, present, past, future.

timid—*Syn.* fearful, shy, diffident, timorous, afraid, humble, frightened, nervous, shaky, apprehensive, wavering, faltering. *Ant.* brave, bold, courageous, undaunted, resolved, determined, resolute, daring, unafraid, fearless.

tire—*Syn.* weary, exhaust, harass, fatigue, irk, strain, overwork. *Ant.* refresh, invigorate, inspirit, regale, enliven, freshen, stimulate, incite, energize, inspire, encourage, amuse, entertain, divert, interest, relax, relieve, rest, restore, rouse.

tolerate—*Syn.* permit, allow, suffer, endure, admit, let, abide, indulge, concede, recognize, accord, license, authorize, warrant, sanction, submit, stand, bear, swallow. *Ant.* prohibit, inhibit, forbid, taboo, disallow, hinder, prevent, restrict, veto, disapprove, deprecate, censure, remonstrate, protest, check, preclude, restrain.

topic—*Syn.* theme, subject, text, thesis, material, proposition, resolution, motion, argument, point, matter, problem, division, head, issue.

torture—*Syn.* pain, anguish, agony, torment, rack, pang, ache, twinge, suffering. *Ant.* enjoyment, delight, gratification, comfort, bliss, pleasure.

tough—*Syn.* stubborn, hardened, refractory, tenacious, strong, firm, seasoned, hard, unyielding, resisting, difficult, coherent, savage, uproarious, fierce, brutal, ferocious, onerous, intricate. *Ant.* mild, amendable, gentle, kind, good, tractable, yielding, complaisant, compliant, submissive, dutiful, obedient, docile, controllable, quiet, deferential, subservient, passive.

trace—*Syn.* sign, mark, impression, trail, remains, vestige, track, remnant, token, record, indication, index, indicator, symbol, scent, wake, representation, monument, memento, characteristic. *Ant.* obliteration, deletion, extinction, cancellation, suppression, oblivion, destruction, demolition, abolition, dissolution, devastation.

trade—*Syn.* business, exchange, barter, traffic, speculation, sales, commerce, dealing, employment, office, occupation, calling, profession, line, job, situation, position, trading, undertaking, pursuit, province, function, craft, vocation, affair, concern, case, matter, art, handicraft, work transaction, duty, avocation.

train, *n.*—*Syn.* series, sequel, sequence, trail, procession, retinue, line, tail, succession, attendants, henchmen, retainers, followers, following.

train, *v*—*Syn.* lead, accustom, habituate, drill, exercise, practice, discipline, instruct, bend, educate, aim, direct, teach, prepare, qualify, initiate, familiarize with, inculcate, indoctrinate, implant, guide, school, enlighten, prime, coach, inform, equip. *Ant.* misguide, misrepresent, mislead, misdirect, pervert, deceive.

trammel—*Syn.* impede, hinder, obstruct, hamper, shackle, fetter, restrain, check, encumber, cramp, retard, oppose, incommode, discompose, thwart, frustrate, gag, bind, tie. *Ant.* help, assist, succor, encourage, animate, incite, inspirit, stimulate, aid, advance, sustain, support, relieve, uphold, serve, minister to, nurtur, tend, oblige.

tranquil—*Syn.* calm, peaceful, unruffled, quiet, still, hushed, undisturbed, restful, composed, smooth, tame, untroubled, pacific, gentle, soft, low, soothing. *Ant.* noisy, tumultuous, violent, rough, clamorous, blaring, disturbing, furious, distracting.

transact—*Syn.* do, act, perform, accomplish, treat, negotiate, conduct, achieve, execute, work, operate, officiate. *Ant.* idle, lounge, dawdle, slouch, lag, loiter, inactive.

transaction—*Syn.* doing, proceeding, business, act, affair, matter, deed, action, event, happening, deal, sale, buying, purchase, disposal.

transcendental—*Syn.* primordial, original, intuitive, intellectual, beyond, grasp, unintelligible, innate, vague, obscure, fantastic. *Ant.* plain, clear, evident, obvious, intelligible, manifest, distinct, transparent, definite, positive, simple.

transient—*Syn.* brief, transitory, temporary, passing, momentary, short, fleeting, impermanent. *Ant.* lasting, permanent, durable, enduring, persistent, chronic, perpetual, unending, incessant.

travel—*Syn.* journey, tour, voyage, expedition, excursion, pilgrimage, trip, tramp, ramble, wandering, itinerary, march, migration, exodus, course, circuit. *Ant.* rest, cessation, sleep, slumber, stop, pause, halt, inaction, stability, disconntinuance.

treacherous—*Syn.* false, faithless, treasonable, unfaithful, unntrustworthy, unreliable, deceitful, malicious, venomous, base, inglorious, evil, ignominious, disloyal. *Ant.* true, faithful, trustworthy, reliable, dependable, friendly, affectionate, kind, loving.

trenchant—*Syn.* sharp, keen, severe, cutting, critical, energetic, emphatic, assertive, vigorous, strong, powerful, important, ironical, pointed, intense, vivid, poignant, positive, salient, significant, spirited. *Ant.* weak, feeble, vacillating, light, unimportant, shallow, simple, unimpressive, obscure, ambiguous, diffuse, pointless.

trite—*Syn.* hackneyed, common, commonplace, ordinary, dull, stupid, old, ancient, stale, familiar, known. *Ant.* fresh, keen, sharp, interesting, new, novel, appealing, moving, proper, opportune, becoming.

triumph, *n.*—*Syn.* victory, conquest, mastery, achievement, ovation, exultation, success, boast, celebration, gain, advantage. *Ant.* defeat, vanquishment, repulse, loss, rout, ruin, destruction, calamity, catastrophe, reverse, setback, disaster.

trivial—*Syn.* petty, trifling, small, piddling, insignificant, frivolous, unimportant, diminutive, slight, scanty, meager, inappreciable, inconsiderable, minute, unessential, paltry, worthless. *Ant.* great, large, massive, ponderous, heavy, important, serious, grave, consequential, mighty, ample, significant, essential, vital, useful.

true—*Syn.* real, accurate, veracious, reliable, trustworthy, straight, honorable, honest, dependable, sincere, exact, correct, actual, sincere, precise, factual, literal, positive, absolute, legitimate, definite, valid. *Ant.* false, fickle, disloyal, fictional, lying, fabulous, mythical, ideal, imaginary, incorrect, erroneous, illusive, illusory, wrong, inaccurate, inexact.

trust, *n.*—*Syn.* belief, confidence, credit, faith, hope, dependence, assurance, reliance, conviction, security, benefit, interest. *Ant.* disbelief, distrust, doubt, scruple, suspicion, incredibility, skepticism, debt, default, surrender, dereliction, renunciation.

trust, *v.*—*Syn.* believe, credit, consider, esteem, confide in, depend upon, intrust. *Ant.* distrust, disbelieve, doubt, impugn, assail, discredit, scruple, hesitate.

trustworthy—*Syn.* reliable, honest, honorable, true, veracious, candid, sincere, steady, constant, square, decent, incorrupt, reputable, respectable, sincere. *Ant.* faithful, unreliable, corrupt, underhand, irregular, unsteady, dishonest, infamous.

truth—*Syn.* veracity, probity, honor, sincerity, candor, openness, honesty, fidelity, verity, authenticity, accuracy, exactness. *Ant.* falsehood, lying, prevarication, fabrication, falsification, deception, invention, evasion.

try—*Syn.* attempt, assay, endeavor, aim, strive, risk, tackle, test, experiment, venture, adventure, speculate, use, handle, manipulate. *Ant.* leave off, cast aside, prejudge, neglect, avoid, shun.

tumultuous—*Syn.* turbulent, violent, boisterous, disorderly, uproarious, lawless, riotous, noisy, excited, rowdy, rough, raging, clamorous, passionate, uncontrolled, shaking, tremulous, rebellious, demonstrative, vociferous. *Ant.* peaceful, quiet, restful, muffled, tame, subdued, unexcited, silent, modest, pacific, moderate, still, calm, unruffled, passive, composed.

type—*Syn.* symbol, emblem, figure, character, letter, representative, representation, sign, sort, kind, pattern, form, class, model, standard, original, example, sample, copy, design, genus, species, variety, caste, clan, sept, breed, assortment, cast, mould, shape. *Ant.* amorphism, misproportion, deformity, monstrosity, abnormality, deviation, malformation, distortion, unconformity, peculiarity, teratism, freak, anomaly, anomalousness, shapelessness.

tyro—*Syn.* novice, beginner, learner, neophyte. *Ant.* expert, proficient, adept, scholar, connoisseur, master, teacher, guide, leader, tribune, *doyen [Fr.],* seer, wizard, genius, prodigy, veteran, old stager, sage, thinker, star.

ugly—*Syn.* homely, plain, unsightly, unseemly, offensive, hideous, forbidding, dour, unshapely, unpleasant. *Ant.* beautiful, handsome, nice, fair, pretty, lovely, charming, captivating, fascinating, graceful, elegant, radiant, splendid, appealing, attractive.

umbrage—*Syn.* dissatisfaction, displeasure, resentment, offense, hatred, contempt, harsh feeling, estrangement, grudge, antipathy, bitterness, resentment, aversion, alienation, enmity, malice, detestation, animosity, spite. *Ant.* love, sympathy, affection, esteem, admiration, respect, regard, tenderness, friendliness, amity, good-will, unselfishness, consideration.

umpire—*Syn.* arbiter, arbitrator, judge, referee, justice, moderator, mediator, negotiator, settler. *Ant.* partisan, adherent, follower, client, sympathizer, enemy, foe, opponent.

unanimity—*Syn.* accord, agreement, unity, unison, concord, concordance, sympathy, aptitude. *Ant.* discord, disagreement, dissonance, break, shock, jar, jostling, quarrel.

uncouth—*Syn.* ungainly, awkward, odd, strange, ungraceful, vulgar, boorish, rude. *Ant.* handsome, symmetrical, easy, graceful, shapely, pleasing, elegant, refined, genteel, courteous.

understand—*Syn.* comprehend, learn, apprehend, know, perceive, discern, recognize, conceive, imply, interpret. *Ant.* misunderstand, misconstrue, misinterpret, garble, muddle, twist, render, obscure, mix, confuse.

understanding—*Syn.* intellect, intelligence, reason, knowledge, mind, comprehension, mentality, capacity, conception, wisdom. *Ant.* unwisdom, foolishness, aberration, incapacity, stupidity, simplicity.

undoing—*Syn.* ruin, ruination, downfall, reversal, destruction, misfortune, trouble, grief, catastrophe, casualty, accident, mishap, infliction, adversity, reverse, blow, trial, loss. *Ant.* prosperity, fortune, blessing, enjoyment, renown, glory, delight, success, triumph, victory, advantage.

uneasy—*Syn.* restless, disturbed, anxious, troubled, fearful, timid, apprehensive, nervous, frightened, shaky, fearful, suspicious, unsettled, irritable. *Ant.* steady, firm, sober, constant, staid, dismayed, calm, cool, collected, settled, stable, immutable, content, resigned.

unequal—*Syn.* uneven, irregular, unlike, inadequate, different, disparate, unbalanced, wanting, lacking. *Ant.* equal, balanced, even, full, sufficient, same, matched, equivalent, coequal, invariable, regular, constant, steady, unchanging.

unfortunate—*Syn.* unlucky, disastrous, calamitous, unhappy, wretched, miserable, undone, lost, abandoned, deserted, ruined. *Ant.* fortunate, happy, successful, healthy, triumphant, affluent, advantageous, beneficial, lucky.

ungainly—*Syn.* clumsy, awkward, unskilled, unfit, unweildly, bungling, unhandy, slovenly, gawky, unqualified, green, inept, stiff, rough, ungracious, unmannerly, brutish, brutal, boorish, bearish. *Ant.* smart, quick, active, neat, attractive, refined, expert, appealing, comely, fair, dainty, fit, alert.

uniform—*Syn.* even, alike, symmetrical, equal, regular, agreeing, consistent, unchanging, homogeneous, unvarying, normal, constant, stable, steady. *Ant.* irregular, uneven, distorted, askew, awry, crooked, misproportioned, grotesque, jumbled, confused, twisted.

union—*Syn.* unity, unification, unison, oneness, junction, combination, conjunction, cooperation, coalition, concert, connection, concord, alliance, harmony, association, attachment, agreement, unanimity, conjugation, blending, absorption, amalgam, compound, amalgamation. *Ant.* difference, divergence, opposition, disagreement, discord, disunity, incongruity, disparity, inequality, disproportion, variance, conflict, separation, division, rupture, break.

unique—*Syn.* rare, uncommon, choice, different, unlike, original, unparalleled, individual, unusual, remarkable, sole, bizarre, outlandish. *Ant.* common, commonplace, ordinary, normal, everyday, regular, resembling, close, twin, equal, conventional, customary, universal, prevailing.

universal—*Syn.* general, entire, whole, complete, comprehensive, total, unlimited, all, sweeping, widespread, prevailing. *Ant.* special, private, individual, sectional, distinctive, unique, limited, narrow, particular, definite, certain, partial, singular, restricted, bounded, confined, small, circumscribed, terminable, defined, ringed.

unseemly—*Syn.* unfit, undesirable, unsuitable, inept, objectionable, inappropriate, inopportune, improper, gross, ungraceful, unkempt, uncouth. *Ant.* desirable, expedient, acceptable, convenient, fitting, becoming, seemly, practicable, refined, cultured, polished, suave, courteous, artistic, cultivated, correct, proper, decorous, right, worthy, commendable, righteous, moral, admirable, deserving.

urgent—*Syn.* pressing, compelling, necessary, imperative, important, serious, momentous, required, salient, impressive, chief, paramount, essential, critical, vital, hasty. *Ant.* slow, dilatory, unnecessary, trifling, trivial, slight, unimportant, unessential, irrelevant, petty, frivolous, immaterial, insignificant, uninteresting, inconsiderable, common, subordinate.

usual—*Syn.* general, habitual, normal, accustomed, frequent, familiar, ordinary, prevalent, regular, common, public, prevailing, customary, conventional, formal, recognized. *Ant.* unusual, rare, infrequent, strange, unconventional, odd, unique, extraordinary, remarkable, noteworthy, abnormal, exceptional, unaccustomed.

usurp—*Syn.* assume, arrogate, appropriate, seize, assume, claim, encroach, take, exact, wrest, oppress, override, trample, violate, dominate. *Ant.* indulge, tolerate, spare, restore, recoup, compensate, indemnify, reinstate, return, allow, grant, permit, exempt, concede.

utility—*Syn.* use, usefullness, service. advantage, convenience, benefit, expediency, profit, avail, favor, efficacy, adequacy. *Ant.* disadvantage, unfitness, inefficiency, disservice, ineptitude, uselessness.

utter, *v.*—*Syn.* speak, express, talk, articulate, pronounce, issue, voice, declare, say, assert, enunciate, deliver, emit, vocalize, recite, proclaim, acclaim, disclose, divulge, reveal, inform, tell, diffuse. *Ant.* muffle, suppress, keep secret.

utterly—*Syn.* completely, entirely, totally, fully, wholly, altogether, quite, exclusively, absolutely, unreservedly, assuredly, positively.

vacant—*Syn.* void, unoccupied, idle, uncrowded, unfilled, deserted, null, absent. *Ant.* full, filled, occupied, substantial, tangible, corporeal, solid, tenanted, congested, wise.

vagrant, *a.*—*Syn.* idle, wandering, roaming, traveling, roving. *Ant.* steady, staid, stable, sober, settled, fixed, stationary.

vague—*Syn.* uncertain, unsettled, indefinite, unsure, dubious, indeterminate, undefined, questionable. *Ant.* certain, sure, definite, real, doubtless, true.

valiant—*Syn.* brave. bold, courageous, daring, dauntless, intrepid, gallant. *Ant.* cowardly, fearful, afraid, shy, timid.

valid—*Syn.* sound, cogent, sufficient, substantial, real, authentic, genuine, legitimate, accurate, adequate. *Ant.* erroneous, erring, fallacious, false, dubious, uncertain, deceptive.

valor—*Syn.* bravery, courage, prowess, intrepidity, boldness, gallantry, heroism, fearlessness, chivalry. *Ant.* fear, cowardice, fright, dismay.

value, *n.*—*Syn.* worth, price, esteem, consideration, estimate, valuation, appreciation, charge, cost.

value, *v.*—*Syn.* esteem, estimate, reckon, assess, appraise, prize, treasure, appreciate, figure, compute. *Ant.* condemn, discard, relinquish, repudiate, abrogate, surrender, drop, renounce, abandon.

vanity—*Syn.* ostentation, display, show, conceit, pretension, assurance. *Ant.* modesty, diffidence, humility, unpretentious, timidity.

variance—*Syn.* change, fluctuation, deviation, modification, mutation, diversity, inconsistency. *Ant.* union, unity, sameness, equality, facsimile, agreement, harmony, unanimity, consistency.

variety—*Syn.* diversity, difference, medley, mixture, diversification, division, sort, species. *Ant.* monotony, unit, individual, identity.

vast—*Syn.* huge, colossal, spacious, enormous, mighty, bulky, great, large, unlimited, ample, extensive, expansive. *Ant.* small, little, narrow, confined, limited, petty, insignificant, paltry, slight, inconsiderable.

venerable—*Syn.* old, aged, serious, sage, wise, honored, esteemed. *Ant.* young, inexperienced, immature.

venom—*Syn.* poison, bane, malice, enmity, resentment, rancor. *Ant.* antidote, remedy, cure, panacea.

venture, *n.*—*Syn.* risk, hazard, peril, stake, chance, speculation, dare, experiment, trial, attempt, investment. *Ant.* intention, purpose, design, determination, decision, resolution.

venture, *v.*—*Syn.* attempt, essay, experience, try, speculate. *Ant.* plan, devise, reason, scheme, consider, meditate.

veracity—*Syn.* truth, accuracy, credibility, honesty, candor. *Ant.* lying, trickery, artifice.

verbal—*Syn.* oral, spoken, literal, vocal, unwritten, nominal, declamatory, talkative.

verdict—*Syn.* judgement, finding, decision, sentence, decree, result, conclusion. *Ant.* misjudgement, misconception, quirk, prejudice.

vibrate—*Syn.* swing, undulate, wave, sway, thrill, oscillate, quiver, fluctuate, alternate. *Ant.* stop, rest, pause, hold, close, cease, terminate, end, discontinue.

vice—*Syn.* corruption, depravity, immorality, crime, evil, defect, fault, lust. *Ant.* virtue, goodness, honor, decency, integrity.

vicious—*Syn.* corrupt, bad, base, degenerate, contrary, harmful, obnoxious. *Ant.* virtuous, good, gentle, innocent, upright, decent, noble, true, praiseworthy.

victory—*Syn.* conquest, triumph, success, achievement. *Ant.* defeat, retreat, rout, disaster, destruction, overthrow, failure, blunder.

vigilant—*Syn.* wary, watchful, cautious, alert, guarded, stealthy. *Ant.* careless, negligent, unwary.

violent—*Syn.* furious, vehement, angry, raging, mad, frenzied, turbulent, rampant. *Ant.* gentle, mild, tender, kindly, humble, quiet, smooth, composed.

virtue—*Syn.* chastity, sanctity, purity, morality, goodness, rectitude, honor, honesty, decency. *Ant.* vice, evil, dishonesty, fraud, outrage.

vision—*Syn.* phantom, apparition, image, shadow, ghost, wraith, dream. *Ant.* reality, substance, body, solidity, matter, fact, truth.

vision—*Syn.* sight, optics, glance, glimpse, peek, gaze, stare, view, look, survey, inspection, examination. *Ant.* blindness, darkness.

volatile—*Syn.* light, subtle, buoyant, sublimated. *Ant.* heavy, ponderous, serious, unwieldy.

vouch—*Syn.* assert, aver, attest, warrant, affirm, confirm, guarantee, declare, testify, assure, contend. *Ant.* deny, repudiate, discard, recant, rebut, confute, controvert.

vulgar—*Syn.* common, ordinary, uncouth, rude, uncultured, unpolished, rough, ignorant, inelegant, lowborn, offensive, impudent, impertinent, profane, dirty, nasty, boorish, clownish, plebeian, odious. *Ant.* refined, polite, polished, cultured, learned, accomplished, civil, elegant, graceful.

wait—*Syn.* tarry, linger, await, expect, adjourn, dally, idle. *Ant.* forestall, anticipate, hurry, quicken, accelerate, urge, spur, goad.

wander—*Syn.* roam, stray, range, rove, ramble, walk, move, shift, drift, glide, roll, roll on, journey, tramp, jog, digress, diverge, meander, rave. *Ant.* stay, pause, wait, remain, rest, repose, tarry, stick, halt, stop.

want—*Syn.* need, privation, penury, insufficiency, dearth, emptiness, depletion. *Ant.* plenty, profusion, abundance, wealth, riches, property, affluence, luxury, cornucopia.

wary—*Syn.* circumspect, cautious, alert, prudent, guarded, careful, vigilant. *Ant.* careless, thoughtless, unwary, impetuous, imprudent, impulsive, heedless, wanton, foolhardy.

waste—*Syn.* squander, destroy, scatter, spend, wither, decay, spoil, misuse, abuse, lose, exhaust, consume, deplete, empty. *Ant.* increase, serve, preserve, supplement, accomplish, achieve, provide, supply, provision, revive, render, useful, use.

wasteful—*Syn.* extravagant, squandering, careless. *Ant.* saving, hoarding, stingy.

way—*Syn.* path, track, street, avenue, road, course, lane, gateway, entrance, passage, plan, manner, form, process, procedure.

weak—*Syn.* feeble, infirm, soft, flaccid, relaxed, soft, fragile, delicate, sound, languid, shaky, faint, powerless. *Ant.* strong, stout, vigorous, muscular, robust, sturdy, husky, virile, potent, hard, sturdy, lusty, mighty, energetic.

wealth—*Syn.* money, riches, property, assets, affluence, pelf, possessions, prosperity, substance, goods, fortune, plenty. *Ant.* poverty, privation, want, scarcity, destitution, dearth, insufficiency.

wearisome—*Syn.* vapid, insipid, dull, sluggish, apathetic, phlegmatic, laborious, strenuous, drooping, difficult, heavy, troublesome. *Ant.* exhilarating, refreshing, stimulating, entertaining, charming.

weary—*Syn.* fatigue, tire, irritate, worry, vex, anger, bother, bore, fret, chafe, grieve, distress, displease, irk, exhaust, overburden, dishearten, deject, strain, dispirit. *Ant.* refresh, comfort, gladden, rejoice, regale, invigorate, inspire, animate, strengthen, revive, arouse, praise, calm.

weight—*Syn.* gravity, burden, load, ballast, mass, contents, freight, influence, domination, power, control. *Ant.* levity, lightness, buoyancy, volatility, nothingness, immateriality, unimportance, impotence.

well-being—*Syn.* happiness, prosperity, welfare, fortune, blessing, luck, success, health, affluence, riches, wealth. *Ant.* adversity, misfortune, trouble, hardship, poverty, sickness, calamity, catastrophe, blow, trial, sorrow, setback, drawback.

whole—*Syn.* entire, complete, total, integral, all, aggregate, full, absolute, undivided, inclusive. *Ant.* part, partial, incomplete, fractional, sectional, divided, imperfect, insufficient, wanting, short, broken, reduced.

wicked—*Syn.* iniquitous, nefarious, vile, wrong, vicious, erring, dissolute, disorderly, disreputable, corrupt, immoral, malevolent, base, foul, gross, atrocious, scandalous, infamous. *Ant.* good, kind, loving, affectionate, innocent, stainless, sterling, upright, fine, pure, laudable, excellent, admirable.

winning—*Syn.* attractive, charming, fascinating, enchanting, dazzling, nice, captivating, alluring, pleasing, lovable, courteous, sweet, amiable, agreeable. *Ant.* repulsive, repellent, terrible, frightful, revolting, annoying, aggravating, irksome, wearisome, unbearable.

wisdom—*Syn.* prudence, foresight, sagacity, acumen, intelligence, discernment, good judgement, capacity. *Ant.* folly, foolishness, absurdity, nonsense, stupidity, misjudgement, miscalculation.

wit—*Syn.* humor, jest, fun. *Ant.* solemnity, sobriety, gravity, seriousness, stolidity.

wonder, *n.*—*Syn.* amazement, bewilderment, astonishment, surprise, sensation, prodigy, marvel, miracle. *Ant.* expectation, anticipation, steadiness, commonness, imperturbability, calmness, stolidity.

work—*Syn.* labor, task, toil, performance, accomplishment, achievement, deed, action, production. *Ant.* idleness, ease, leisure, relaxation, rest, respite, halt, stop, interruption, intermission.

worthless—*Syn.* useless, insignificant, unessential, trivial, paltry, unserviceable. *Ant.* valuable, precious, useful, important, beneficial.

worthy—*Syn.* good, true, honorable, reliable, trustworthy, dependable, noble, virtuous, moral, pure, upright, righteous, decent, incorrupt, incorruptible, meritorious, creditable. *Ant.* unworthy, bad, evil, reprehensible, untrustworthy, deceitful, immoral, dishonest, corrupt.

wrong—*Syn.* sin, bane, turpitude, transgression, oppression, persecution, tyranny, abuse, hate, inhumanity, partisanship. *Ant.* right, justice, righteousness, honesty, decency, integrity.

X-ray—*Syn.* Rontgen rays, radioactivity, radium emanation, ultra-violet rays, cathode rays.

x, y, z—*Syn.* unknown quantities, the Great Unknown, unexplored ground, prehistoric time, the Great long ago. *Ant.* the present.

youth—*Syn.* boy, youngster, hopeful, girl. *Ant.* old.

youthful—*Syn.* young, budding. *Ant.* old, aged, elderly, ripe.

Hereafter, the Dark Ages, virgin soil, *terra incognita [L.].*

yawn—*Syn.* gape, open wide, vent, be fatigued, droop, flag, puff, gasp, be tired, be sleepy. *Ant.* close, close the mouth, shut the mouth, pucker the lips, be active, be brisk.

yearn—*Syn.* desire, crave, long for, fret, grieve, pine, languish, wish. *Ant.* content.

yell—*Syn.* cry, shout, yelp, roar, howl, shriek. *Ant.* keep quiet, refrain, suppress, whisper.

yes—*Syn.* assent, acquiescence, affirmation, accord, avowal. *Ant.* no, dissent.

yet—*Syn.* nevertheless, however, besides, furthermore, now, still, but.

yield—*Syn.* surrender, give, accede, relinquish, abidicate, quit, succumb, grant, bestow. *Ant.* deny, protest, disallow, reject, withstand, resist, disapprove, refuse.

yielding—*Syn.* productive, conceding, pliant, soft, flexible, resilient. *Ant.* unproductive, barren, tough, defiant, fierce, unbending.

yoke—*Syn.* connect, harness, unite, attach, tie, strap, hitch, fasten, secure. *Ant.* sever, disunite, untie, liberate, free, release, set free, detach, disjoin, separate.

yore—*Syn.* the past, past times, old times, days gone by, antiquity,

zeal—*Syn.* ardor, eagerness, fervor, activity, hustle, bustle, intensity, spirit, industry. *Ant.* apathy, coldness, carelessness, laziness, slowness, inaction, lethargy.

zealot—*Syn.* partisan, fanatic, visionary, enthusiast. *Ant.* *(slang)*, quitter.

zenith—*Syn.* top, pinnacle, summit, culmination, highest point, maximum, apex, elevation, acme. tip. *Ant.* base, lowest point, nadir, bedrock, floor, bottom.

zero—*Syn.* nothing, naught, cipher, unreality, nonenity, blank, void, phantom, shadow. *Ant.* something, anything, matter.

zest—*Syn.* taste, pleasure, delight, desire, savor, enhancement, tang, nip. *Ant.* distaste, disgust, detriment, sourness, tastelessness, flat, acerbity.

zigzag—*Syn.* oblique, inclined, sloping, awry, crooked, twisted, crinkled. *Ant.* straight, direct, even, unbent, true, normal.

zone—*Syn.* belt, region, district, territory, section, quarter, area, inclosure, ground, country, dominion, band, latitude, sector.

WORD FORMATION

ROOTS AND DERIVATIVES

Like all other things words had a beginning. Almost every word in the English language can be traced back to its beginning or origin, to the source from whence it came. The beginning, origin or source of a word is called its *root.* The root is the fundamental or primary element, the part from which the word springs, as the stem from the root of a tree.

Words may be divided into two classes, *primitives* and *derivatives.* Primitives are words that cannot be reduced to simpler forms, in fact they are root words. Derivatives are words formed by modifying the root or primitive word in some way, as by the addition of a prefix or suffix, either of which may be called an affix. A prefix is a word, or part of a word, as a syllable or letter, placed *before* the main body of a word to modify its meaning. A suffix is part of a word, a particle, placed after the root of a word to modify its meaning. The *stem* is the part of the word upon which inflections are based.

A large number of prefixes, especially of Latin and Greek origin, are used in the formation of English words. The following is a partial list of the principal ones:—

English has built largely on the old Greek roots and still continues to utilize them as foundations upon which to construct new terms. Many, indeed most, of the words recently coined to meet the demands of scientific progress for expression in English have been based on the tongue words used in ancient Hellas more than two thousand years ago. In the following table are some words, now standard in English, which were derived from the old-time Greek root:—

GREEK ROOTS AND DERIVATES

aer, the *air,* aeroplane, aerostat
agon, *a contest,* agony, antagonist
allos, *another* allopathy, allegory
angelos, *messenger,* angel, evangelist
anthos, a *flower,* anthology, anthologist
anthropos, a *man,* philanthropy, misanthropy
arche, *rule,* or *beginning,* archbishop, monarch, archaic
aristos, *best,* aristocracy, aristocrat
aster, astron, a *star,* astronomy, astrology, asteroid
atmos, *vapor,* atmosphere, atmology
autos, *self,* autocrat, autograph, automobile
ballo, *I throw,* symbol, hyperbole
bapto, *I dip,* baptise, baptism, baptistry
biblos, biblion, a *book,* Bible, bibliography, bibliomania
bios, *life,* biology, biography, amphibious
cheir, the *hand,* chiropodist, chirography, chirurgeon
chromos, *time,* chronicle, chronology, chronic
daklulos, a *finger,* dactyl, dactylography
deka, *ten,* decade, decalogue, decagon
demos, the *people,* democrat, demagogue, epidemic
dendron, a *tree,* rhododendron, dendrology
doxa, *opinion,* doxology, dogma, orthodox
dunamis, *power,* dynamite, dynamics
eidos, *form,* kaleidoscope, spheroid
eikon, an *image,* icon, iconoclas
electron, *amber,* electric, electricity, electrotype
ergon, a *work,* energy, chirurgeon (surgeon, archaic)
eu, *well,* euphony, evangel, eucharist
gamos, *marriage,* polygamy, bigamy, monogamy
gaster, the *stomach,* gastric, gastronomy
ge, the *earth,* geography, geology, geometry
glossa, the *tongue,* glottis, glossary
gramma, a *letter,* monogram, diagram, grammar
grapho, *I write,* biography, telegraph
gyne, a *woman,* gynecology, misogyny
haima, *blood,* hemorrhage, hemorrhoid
helios, the *sun,* heliography, heliotrope
hepta, *seven,* heptarchy, heptagon, heptachord
hieros, *sacred,* hieroglyphic, hierarchy
hippos, a *horse,* hippopotamus, hippology
hodos, a *way,* method, exodus, period
homos, the *same,* homogenous, homologous, homeopathy
hydor, *water,* hydraulics, hydrogen, hydrophobia
ichthus, a *fish,* ichthyology, ichthyophagy, ichthyoid
isos, *equal,* isotherm, isoceles, isocracy
kakos, *bad, evil,* cacophony, cacogenic, cacodemon
kardia, the *heart,* cardiac, cardialgia, carditis
kosmos, the *world, order,* cosmology, cosmogony, cosmopolitan
krino, *I judge,* critic, criterion, hypocrite
kyklos, *circle, ring,* cycle, cyclopedia, cyclone
kuon, a *dog,* cynic, cynical, cynicism
lithos, a *stone,* lithograph, monolith, aerolite
logos, *word, discourse,* monologue, dialogue, trilogy
methon, a *measure,* diameter, barometer, thermometer
mikros, *small,* microscope, microphone, microcosm
misos, *hatred,* misogyny, misanthrope
monos, *alone,* monologue, monosyllable
morphe, *shape,* amorphous, metamorphosis
mythos, a *fable,* myth, mythical, mythology
naus, a *ship,* nautical, navigation, argonaut

nekros, *dead,* a *dead body,* necropolis, necrology necromancy
neos, *new,* neophyte, neology, neologism
neuron, a *nerve,* neuritis, neuralgia, neuropath
nomos, a *law,* Deuteronomy, autonomy, astronomy
nosos, *disease,* nosology, nosologist, nosography
oide, a *song,* ode, prosody, palinode
oikos, a *house,* economy, ecology, ecologist
onoma, onyma, a *name,* synonym, patronymic, anonymous
orthos, *right,* orthodox, orthography, orthoepy
pais, a *child,* pedagogue, pediatrics
pan, *all,* pandemic, panoply, panorama
pathos, *feeling,* pathetic, sympathy, apathy
pente, *five,* pentagon, pentameter, pentarchy
petra, a *rock,* petrify, petrography, Peter
phaino, *I show,* phantom, phenomenon, fancy
philos, *loving, fond of,* philosophy, philology, philanthropy
phobos, *fear, dread,* hydrophobia, claustrophobia
phone, *sound,* microphone, telephone, phonetic
phos, *light,* phosphorescent, photography, photometer
physis, *nature,* physiology, physiography, physician
poieo, *I make,* poem, poet, pharmacopoeia
polis, a *city,* politics, police, metropolis
polys, *many, much,* polyandry, polygamy, polygon
pous, a *foot,* chiropodist, pediatrist, antipodes
potamos, a *river,* hippopotamus, transpotamian
protos, *first,* prototype, protoplasm, protocol
pseudes, *false,* pseudonym, pseudepigrapha
psyche, *soul, mind,* psychology, psychiatry, psychoanalysis
pyr, *fire,* pyrotechnics, pyrology, pyromaniac
rheo, *I flow,* rhetoric, pyorrhea, catarrh
skopeo, *I see,* microscope, telescope, fluoroscope
sophia, *wisdom,* sophist, philosophy, theosophy
sphaira, a *sphere,* hemisphere, planisphere
stello, *I send,* apostle, epistle, epistolary
stratos, an *army,* stratagem, strategy, strategist
strepho, *I turn,* apostrophe, catastrophe
techne, *art,* skill, craft, technical, technician
tele, *after, distant, end,* telegraph, telescope, telelectric
theos, *God,* theist, atheist, theocracy
therme, *heat,* thermometer, thermal, isothermal
topos, a *place,* topical, toponym, topography
treis, *three,* tripod, trinity, triangle
trepo, *I turn,* heliotrope, tropic, tropism
typos, *mark, impression,* type, stereotype, linotype
zoon, an *animal,* zoology, zootomy, epizootic

GREEK PREFIXES

a, an, *not, without*
amphi, *on both sides*
ana, *back, again, up*
anti, *oppose, against*
ap, apo, *from, away from:* also aph-
arch, archi, *chief*
auto, *self*
caat, cata, *down:* also cath-
dia, *through*
di, dis, *twice*
dys, *ill*
ec, *out of:* also ex-
en, *in:* also el, em-
endo, *in*
ep, epi, *upon*
eu, *well:* also ev-
hemi, *half*
hyp, hypo, *under*
hyper, *over, above*
met, meta, *after, over*
mon, mono, *alone, one, single*
ortho, *right*
pan, *all*
par, para, *beside*
peri, *round, around*
pro, *before*
pros, *towards*
proto, *first*
sy, syn, *with, along with:* also syl-

LATIN PREFIXES

a, ab, abs, *from, away from*
ad, *to:* become ac, af, ag, al, an, ap, ar, as, at- to assimilate with the first consonant of the root word, for the sake of euphony
am, amb, ambi, *about, around*
ante, *before*
bi, bis, *twice*
com, *with together:* also co, col, con, cor, for euphony
contra, *against:* also contro, counter-

de, *down*
dis, *apart, asunder*
ex, *out of, from, off:* also e, ef-
extra, *beyond*
in, *in, into:* also em, en, il, im, ir-
in, *not:* also ig, il, im, ir-
inter, *between, within:* also intro-
male, *bad, ill:* also, mal-
non, *not*
ob, *against, in the way of:* also oc, of, op-
per, *through:* also par, pel-
post, *after*
prae, pre, *before*
praeter, preter, *beyond, past*
pro, *before, in front of, forward, for, in behalf of*
re, *back, again:* also red-
retro, *backward*
se, *aside, apart:* also sed-
semi, *half*
sub, *under:* also suc, sud, suf, sug, sum, sup, sur, sus-
super, *above, over*
trans, *beyond, through, across*
ultra, *beyond*
un, uni, *one*
vice, *in the place of*

A large percentage of English words come from the Latin and Greek. Most of the modern words, especially technological and scientific terms, that have been incorporated into English have been compounded directly from these two languages. The following is a list of a number of the Latin roots, with some of the words in common use that have been derived from them:—

LATIN ROOTS AND DERIVATIVES

acer, sharp, acrid, acrimony, vinegar
aedes, a *building,* edifice, edify
ager, a *field,* agriculture, agrarian
ago, *I act,* action, agent, agitate
alo, *I nourish,* aliment, alimentary
alter, *another,* alternate, alteration
altus, *high,* altitude, exalt
amo, *I love,* amorous, amiable
anima, *breath, life,* animal, animate
animus, *mind,* unanimous, magnanimity
annus, a *year,* annual, anniversary, biennial
antiquus, *ancient,* antique, antiquity
appello, *I call,* appeal, appellation
aqua, *water,* aquatic, aqueduct, aquarium
arbor, a *tree,* arboreal, arborage, arboriculture
arcus, a *bow,* arcade, archer
ars, *art,* artist, artisan, artifice
audio, *I hear,* audible, audience, auditory
augeo, *I increase,* auction, augment
barba, a *beard,* barb, barber
bellum, *war,* bellicose, belligerent
bis, *twice,* bisect, biscuit
brevis, *short,* brevity, abbreviate
cado, *I fall,* accident, decadence
canis, a *dog,* canine
cano, *I sing,* canticle, chant
cavus, a *hallow,* cave, cavity, excavate
cedo, *I go, yield,* cede, accede, precede
cito, *I call, summon,* cite, recite, citation
civis, a *citizen,* civil, civilian, civic
clamo, *I cry out,* exclaim, exclamation, proclamation
clarus, *clear,* clarify, clarion, declare
claudo, *I shut,* exclude, seclusion
clino, *I bend,* incline, decline
coelum, *heaven,* celestial
colo, *I tell,* cultivate, culture
cor, the *heart,* cordial, courage
corona, a *crown,* coronet, coronation
credo, *I believe,* creed, credible, incredulous
cresco, *I grow,* increase, decrease, crescent
crux, a *cross,* crucify, crucifix, cruciform
culpa, a *fault,* culprit, culpable
cura, *care,* curate, accurate
decem, *ten,* decimal, decimate, December
dens, a *tooth,* dental, dentist, indent
dexter, *right-handed,* dexterity, dexterous
dico, *I say,* dictation, verdict, diction
dies, *a day,* diurnal, diary
dignus, *worthy,* dignity, indignity, dignify
doceo, *I teach,* docile, doctrine
domus, a *house,* domicile, domestic
duco, *I lead,* induct, educate, ductile
durus, *hard, lasting,* durable, duration, endure
ego, *I, egotist,* egoist, egoism
emo, *I buy,* redeem, exemption, preemption
erro, *I wander,* errant, error, aberration
esse, *to be,* essence, essential
facilis, *easy,* facile, facilitate, facility
fames, *hunger,* famine, famish
felix, *happy,* felicity, felicitous
femina, a *woman,* feminine, effeminate
fido, *I trust,* confide, fidelity, confident
finis, the *end,* finite, infinite, finish
fluo, *I flow,* flux, fluid, fluent
folium, a *leaf,* foliage, portfolio
fortis, *strong,* fortify, fortress, fortitude
frango, *I break,* fragile, fraction
frater, a *brother,* fraternal
frons, the *forehead,* front, frontal, frontier
fumus, *smoke,* fumigate, fumigation
fundus, the *bottom,* foundation, founder, profound
gelu, *frost,* gelid, congeal, gelatin
gens, a *race, people,* gentile, generation, gender
gradus, a *step,* grade, gradient, degrade
gravis, *heavy,* grave, gravity, grieve
grex, a *flock, herd,* aggregate, congregate, gregarious
habeo, *I have,* habit, habitual, inhabit
haereo, *I stick,* adhere, cohere, cohesion
halo, *I breathe,* inhale, exhale
homo, a *man,* homage, human, homicide
hostis, an *enemy,* hostile, hostility
humus, *earth, soil,* humble, exhume
ignis, *fire,* ignite, ignition, igneous
impero, *I command,* empire, imperial, imperative
insula, an *island,* insular, peninsula
ira, *anger,* irate, ire
judex, *judge,* judicial, judiciary
jungo, *I join,* juncture, junction
jus, *right,* justice, jurisdiction
lapis, a *stone,* lapidary, dilapidated
laus, *praise,* laudation, laudable
lavo, *I wash,* lave, lavatory
laxus, *loose,* lax, laxity, relax
lego, *I gather, read,* collect, lecture, legible
lego, *I send,* legate, delegate
lex, a *law,* legal, legitimate
liber, *free,* liberty, liberate, liberal
libra, a *book,* library, librarian
lignum, *wood,* ligneous, lignite, lignify
ligo, *I bind,* ligament, liable, religion
litera, a *letter,* literal, literary, literature
locus, a *place,* local, location, allocate
loquor, *I speak,* elocution, eloquent, loquacious
lumen, *light,* luminary, luminous, illuminate
luna, the *moon,* lunacy, lunatic, lunar
luo, *I wash,* ablution, dilute

lux, *light,* lucid, lucidity, elucidate
macula, *spot, stain,* immaculate, maculate
magnus, *great,* magnify, magnitude, magnificent
malus, *bad, evil,* malevolent, malady
manus, the *hand,* manual, manufacture, manuscript
mare, the *sea,* marine, maritime, mariner
Mars, *God of War,* martial, Matian
medius, *the middle,* median, medium, intermediate
memor, *mindful,* memory, memorial
mens, the *mind,* mental, mentality
mergo, *I dip,* emerge, immersion
miles, a *soldier,* military, militant, militia
miror, *I admire,* miracle, admirable
mitto, *I send,* commit, remit, mission
moneo, *I warn,* monitor, monition
mons, a *mountain,* ultramontane, promontory
mors, *death,* mortal, immortal, mortify
moveo, *I move,* motion, motive, motor
multus, *many,* multitude, multiply
munus, a *gift,* munificent, remunerate
murus, a *wall,* immure, mural
muto, *I change,* mutable, transmute
narro, *I relate,* narration, narrative
nascor, *to be born,* nascent, natal, native
navis, a *ship,* navy, naval, navigation
nihil, a *nothing,* annihilate, nihilist
noceo, *I injure,* noxious, innocent, innocuous
nomen, a *name,* name, nominal, nomination, cognomen
norma, a *rule,* normal, abnormal, enormous
novus, *new,* novel, renovate, novice
nox, *night,* nocturnal, equinox
nudus, *naked,* nude, denude
nuntio, *I declare,* announce, denounce
octo, *eight,* octave, octagon, October
oculus, the *eye,* ocular, oculist
odi, *I hate,* odium, odious
omnis, *all,* amnipotent, omniscience, omnibus
onus, a *burden,* onerous, exonerate
opus, *work,* operation, cooperate
orno, *I adorn,* adorn, ornament
oro, *I speak,* orator, oration
ovum, an *egg,* ovate, oval
pando, *I spread,* expand, expanse, compass
pareo, *I appear,* apparent, appearance, apparition
paro, *I prepare,* preparation, repair
pars, a *part,* partial, partition, partner
paseo, *I feed,* pastor, pasture, repast
patior, *I suffer,* patient, passion, passive
pax, *peace,* pacific, pacify
pecco, *I sin,* peccable, peccant
pecunia, *money,* pecuniary, impecunious
pello, *I drive,* compel, repel, impulsive
pendeo, *I hang,* pendant, suspend, suspense
pleo, *I fill,* complete, complement, supplement
poena, *punishment,* penal, penality, penance
pons, a *bridge,* transpontine, pontiff, pontifical
porto, *I carry,* export, report, deportment
primus, *first,* primary, primitive, primrose
probo, *I prove,* probable, approve, improve
proprius, *one's own,* proper, property, appropriate
pungo, *I prick,* puncture, pungent, expunge
puto, *I reckon,* compute, count
quaero, *I ask,* query, inquire, require
quartus, *fourth,* quart, quarter, quartet
radix, a *root,* radicsl, eradicate
rapio, *I seize,* rapine, rapture
rego, *I rule,* regent, regular, rector
rex, *a king,* regal, royal
rideo, *I laugh,* ridicule, deride, risible
rodo, *I gnaw,* rodent, corrode
rogo, *I ask,* interrogation, derogatory
rota, a *wheel,* rotary, rotate, around
rumpo, *I break,* rupture, disruption, eruption
rus, the *country,* rustic, rusticate
sacer, *sacred,* sacrament, sacrilege, sacristan
sanctus, *holy,* sanctify, sanctuary, saint
sanguis, *blood,* sanguinary, sanguineous
sanus, *sound,* sane, insane, sanity
sapio, *I taste,* sapid, insipid
scio, *I know,* science, omniscience
scribo, *I write,* scribe, scribble, scripture
senex, *old,* senior, senile, senator
sentio, *I feel,* sense, sentiment, sensual
septem, *seven,* septennial, September
sequor, *I follow,* sequel, sequence, consequence
servio, *I serve,* servant, service, sergeant
signum, a *sign,* signal, significant, designate
socius, a *companion,* social, socialist, society
sol, the *sun,* parsol, solar, solstice
specio, *I see,* inspect, circumspect, spectator
spero, *I hope,* desperate, despair
spiro, *I breathe,* aspire, inspire, conspire
struo, *I build,* structure, construct, construe
suadeo, *I advise,* persuade, dissuade
sumo, *I take,* assume, consume, assumption
tango, *I touch,* contact, tangible, contagious
tempus, *time,* temporal, contemporary
teneo, *I hold,* tenent, tenant, tendril
terminus, *boundary,* terminal terminate, term
terra, the *earth,* terrestrial, subterranean
terreo, *I frighten,* terrible, terrify, terror
timeo, *I fear,* timid, timidity, timorous
traho, *I draw,* tract, traction, contraction
tumeo, *I swell,* tumor, tumid, tumult
umbra, *a shallow,* umbrella, umbrage
unus, *one,* unit, unite, union
urbs, a *city,* urban, urbane, suburban
valeo, *I am strong,* valient, valid, invalid
venio, *I come,* convene, venture, advent
verbum, *a word,* verbal, verbiage, proverb
verto, *I turn,* convert, divert, versatile
verus, *true,* verity, verify, evident
vestis, a *garment,* vestment, vesture, invest
video, *I see,* vision, visit, evident
vinco, *I conquer,* victor, victory, convince
vivo, *I live,* vivid, survive, revive

voco, *I call,* vocal, vocation, revoke
volo, *I will,* volition, voluntary, benevolence
vox, *the voice,* vocal, vocalist
vulgus, *common,* vulgar, vulgate, divulge
vulnus, *a wouind,* vulnerable, invulverable

Suffixes abound in English; there are so many that to list all would be impossible in this book; they comprise noun, adjective, verb and adverb suffixes. The principal noun suffixes are:—

LATIN SUFFIXES

-age, used chiefly in forming abstract nouns.
-al, used in forming action words
-ant, denoting an agent or doer
-ary, denoting *a thing belonging to*
-ate, denoting an *office or function*
-cle, -cule, denoting *diminution*
-ess, denoting *the feminine of*
-et, -ette, denoting *diminution*
-ice, -ise, denoting *quality, condition, act*
-ine, denoting *feminine:* also in forming abstract nouns
-ion, -tion, -sion, in forming abstract nouns
-ment, *instrument of, act*
-mony, *instrument or means of*
-on, -oon, denoting *increase* or *augmentation*
-ory, *place where*
-tude, in forming nouns from Latin adjectives
-ty, *quality, state, condition*
-ure, *action, result of*

GREEK SUFFIXES

-ic, *pertaining to*
-isk, denoting *diminution*
-ism, *act, state, condition:* also in forming abstract nouns
-ist, *a doer, one who does, who practices or professes*
-sis, -sy, *state, condition, action*
-y, used in forming abstract nouns

The root, of course, is the most important part of the word, for not only is it the source but in it is also implied the meaning. In its early period the English language had enough roots of its own on which to base all the words required. For quite a long time, to wit, from the Anglo-Saxon Invasion down to the Norman Conquest, English depended upon the native roots to furnish what words were necessary to carry on social and commercial intercourse. Many words derived from these roots of the Anglo-Saxon period constitute a large part of the language as it is today. The Normans brought over a lot of words—Norman-French—much of which was derived from the Latin and a little from the Greek, so the English began using the words of the Normans as ready-made and to hand, instead of continuing to build new words on native roots, and as time went on more words were taken from other languages. English has put Latin and Greek under heavy tribute to help supply words to serve its purposes and augment its vocabulary.

As just stated, we have many words of pure Anglo-Saxon origin, words which sprang from native roots and which owe nothing whatever to other languages.

In the following list are given some of the old English roots and a few of the words we still retain which were based upon them:

OLD ENGLISH ROOTS AND DERIVATIVES

akr, a *field,* acre, acorn
bacon, to *bake,* baker, batch
beatan, to *strike,* beat. batter, battle
beran, to *bear,* bairn, burden, breed
bindan, to *bind,* bundle, bondage, band
blowan, to *blossom,* blow, bloom
brecan, to *break,* brake, breach, brittle
breowan, to *brew,* brewer, broth, bread
bugan, to *bend,* bow, bough, elbow
byrnan, to *burn, brown, brand*
ceapian, to *buy,* cheap, chop, chap
ceowan, to *chew,* chew, cud, cheek
cleovan, to *cleave,* cleft, clover
cnawan, to *know,* know, knowledge
cwic, *alive,* quick, quicksilver
daelan, to *divide,* deal, dole, dale
deman, to *judge,* deem, doom, kingdom
doan, to *act,* do, deed
dragan, to *draw,* drag, draft, drain
drifan, to *push,* drive, drift
drincan, to *soak,* drink, drench
dripan, to *drip,* dribble, droop, drop
faran, to *go,* fare, ferry, ford
fengan, to *catch,* fang, finger
fleotan, to *float,* float, fleet, flotsman
foda, *food,* fodder, forage, father
freon, to *love,* friend, friendship
galan, to *sing,* gale, nightingale, yell
grafan, to *cut,* grave, carve, groove
gripan, to *seize,* grab, grasp, grope
gyrdan, to *surround,* girdle, garden, yard
haelan, to *heal,* hale, holy, health
hebban, to *raise,* heavy, heave, heaven
hlaf, *bread,* loaf, lord, lady (one who kneads dough)
liegan, to *live,* lie, lair, outlay
magan, to be able, main, mighty, may
mona, *moon,* month, moonshine
nasu, *nose,* nasal, nozzle, nostril
pennan, *to shut up,* pound, impound
pic, *point,* peak, pike, picket
sceapan, to *form,* shape, ship, landscape
sceotan, to *throw,* shut, shot, shoot
sceran, to *cut,* shear, share, shirt
schufan, to *push,* shove, shovel, scuffle
settan, to *set,* seat, settle, saddle
slagan, to *strike,* slay, slaughter, sledge
slipan, to *slip,* slipper, sleeve, slop
snican, to *crawl,* snail, snake, sneak
stearc, *stiff,* strong, strength, strangle
stede, *place,* instead, steady, homestead

stigan, to *climb,* stair, stirrup, sty
styran, to *direct,* steer, steerage, stern
swerian, to *declare,* swear, forswear, answer
taecan, to *teach,* teach, taught, token
tellan, to *account,* teller, tale, talk
techan, to *draw,* tow, tug
thaec, *roof,* thatch, deck
tredan, to *walk,* tread, trade, tradesman
truwa, *good faith,* true, truth, troth
wefan, to *weave,* weaver, woof, web
war, *defense,* war, wary, guard
witan, to *know, wit, witness, wisdom*
wraestan, to *wrest,* wrest, wrestle, wrist

WORDS OFTEN MISPRONOUNCED

abdomen
aborigine
acetic
agile
albino
apropos
avoirdupois
balk
baroque
bayou
blackguard
brooch
buoy
cacao
calk
cayenne
cello
cerebral
chaise lounge
chamois
chantey
chauffeur
chic
cholera
cinchona
clandestine
clapboard
clique
colonel
compote
conduit
consommé
corps
corpuscle
cortege
cotillion
coup
coxswain
crosier
crouton
cuisine
dachshund
debris
debute
devotee
dinghy
diphtheria
dipththong
discern
draught
drought
duodenum
dyspepsia
edifice
egregious
emu
entree
facade
facile
financé
frigate
fuchsia
fuselage
fusillade
gendarme
gentian
gestation
gibber
gladiolus
glazier
glower
gnu
gourmet
granary
guerilla
guillotine
gunwale
habitué
harbinger
heifer
heinous
hirsute
holocaust
hosiery
iguana
imbroglio
inchoate
incognito
indigenous
interstice
inure
irascible
isosceles
isthmus
jodhpurs
joust
khaki
kohlrabi
labyrinth
lascivious
legerdemain
lemur
liaison
lieu
lien
leisure
lineage
liturgy
llama
locale
logy
lorgnette
louver
lucid
lucre
machete
machination
mademoiselle
maestro
mannequin
marijuana
marquis
matinée
mauve
meliorate
mesa
mien
modiste
motif
murrain
myrrh
naïve
naphtha
niche
nihilism
nirvana
nom de plume
nonpareil
nougat
nuance
oblique
ocher
omniscient
onerous
onus
opiate
pachyderm
palsy
paprika
parfait
parquet
paschal
pecan
pellagra
petit
philistine
pimiento
plebeian
pneumatic
poignant
posthumous
precipice
premier
pristine
protégé
pueblo
purulent
quaff
qualm
quay
ragout
regime
renege
reveille
ricochet
rudiment
savoir-faire
short-lived
sleasy
soufflé
specious
suave
subpoena
tarpaulin
thyme
travail
usury
valance
worsted
zealous

PARTS OF SPEECH

English words are divided into eight categories according to their grammatical function. These eight categories, called the parts of speech, are outlined below.

A **noun** is the name of a person, place, or thing. There are several classes of nouns.

A *proper noun* is the name of a specific person, place or thing.

George Washington
Brooklyn Bridge

A *common noun* is the name of a non-specific person, place, or thing.

man town tree dog

An *abstract noun* is the name of an idea or concept.

anger beauty truth

A *collective noun* names a group of individual persons, places, or things.

army herd audience team

A **pronoun** is a word that stands in place of a noun. There are various classes.

A *demonstrative pronoun* points out a person or thing already mentioned.

this that these those

An *indefinite pronoun* gives a general or indefinite impression.

any some none each

A *relative pronoun* refers to an antecedent and at the same time introduces a dependent clause.

who what that which

A *compound relative pronoun* is formed by adding *-ever* or *-soever* to certain relatives.

whoever whichever
whatsoever

An *interrogative pronoun* is used in asking a direct or indirect question.

who which what

A *personal pronoun* stands directly for the name of a person, place, or thing.

I you he it we they

A *compound personal pronoun* is formed by adding *-self* or *-selves* to certain personal pronouns.

herself myself themselves

A *possessive pronoun* indicates ownership.

mine his hers yours theirs

A *reciprocal pronoun* indicates mutual action.

each other one another

A **verb** is a word that indicates action or state of being.

A *transitive verb* is one that requires an object.

An *intransitive verb* expresses action or state of being independent of an object.

An *auxiliary verb* helps establish the form of another verb.

have may can must could

A *copulative verb* connects the predicate idea with the subject

be become seem appear

An **adjective** is a word used to modify a noun or pronoun.

A *descriptive adjective* expresses a quality or condition of the noun or pronoun.

red smooth happy

A *definitive adjective* defines or limits the meaning of the noun or pronoun. This class includes the definite article *the* and the indefinite articles *a* and *an.*

this that the

A *pronomial adjective* resembles a pronoun and may be used as either a pronoun or an adjective.

this that each either
whichever

A *numeral adjective* may be a cardinal, an ordinal, or a multiplicative.

one first single two-fold

A *proper adjective* is one derived from a proper noun.

Roman American English

An **adverb** is a word that modifies a verb or another modifier.

An adverb of *time* answers the question *when?* or *how often?*

now yet today already

An adverb of *place* anwers the question *where?*

in up down back forth

An adverb of *manner* answers the question *how?* This class included adverbs of quality and adverbs of affirmation.

well ill truly verily

An adverb of *degree* answers the question *to what degree?*

much little rather

A **preposition** is a word that expresses some relationship between a noun or pronoun and another word in the sentence.

down by at in behind
up to

A **conjunction** is a word used to connect elements of a sentence or to show relationship between sentences.

A *coordinating conjunction* connects independent words, phrases, or clauses.

and but or

A *subordinating conjunction* indicates the dependence of one sentence element on another.

after before if though
unless while

A *correlative conjunction* is one of two conjunctions that are regularly together.

neither . . . nor either . . . or
both . . . and

An **interjection** is a word that expresses strong or sudden feeling but that has no grammatical relationship with the rest of the sentence.

ah alas bah oh

GUIDE TO SPELLING

The following rules will provide a general guide to correct spelling.

Prefixes

When a consonant ends the prefix and also begins the root element, both letters are retained.

misspell
unnecessary

When the prefix ends in a vowel and the root element begins with a consonant, the consonant is not doubled.

proficient *repeal*

When the prefix ends in a consonant and the root element begins with a vowel, the consonant is not doubled.

disappoint
disappear

Suffixes

Words of one syllable and those accented on the last syllable, if ending in one consonant preceded by one vowel, generally double the consonant when a suffix beginning with a vowel is added.

madder *preferred*
remitted

When the accent falls on a syllable other than the last, the doubling of the consonant does not occur.

visited *reference*

When a suffix beginning with a vowel is added to a word ending in a silent *e*, the *e* is usually dropped.

coming *forgiving*

The *e* is usually kept before a suffix that begins with a consonant.

hopeful
arrangement

When a suffix beginning with *a* or *o* is added to words ending in *ce* or *ge*, the *e* is retained to preserve the soft sound of the *c* or *g*.

serviceable
courageous

When a suffix is added to a word ending in *y* preceded by a consonant, the *y* is usually changed to *i*.

heartily *tardiness*

When a suffix is added to a word ending in *y* preceded by a vowel, the *y* usually remains.

swayed *slayer*

Words ending with a double consonant usually keep both letters before a suffix.

enrolled *installed*
added

Words that end in *l* generally keep that letter when the suffix *-ly* is added.

usually *incidentally*
actually

Words that end in *n* generally keep that letter when the suffix *-ness* is added.

thinness *sternness*
meanness

Words containing ei or ie

Usually *i* follows *l* and *e* follows *c*.

believe *conceive*

It is helpful to remember this jingle.

Write *i* before *e*
Except after *c*
Or when sounded as *a*
As in *neighbor* and *weigh*

Exceptions include *ancient, either, financier, forfeit, inveigle, leisure, neither, seize, weird.*

Plurals

Nouns that do not end in *s* or *es* form their plurals by adding *s*.

cows *books*
horses

Nouns ending with a sibilant *(s, sh, z, zh, ch, j, x)* usually form their plurals by adding *es*.

taxes *churches*
fishes *dresses*

Nouns ending in *f, fe*, or *ff* usually form their plurals by adding *s*.

beliefs *safes* *cliffs*

Nouns ending in *y* preceded by a consonant form their plurals by changing the *y* to *i* and adding *es*.

armies *studies*
follies

Nouns ending in *y* preceded by a vowel form their plurals by retaining the *y* and adding *s*.

plays *keys* *jays*

Nouns ending in *o* preceded by a vowel form their plurals by adding *s*.

duos *ratios*
bamboos

Nouns ending in *o* preceded by a consonant usually form their plurals by adding *es*.

heroes *potatoes*
vetoes

Exceptions include *infernos, halos, Eskimos, solos, zeros, pianos.*

Compounds

Most compound words form their plurals by adding *s* or *es* to the governing word in the compound.

runners-up
mothers-in-law

If the compound is written as one word, the *s* or *es* is added to the end of the word.

bookstores
schoolrooms
cupboards

GUIDE TO PUNCTUATION

The **apostrophe** is used—

To indicate the omission of letters in a contraction and figures in a date.

can't class of '65

To form possessives.

Jim's pencil
the boy's pencils

To form the plural of a letter, number, or abbreviation.

P's and Q's 7's G.I.'s

Brackets are used—

To enclose a parenthetical element already within parentheses.

Moses' treatment of environment (see his "The Question" [3d ed.], II 136) . . .

To correct a mistake.

Amedeo Modiliani [Modigiliani] settled in . . .

To enclose an explanation at the beginning or end of chapters and articles.

[To be continued]

To enclose a clarifying insertion made by someone other than the original author.

It was thought that he [Lawrence] was in . . .

The **colon** is used—

After a complete statement introducing a formal or long quotation, a statement, a question, a closely related illustration, or an explanation.

The entire text is as follows: "The frontier . . ."

fter a salutation in a
iness letter.

r Sir:

xpression of

and
ta-

The **comma** is used—

To set off a brief direct quotation.

He asked, "Are you coming?"

To indicate the omission of a word or phrase.

The apple was good; the pear, poor.

After consecutive coordinate adjectives modifying the same noun.

He ran with a swift, sure gait.

To set off words or phrases causing a distinct break in the continuity of thought.

This was, after all, an important work.

After a long introductory adverbial phrase and after a subordinate clause that precedes the main clause.

By the time the men arrive from the city, the supplies will be lost.

Before coordinating conjunctions joining two independent clauses.

The group embarked last month, and they arrived here yesterday.

To set off a descriptive subordinate clause that follows a main clause.

We will leave, even if it is early.

To set off words, phrases, or clauses that are in apposition or contrast.

Reiner, the conductor, arrived early.

After each unit in a series of three or more words, phrases, or figures and before the coordinate conjunction.

For breakfast we had bacon, eggs, toast, and coffee.

To set off names and words in direct address.

I'm sorry, Manfred, but you must go.

Between identical words.

What the difficulty is, is not known now.

After each unit in a date or address.

On June 6, 1944, the invasion began.

The **dash** is used—

To indicate a sudden change or break in thought or sentence structure.

If you should call—please do so at an early date.

To indicate emphasis, an interruption, or an unfinished word or sentence.

He is the candidate—the candidate we need.

Instead of the comma or parentheses if the clause or phrase is logically and structurally independent from the rest of the sentence.

Should the venture fail—God forbid!—he will be ruined.

The **exclamation point** is used—

To indicate strong emotion, surprise, amusement, or irony.

"No!" he shouted. "What! You did that!"

To indicate a command.

Return to the house at once!

Parentheses are used—

To set off an explanatory or clarifying phrase or clause that is independent of the sentence structure.

The shipment arrived from Volgograd (formerly Stalingrad).

To set off figures or letters indicating divisions or listings within a sentence.

The instructor recommended three methods of painting: (a) watercolor, (b) brush and ink, and (c) oils.

To set off the translation of a foreign word or phrase.

Bienvenido (welcome)

The **period** is used—

At the end of a declarative or imperative sentence.

Come as soon as you can.

With most initials and abbreviations.

Ph.D. ft. A.M.

To indicate omitted material. Use four periods for matter omitted at the end of a sentence; three, for matter omitted within a sentence.

"Faust" was delivered in English . . . at Princeton . . ."

The **question mark** is used—

At the end of a direct question.

How are you?

At the end of a short direct question following a statement.

You are going to town, aren't you?

Within parentheses to indicate irony or to express doubt as to the correctness of the word or statement directly preceding it.

John Jones, 1670(?)-1720 He is an honest(?) man.

Quotation marks are used—

To enclose all direct quotations. When a quotation consists of more than one paragraph or one stanza of poetry, quotation marks are placed before each paragraph or stanza and following the last one.

"The chairman was pleased," he said.

To indicate a quotation within a quotation. Use single marks for this usage.

"The defendant," he added, "had said 'Not guilty' when questioned."

To enclose expressions, colloquialisms, slang, etc., when they are not in keeping with the context.

Two "sticks" of paratroopers left the airplane.

To enclose the titles of short poems, essays, songs, lectures, works of art, etc.

The class read Frost's "The Road Not Taken."

The **semicolon** is used—

Between the clauses of a compound sentence not connected by a coordinating conjunction, especially if a conjunctive adverb is present.

The application was sent to the wrong office; hence there will be a slight delay.

Between the clauses of a compound sentence where a coordinating conjunction is present if one or both of such clauses already contains commas or if emphasis is desired.

The sea, bleak and limitless, rose higher; and still no land was to be seen.

To separate statements so closely related that a comma would be too weak and a period too strong.

War is destructive; peace is constructive.

WORDS OFTEN MISSPELLED

accept
accessible
accommodate
acquaint
adequate
adherent
adjournment
aisle
all right
already
always
analyze
answer
appreciate
argument
bachelor
bankruptcy
basis
beggar
beginning
believe
beneficial
brilliant
brutality
bulletin
buoyant
bureau
business
calendar
camouflage
candidate
carriage
category
cavalry
ceiling
cemetery
cite
committee
competition
complement
compliment
conscious
corps
corpse
courteous
curiosity
deceive
descendant
desert
dessert
disappoint
discipline
dissatisfy
ecstasy
effect
efficient
eighth
embarrass
endurance
enough
environment
erroneous
exaggerate
excel
existence
extraordinary
fallacy
fascinate
fascism
foreign
formally
formerly
friend
furniture
gauge
grievous
guarantee
guard
handkerchief
height
hereditary
humorous
hygiene
hypocrisy
incident
indegestible
initiative
intercede
irrelevant
irresistible
its (vs. *it's*)
kidnapping
knowledge
laboratory
lead
led
leisure
liable
license
literature
livelihood
loose
lose
magazine
maneuver
marriage
material
medicine
medieval
minute
mischievous
misspelled
mortgage
muscle
mysterious
naive
necessary
neither
niece
noticeable
notoriety
occasion
occurred
omission
oneself
optimism
pageant
parallel
parliament
particularly
peasant
perceive
perspiration
piece
prescription
principal
principle
privilege
pronunciation
psychology
quiet
quite
receipt
receive
recommend
reference
referred
reign
restaurant
rhythm
sacrifice
sacrilegious
salary
scarcity
schedule
scheme
scholarly
seize
sergeant
siege
stationary
stationery
subtle
successful
sufficient
superintendent
surprise
syllable
sympathize
systematically
tear
their
thorough
tonight
tournament
tragedy
truly
twelfth
typical
tyranny
unanimous
until
usually
valuable
variety
vegetable
vengeance
village
villain
weather
weird
wherever
whether
whim
wholly
whose
woolen
written
wrote
yacht

PREFIXES AND SUFFIXES

Prefixes and suffixes are word elements that serve a derivative, formative, or inflectional function when combined with root words or other word elements. Listed here are a number of common prefixes and suffixes, together with their meanings and example words.

Prefix	Meaning	Example
ante-	before, preceding	antechamber
anti-	against, contrary to, opposite	antibody, antifreeze
co-	with, together, in conjunction	cooperate, coeducation
dis-	not, a lack of, separation, undoing, depriving of	disfigure, dishonest, displacement
fore-	before in place or time	forecast, forerunner
hyper-	over, above, beyond the normal or ordinary	hypertension, hypercritical
hypo-	beneath, under, less than the ordinary	hypodermic, hypochondria
in-	not, within, in, on, toward	inactive, inside
inter-	between, among, together, mutual	intercede, interstate
micro-	small, petty, enlarging, a millionth part of a unit	microcosm, microphone, microliter
mis-	wrongly, wrong, bad, ill	mispronounce, misconduct
non-	not	nonsense
post-	after in time or position	postscript, postclassical
pre-	before in time, position, or degree	preview, prepaid
pro-	before, in front, forth, in place of, according to	proceed, proclaim, produce
re-	back, again	recede, reconstitute
semi-	half, partly, occurring twice, incompletely, in low degree	semipermeable, semiweekly, semiautomatic
sub-	under, below, beneath	subhuman
super-	above, over, surpassing	superstructure, supernatural
tele-	far, operating at a distance	telegraph, television
trans-	over, across, beyond, through, on the other side of	transportation, translate, trans-Canadian
un-	not, opposing, the reverse of	unacceptable, unfriendly

Suffix	Meaning	Example
-able	capable of being, able to, tending to	readable, perishable
-ance	the action of, the fact of	assistance, reliance
-ant	possessing the quality of one that, a person or thing that	brilliant, servant, defiant
-ary	belonging to, pertaining to, joined with	revolutionary, functionary
-dom	the office, title, domain or territory of, the state of being, a total of those who are	kingdom, freedom, officialdom, wisdom
-ed	possessing, provided with, having characteristics of	honored, jointed, bigoted
-ence	the state or quality of being	dependence, occurrence
-er	a person or object that, a person living in, a degree of	grocer, New Yorker, harder
-ful	that which fills, tending, to, characterized by, full of	handful, cheerful, hopeful
-ft	to make into, become like, cause to be	solidify, rectify
-hood	a state or character of being	boyhood, falsehood
-ic	of, belonging to, like	historic
-ing	the act of, that which results from the act	drinking, roofing
-ion	the act or process of doing, the state or condition of being	revulsion, ambition, promotion
-ish	somewhat, suggestive of, like	whitish, boyish
-ist	one who does or professes	pianist, atheist
-ive	having the quality of, having a tendency to	extensive, responsive
-less	without, unable to, beyond the range of	formless, countless
-let	small, something worn on	pamphlet, armlet
-like	similar to	apelike, childlike
-ly	similar to, characteristic of, every	brotherly, annually
-ment	the act of doing, the result of doing, the state of being	encouragement, amazement, argument
-ness	the quality or state of being	goodness, dimness
-or	the quality of being, the person or thing that does	ardor, auditor, visitor
-ous	full of, having, similar to	dangerous, nebulous
-ship	state or quality, an office or position, skill, something showing a state or quality	friendship, instructorship, craftsmanship, championship, fellowship
-ty	the state or quality of being	loyalty, oddity
-ward	in the direction of, toward	windward, upward
-y	similar to, full of, somewhat, tendency to, the state of being	downy, honesty, wary

Printed in the U.S.A.